RELIGION AND TRADE IN NEW NETHERLAND
Dutch Origins and American Development

RELIGION AND TRADE
IN NEW NETHERLAND

Dutch Origins and American Development

GEORGE L. SMITH

Cornell University Press | ITHACA AND LONDON

Cornell University Press gratefully acknowledges
a grant from the Andrew J. Mellon Foundation that
aided in bringing this book to publication.

First published 1973 by Cornell University Press.
Published in the United Kingdom by Cornell University Press Ltd.,
2-4 Brook Street, London W1Y 1AA.

International Standard Book Number 0-8014-0790-7
Library of Congress Catalog Card Number 73-8403

Printed in the United States of America by York Composition Co., Inc.

*For my mother and my father
who love New York State*

Contents

Preface

Between 1600 and 1800 the place of religion within Euro-American society altered radically. In the early seventeenth century the church still dominated society in every aspect. It dominated society physically. Its spires rose above nearly every village square and city marketplace. The church dominated society metaphysically. Its professional clergy possessed and purveyed the "correct" understanding of the universe. And society listened. Sermons were not only heard on Sunday mornings; they were discussed on Sunday afternoons. The metaphysic of the church was the metaphysic of the world, and preachers and sermons made a real difference in people's lives. The church dominated society educationally. Schools were more a function of the church than of the state, and education was virtually synonymous with religious education. The church dominated ethically in every aspect of society's life. Robert Keayne, that troubled merchant of first-generation Boston, thought that the church had misjudged his commercial practices as usurious, but he never doubted that mercantile practices as such ought to be open to ecclesiastical scrutiny. Both the church and the people expected religious control of economic affairs. It was that kind of world. Finally, the church dominated society legally and politically. To "own the covenant" of the church—either implicitly or explicitly, depending on the society—was to claim one's rightful place in the functioning social organism. Explicitly to disown the ecclesiastical covenant was to bring upon oneself both ecclestiastical and civil disabilities.

By the end of the eighteenth century this picture had changed almost beyond recognition—especially in that part of North America which had meanwhile become the United States. Sunday morning's metaphysics lesson, now obtainable in any one of a number of competing architectural and theological packagings, was heard by fewer people and believed by even fewer. Education was increasingly the function of a state that recognized any number of ecclesiastical covenants while itself embracing none. The economic entrepreneur had gone his own ethical (or unethical) way, while the church's sphere of ethical concern had been sharply reduced to matters of private morality and public charity.

What happened is often referred to by historians of culture and theologians as secularization. The term is fine as far as it goes, but the workaday church historian is inclined to ask whether it does not obscure at least as much as it explains. He wants to know more pedestrian things. Why did so many varieties of the Christian metaphysic come to compete in North America? How did the economic entrepreneur manage to wriggle out of the ethical grasp of the church? Who let it happen and why?

In recent years several books have appeared that suggest that the answers to such questions are to be sought very early in the American colonial experience. Sumner Chilton Powell's *Puritan Village* revealed first-generation Puritans who were more interested in land ownership and less interested in sermons than we had previously supposed. Bernard Bailyn's *New England Merchants in the Seventeenth Century* and Darrett Rutman's *Winthrop's Boston* showed that if John Winthrop and Robert Keayne lived in uneasy tension between commerce and covenant, their Bostonian descendants soon resolved the tension by forgetting about covenant. Frederick B. Tolles's *Meeting House and Counting House* argued that in Philadelphia success spoiled the Quakers and that Friends were soon spending more time in the counting house than in the meeting house.

What these books have done—each in its own way—is to expose the ecclesiastical intentions for New England and Pennsylvania for what they were, namely, oligarchic. Even in the early seventeenth century the vision of a covenanted society built organically around the church was the vision of an elite ecclesiastical minority. "Secular" intentions were also present in the American experiment from the very beginning, and in the long run they prevailed, not because American colonists were in any profound sense anticlerical but because two of the elements of secularism—commerce and pluralism—were more functional to the job of colonizing than was the ecclesiastical vision. They were forms of social organization better suited to clearing land and populating it.

This work attempts to place the story of religion in New Netherland against the backdrop of the colony's commercial beginnings. It is axiomatic for gestalt psychologists that an object is likely to be perceived differently when placed against a different background. My thesis is that New Netherland's religious experience assumes a different aspect when seen within the context of the intentions held for the colony by its economic underwriters. I conclude that New Netherland—New York—was very secular very early. The spirit of commerce was prevalent in the colony from the very outset, and over the outraged cries of Reformed *predikanten* it soon created within the colony a de facto religious pluralism.

It should be noted that, although this is a book about New Netherland, approximately half of the text deals with the Netherlands. We are, I think, finally beginning to realize that what usually passes for "American history" is often the history of Europeans in America. And what is true of American history in general is true *a fortiori* of American colonial history. As I became immersed in the research for this book I soon realized that

I would never understand religion and its social matrix in New Netherland unless I could go to the Netherlands and study the original version of the problem. This I was fortunate enough to be able to do.

Grateful acknowledgment is expressed to AMS Press for permission to quote the poetry of Andrew Marvell; and to the *Journal of Presbyterian History* for permission to reproduce portions of the author's previously published article, "Guilders and Godliness: The Dutch Colonial Contribution to American Religious Pluralism."

To name all the persons who have helped make the book a reality would extend this introduction to an unrealistic length. There are three, however, without whom the book would never have been completed. His insight exceeded only by his patience, Martin E. Marty of the University of Chicago Divinity School encouraged and criticized, coaxed and prodded. Max Weber's *The Protestant Ethic and the Spirit of Capitalism* served as the heuristic tool with which I first conceived the shape for this study, and Charles R. Boxer's *The Dutch Seaborne Empire* provided what I regard as a helpful corrective to Weber at several points.

There are others who were far too helpful and kind to go unmentioned. The Arie van Proeyen family of Chicago, Illinois, put in many long hours teaching Dutch to my wife and me. Simon Hart of the Amsterdam Municipal Archives was a wonderful host and a virtuoso on the history of "his" city. The Leo van Klaveren, Simon Wynia, and Jan Brouwer families, by their friendship and hospitality throughout a whole year of study in the Netherlands, contributed more to this book than any of them probably suspects.

The editorial staff of Cornell University Press often converted my futile efforts into authentic English prose. Bryan Feille, Ernest Beckham, and John Loucks—graduate students of the variety that causes teachers to rejoice—constructed the index and helped read proof. Gloria Young and Bobbie Tucker typed and retyped the manuscript and aided in the final preparation in numerous ways beyond the call of duty.

Finally, it was my wife, Margaret, with her Dutch ancestry and deep desire to understand other cultures who led me into this project and sustained me throughout it. It is, in a very real sense, her book.

GEORGE L. SMITH

Fort Worth, Texas

RELIGION AND TRADE IN NEW NETHERLAND
Dutch Origins and American Development

1. Introduction

When young William II of Orange died suddenly of the small-pox in November 1650 leaving only a pregnant wife as his successor, Oliver Cromwell's English Independent party acted swiftly in hopes that the Dutch States-General could be persuaded to join forces with England in a Protestant crusade to defeat Spain and Portugal and split the colonial spoils. The Dutch, however, wanted no part of the scheme for two reasons: the Dutch Reformed Church distrusted the nonpresbyterian form of English Independency, and the merchant magistrates of Holland had no intentions of sharing their lead in European trade with English entrepreneurs. Cromwell's ambassadors were jeered in the streets of The Hague in March 1651, and sent home empty-handed by the States-General. When he heard the news the Lord Protector is said to have lamented that "the Dutch love gain more than Godliness."[1]

Cromwell was not the only foreigner so to evaluate Dutch motivation during the course of the seventeenth century, and indeed the Dutch themselves acknowledged the commercial character of their own national and colonial enterprises. Joost van den Vondel, the greatest poet of the Dutch Golden Age, wrote that "we Amsterdammers travel wherever profit drives us."[2] By

[1] "Memorandum on Cromwell's Anglo-Dutch Policy," *English Historical Review*, 21 (1906), 320. Cited in C. R. Boxer, *The Dutch Seaborne Empire* (New York: Alfred A. Knopf, 1965), p. 113.

[2] Joost van den Vondel, "Blyde Inkomst der Allerdoorluchtighste

1

the opening of the seventeenth century, mercantilism had blossomed as an economic system in Western Europe, and the Netherlands held a position of supremacy in the international commercial rivalry generated by that system.[3]

The question to be investigated here is what this thoroughgoing commercialism meant for the relationship of church and state in the Dutch colonial empire, particularly in the colony of New Netherland from 1609 to 1664. It is a question which, for a variety of reasons, has been left not only unanswered but even unasked. Serious historians of the American colonial period have dealt relatively little with New Netherland. Such neglect is in part understandable, for one finds in the documentary leavings of the colony no such profound testimony of a theological and literary elite as in New England, Rhode Island, or even Pennsylvania. It is regrettable that because of this failure on the part of historians New Netherland's history has become, as Thomas Condon puts it, "a jumble of archetypal heroes, villains, and buffoons whose exploits have been better suited to the art of a Washington Irving or a Kurt Weill than to the art of an historian."[4] More to be regretted, however, is that those church historians who have chronicled the colony's religious history have pursued their craft so unaware of the important—indeed, decisive—implications of Dutch commercialism for their subject. Church historians have held rather uncritically to the idea that the place of religion in the total social, political, and intellectual construct of New Netherland was about as central as that enjoyed by religion in the other North American colonial ventures roughly contemporaneous with it. Such a notion has been the

---

Koninginne, Maria de Medicis t' Amsterdam," in *De Werken van Vondel* (Amsterdam: Maatschappij voor Goede en Goedkoope Lectuur, 1929), 3, 629 [my translation].

[3] S. G. Nissenson, *The Patroon's Domain* (New York: Columbia University Press, 1937), p. 3.

[4] *New York Beginnings: The Commercial Origins of New Netherland* (New York: New York University Press, 1968), p. 126.

source of much confusion and wrong-headed thinking about religion in New Netherland.

It would be naive to argue without further qualification that people came to Massachusetts Bay in the early seventeenth century to express religious conviction while people came to Manhattan Island to get rich. This thesis, while it might contain a kernel of truth, would be both doctrinaire and foolish, because it fails to take account of the intricacy of all human motivation and the inaccessibility of historical data on the subject. Edwin Scott Gaustad writes on the problem of the historical investigation of motivation: "Motives are always complex and obscure—our own no less than those we plumb for in others. Complexity is confounded when the historian must sift the always fragmentary evidence from centuries past, hoping to discern not only what happened but why."[5]

Anyone at all familiar with the literature of the seventeenth-century European colonial propagandists knows that a mixture of motives was the rule, not the exception. Gaustad's remark about the complexity of human motives is made in the context of an introduction to two works of English colonial-expansion propaganda—*A Discourse How Hir Majestie May Annoy the King of Spayne* by Sir Humphrey Gilbert and *A Discourse on Western Planting* by Richard Hakluyt. Both discourses reveal a complex of motivation, but in the main Gilbert's argument is economic while Hakluyt's is religious.

Gilbert maintained that Queen Elizabeth, to whom his essay was addressed, had a primary responsibility "to seeke the kingdome of heaven, because no state or common weale can florishe, where the first and principall care is not for goddes glorie, and for thadvaunsing of the pollisies of his spirituall kingdom." But in the contemporary situation this meant that Elizabeth had a bounden duty to do battle against papist Spain and Portugal ("it

---

[5] Gaustad, ed., *Religious Issues in American History* (New York: Harper and Row Forum Books, 1968), p. 1.

is more then tyme to pare theire nayles by the stumpes"). The power of Spain and Portugal could best be undermined "by the farther weakening of theire navies, and by preserving and increasing of your owne." Gilbert then outlined his plan for privateering against Iberian shipping in the Atlantic and concluded with this sanguine prospectus:

if your highness will permit me, with my associates eyther overtly or covertly to perfourme the aforesaide enterprise: then with the gayne thereof there may be easely such a competent companie transported to the W.I. [West Indies] as may be hable not only to disposses the S. [Spaniards] thereof, but also to possesse for ever your Majestie and Realme therewith, and thereby not only be countervaile, but by farr to surmounte with gaine, the aforesaid supposed losses: besides the gowld and silver Mynes, the profit of the soyle, and the inward and outward customs from thence, By which meanes your highnes doubtfull frendes, or rather apparaunte enemyes, shall not be only made weake and poore, but therewith your selfe, and Realme made strong and rich, both by sea, and by lande, as well there, as here. And where both is wrought under one, it bringeth a most happy conclusion.[6]

Hakluyt's discourse was also belligerent toward the papist Iberian powers. The Spanish and Portuguese missionaries, he argued, have drawn the native infidels "oute of Sylla into Charibdis, that is to say, from one error into another." But on the whole, Hakluyt took a different, more purely evangelical line. The subtitle of his first chapter is "that this Westerne discoverie will be greately for thinlargemente of the gospell of Christe, whereunto the princes of the Reformed Religion are chefely bounde." It was profoundly disturbing to Hakluyt that "the people of that parte of America from 30. degrees in Florida northewarde unto 63. degrees (which ys yet in no Christian princes actuall possession) are idolaters." And he couched his whole plea for English colonial expansion in terms of response to the spiritual need of these poor infidels: "Nowe the meanes to sende such as shall labour effectually in this business ys, by plantinge one or twoo colonies of our nation

6 *Ibid.*, pp. 4, 5, and 8.

upon that fyrme, where they may remaine in saftie, and firste learne the language of the people nere adjoyninge (the gifte of tongues beinge nowe taken awaye), and by little and little acquainte themselves with their manner, and so with discretion and myldenes distill into their purged myndes the swete and lively liquor of the gospel."[7]

From the beginning the English colonial enterprise showed a mixture of motivation. In the Netherlands the pamphlets of Willem Usselincx, conceiver of and leading propagandist for the Dutch West India Company, manifest the same kind of mixture within Dutch colonial theory, and it is interesting that with Usselincx the religious and economic motives have approximately equal weight. Usselincx began his ardent agitation for the formation of a Dutch "West India" company as early as 1591, but after his plans were temporarily thwarted in 1609 by the signing of the truce with Spain at Treves he began to propagandize even more vehemently. In the final months of 1618, when it appeared that the truce might run out and hostilities with Spain be renewed, Usselincx submitted to the States-General a proposal concerning the structure and purposes of a "West India" company. In this proposal he put forth the general rationale for establishing such a company:

Inasmuch as we know that for several years past there have been discovered many rich lands and islands—both in Africa-America and in *Terra Australis* or *Magellanica*—and that these lands are for the most part inhabited by many different peoples, tribes, and nations. And inasmuch as it may be hoped that from this discovery of lands and knowledge of peoples will come not only a great growth and increase in shipping, trade, and commerce (which, next to God, have always been primarily responsible for the welfare of these united provinces and the well-being of their inhabitants), but also the furtherance of the saving Gospel of our Lord Jesus Christ and the bringing of many thousands of men to the light of truth and to eternal salvation. For these reasons, desiring to demonstrate the great inclination we have always had to promote the honor of God by

[7] *Ibid.*, pp. 13, 10, and 11.

the proclamation of the holy Gospel, and desiring also to provide
that the inhabitants of the United Netherlands should benefit not
only from their previous shipping and commerce but also, so far as
possible, from an increase in that welfare and trade, . . . we have
resolved that the shipping, commerce and trade in the West Indies,
Africa and the southern part of the world shall hereafter be prose-
cuted only by the unified strength of the Dutch citizenry, and to this
end there shall be created a general Company.[8]

It is important for understanding the nature of the Dutch West
India Company to note that the patent or *octroy* upon which the
Company was finally founded in June 1621 deviated radically
from Usselincx's proposal exactly at the point of the role of religion. The 1621 charter did not even mention religion.[9] Nevertheless, the prominence of Usselincx in the total picture of Dutch
thinking about colonies means that Dutch motives were mixed
too, though mercantilism finally dominated.

Generally speaking, then, a mixture of religious and economic
motivations characterized both the English and the Dutch colonial enterprises. And yet, when one begins to be specific about
New England and New Netherland, striking differences emerge.
Bernard Bailyn, in *New England Merchants in the Seventeenth
Century,* demonstrates the presence in Massachusetts of a real
mercantile mentality at a surprisingly early date. By the mid-
1630's there were in Boston men like Robert Keayne who "start-
ing as a Butcher's son in Windsor . . . had risen through ap-
prenticeship in London to prominence as a merchant tailor."[10]

---

[8] Appendix 2 in O. van Rees, *Geschiedenis der Staathuishoudkunde in
Nederland tot het Einde der Achttiende Eeuw* (Utrecht: Kemink, 1865),
2, 384–385 [my translation].

[9] The West India Company charter is published in full in Johannes de
Laet, *Jaerlyck Verhael van de Verrichtingen der Geoctroyeerde West-
Indische Compagnie,* ed. by S. P. l'Honoré Naber and J. C. M. Warnsinck,
4 vols. (The Hague: Nijhoff, 1937), 1, 6–31.

[10] Bailyn, *The New England Merchants in the Seventeenth Century*
(New York: Harper and Row, 1964), p. 41. Several excellent recent
monographs such as Sumner Chilton Powell, *Puritan Village* (Garden
City, N.Y.: Doubleday Anchor, 1965), and Darrett B. Rutman, *Winthrop's Boston* (Williamsburg, Va.: University of North Carolina Press,

That Keayne and other men like him were present in the New England picture so early raises some interesting questions about the "purity" of the great Puritan experiment. And the friction between these early New England merchants and the civil and ecclesiastical authorities of the colony indicates an awareness on the part of important Puritans themselves that the strongly commercial interests of these men were somehow incompatible with the prodigious effort of the Puritan community to erect the pure Church of God on earth. In 1639 the Massachusetts General Court indicted and convicted Keayne for usurious business practices, "taking above six-pence in the shilling profit; in some above eight-pence; and in some small things, above two for one."[11] Keayne was fined 100 pounds, and the church then added its punishment to the civil one. In Keayne's own words, the elders instituted an "exquisite search" of his business practices, the outcome of which was public rebuke "in the name of the Church for selling his wares at excessive Rates, to the Dishonor of Gods name, the Offence of the General Cort, and the Publique scandall of the Cuntry."[12] The first Puritan generation was not very sympathetic to Keayne and what he represented. John Winthrop writes that "the cry of the country was . . . great against oppression, and some of the elders and magistrates had declared . . . detestation of the corrupt practice of this man (which was the more observable, because he was wealthy and sold dearer than most other tradesmen, and for that he was of ill report for the like covetous practice in England, that incensed the deputies very much against him)."[13]

1965), have offered unimpeachable evidence that self-aggrandizement was present in an intense form in Sudbury and Boston at a very early date. This evidence does not, however; vitiate the argument that the original *intention* for New England (spokesmen: Winthrop, Bradford, et al.) was religious—was "a city upon a hill."

[11] John Winthrop, *History of New England,* ed. by J. K. Hosmer, 2 vols. (New York: Scribner's, 1908), 1, 315.

[12] "The Last Will of Robert Keayne," as cited in Bailyn, p. 42.

[13] 1, 315–316. The whole Keayne episode was extremely complex, with

Some of the later New England leaders were even more explicit in their disclaimers of trade as a motivation for the Puritan experiment. In his 1663 election-day sermon, *The Cause of God and His People in New England,* John Higginson reminded his congregation:

My fathers and Brethren, this is never to be forgotten, that New-England is originally a plantation of Religion, not a plantation of trade.

Let Merchants and such as are increasing Cent per Cent remember this. Let others that have come over since at several times understand this, that worldly gain was not the end and designe of the people of New England, but Religion. And if any man amongst us make Religion as twelve, and the world as thirteen, let such an one know he hath neither the spirit of a true New-England man nor yet of a sincere Christian.[14]

Increase Mather put it this way in his *Necessity of Reformation* of 1679: "It was in respect to some worldly accommodation that other Plantations were erected, but Religion and not the World was that which our Fathers came hither for. . . . Pure Worship and Ordinances without the mixture of humane Inventions was that which the first Fathers of this Colony designed in their coming hither. We are the Children of the good old Non-Conformists. . . . And therefore that woful neglect of the Rising Generation which hath bin amongst us, is a sad sign that we have in great part forgotten our Errand in this Wilderness."[15]

Both Higginson and Mather, of course, were delivering jeremiads against the corrupt and wicked ways of a later Puritan generation. The very fact that New England in 1663 and 1679 needed to be reminded that its main rationale was religious is

---

many doubts and agonies on both sides. Much later in his life Keayne constructed a lengthy and tortured apologia in which he attempted to demonstrate that the profits he had taken were not inconsistent with a godly life. According to Keayne, Winthrop also had second thoughts about the action of the court and was inclined to think that the punishment had been too harsh.

[14] Quoted in Bailyn, p. 140.
[15] Quoted in Bailyn, pp. 140–141.

evidence that that rationale had become at least slightly obscured. Higginson and Mather can scarcely be taken prima facie as indications of New England's spirituality. What their words do indicate, however, is the essential spirituality of the Puritan intention. In a time of "woful neglect" on the part of the "Rising Generation," in a time of ideological uncertainty, the conceptual foundation of the colony was re-examined by these men and found to have been religious in character—"We are the Children of the good old Non-Conformists."

As time went on, trade and commerce came gradually to displace religion at the center of New England life. Bailyn carefully chronicles the metamorphosis. In the beginning, however, religion was the center. Perry Miller writes of Virginia—and the statement applies *a fortiori* to New England—that the early colony represented "not a mercantile investment but a medieval pilgrimage."[16]

This was precisely where the Dutch colony of New Netherland differed from its English sister colonies; the Puritan intention for New England was religion, the Dutch intention for New Netherland was trade. Thomas Condon argues convincingly on behalf of "the commercial origins of New Netherland." Depending upon the Dutch archival researches of Simon Hart, Condon shows that Dutch ships were trading and privateering in Newfoundland by 1600, and were carrying on a vigorous and sometimes illicit fur trade in New France by 1605. All this, of course, occurred before Henry Hudson's "discovery" voyage in 1609 for the Dutch East India Company.[17]

[16] *Errand into the Wilderness* (New York: Harper and Row, 1964), p. 101.

[17] In his epilogue, Condon concludes that "the West India Company initially undertook settlement of New Netherland not with any grand design in mind to transplant a truly Dutch society there, but in an attempt to make its investment in New Netherland pay off" (p. 179). Simon Hart, *The Prehistory of the New Netherland Company* (Amsterdam: City of Amsterdam Press, 1959). For the story of Dutch trade in Newfoundland and New France, see Condon, p. 7.

After Hudson's voyage, the Dutch presence gradually increased in that area of North America later to be designated as "New Netherland" and later still as "New York." Three Amsterdam merchants banded together and sent a ship to the Hudson River area for fur trading each year from 1611 to 1613. This "company," known as the van Tweenhuysen Company from its leading financial supporter Lambert van Tweenhuysen, was soon joined in the Hudson fur trade by several other mercantile companies, underwritten for the most part by Amsterdam capital. The Hans Claeszoon Company, the Witsen Company, and the Brouwer Company were three of these, the latter being financed by merchants in the city of Hoorn. The competition resulting from this sudden appearance of a number of trading companies, all interested in Hudson River beaver pelts, had a deleterious effect on the trade. Purchase price in North America went up, while sale price on the Amsterdam Bourse tended to drop as the market became glutted. Wise business minds in the Netherlands realized that only some kind of monopoly could ultimately save the Hudson fur trade. Consequently on October 11, 1614, the principal merchants of the previously mentioned companies joined to form the New Netherland Company, and were granted by the States-General a patent of monopoly on the New Netherland trade for three years beginning January 1, 1615. After the expiration of this charter, December 31, 1617, the New Netherland Company was unable to obtain a renewal from the States-General, with the result that the New Netherland fur trade became again less profitable—once more due to extensive competition.[18]

All this time, sentiment had gradually been building in the Netherlands for the formation of a mercantile-military vehicle which would enable the Dutch, should the truce end in 1621 as

---

[18] Condon, pp. 13–14, 19–20, 23. For another discussion of the *voorcompagnieën* (fur-trading companies), see Van Cleaf Bachman, *Peltries or Plantations: The Economic Policies of the Dutch West India Company in New Netherland, 1623–1639* (Baltimore: Johns Hopkins Press, 1969), pp. 3–24.

seemed likely, greatly to "annoy the king of Spayne" (in Humphrey Gilbert's words).[19] The truce did end, and on June 3, 1621, the Incorporated West India Company came into being. As Condon points out, the idea of a West India Company which would hold a Dutch trade monopoly over the entire western hemisphere had diverse roots.[20] The company charter, as it was drawn up in 1621, expressed this diversity of thinking, and it is therefore somewhat misleading to characterize the West India Company primarily as a military and political venture.[21] The company was equally interested in trade and in offensive military strategy. The charter provided that two sets of books should be kept—"one relating to trade and one relating to war, each separate."[22]

After 1621, then, the fate of New Netherland lay in the hands of this gigantic Dutch West India Company (W.I.C.), whose assets in 1626 totaled twelve and one-half million guilders plus a fleet of eighty ships. New Netherland was by no means the center of the W.I.C.'s attention, but on the other hand the W.I.C. directors had no intention of dropping the Dutch claim to this North American territory.[23] The W.I.C.'s attitude toward New Netherland remained essentially what the attitude of the early Dutch merchants there had been: "The Amsterdam merchants

[19] Four very good discussions of the historical conditions leading to the establishment of the W.I.C. in 1621 are W. R. Menkman, *De West-Indische Compagnie* (Amsterdam: Van Kampen, 1947), pp. 1–41; van Rees, 2, 72–143; J. Franklin Jameson, "Willem Usselincx," *American Historical Association Papers,* vol. 2, no. 3 (1887); and Bachman, pp. 3–43.

[20] Pp. 37–61.

[21] This has been attempted; see, for example, Boxer, pp. 24–25, 48–50.

[22] A. J. F. van Laer, ed. and trans., *New York State Library Van Rensselaer Bowier Manuscripts* (Albany, 1908), p. 99. Cited in Condon, p. 58.

[23] W. J. van Hoboken, "De West-Indische Compagnie en de Vrede van Münster," *Tijdschrift voor Geschiedenis,* vol. 70 (Groningen: Noordhoff, 1957), argues very convincingly that Brazil was the area upon which the W.I.C. staked all its long-range financial hopes.

engaged in the [New Netherland fur] trade were primarily interested in furs and profits. And they never lost sight of these objectives whether operating in New Netherland or maneuvering at home."[24] Turning a profit was the basic aim; the idea of establishing an outpost of Dutch society in North America was never first in the minds of the directors of the W.I.C. Only as it became clear that New Netherland could not be profitably maintained apart from the undertaking of permanent colonization did the W.I.C. embark upon such a project. Still in search of profit from its investment, the W.I.C., beginning in 1629 with the "patroonship" idea, launched a series of experiments to attract immigrants to New Netherland, not, however, with any marked success. Indeed, the inability of the company to populate the region densely was one of the chief reasons for its fall to the English in 1664.

What, then, did this emphasis on commercialism mean for the religious development of New Netherland? For one thing, it meant that although there were Dutch fur traders scattered throughout the territory beginning in 1611, and settlers from 1624, it was not until 1628 that the first Reformed *predikant* (preacher) arrived. And even after the Reformed Church—the established church in the homeland—came to the colony, it had great difficulty attaining the central position in the colony's social, intellectual, and moral life. Interestingly, as late as 1642 a Dutch visitor in New Amsterdam was upbraiding the Director-General about the shoddiness of the church building in the settlement. This, the visitor argued, was certain to appear particularly scandalous to the English passing through, for "the first thing which the English in New England built, after their dwellings, was a fine church, and we ought to do so too."[25]

[24] Condon, p. 37.

[25] J. F. Jameson, ed., *Narratives of New Netherland* (New York: Scribner's, 1909), p. 212. The visitor was David Pieterszoon de Vries, a merchant-sailor born in Rochelle, France, who lived most of his life in North Holland. He became a patroon in New Netherland in 1630, and

Most important, however, New Netherland's commercial character gave birth, very early, to a situation of religious pluralism and the accompanying de facto toleration of a wide variety of religious viewpoints. Already in 1643 a Jesuit priest visiting at New Amsterdam observed, "No religion is publicly exercised but the Calvinist, and orders are to admit none but Calvinists, but this is not observed; for besides the Calvinists there are in the colony Catholics, English Puritans, Lutherans, Anabaptists, here called Mnistes, etc."[26] The growing desire of the Dutch W.I.C. to populate the province added Jews and Quakers to this religious mélange. The Reformed *predikanten* themselves, in 1655, admitted the presence in New Netherland of "Papists, Mennonites and Lutherans among the Dutch" as well as "many Puritans or Independents, and many atheists and various other servants of Baal among the English."[27]

Historians have long recognized that the rise in the seventeenth century of religious toleration and even religious liberty in the so-called Middle Colonies (Maryland, New York, and Pennsylvania) exerted a decisive influence on the history of church-state relations in America. In his definitive study of those relations, Anson Phelps Stokes gives a broad overview of "the three-fold colonial tradition."[28] Church-state relations developed in

---

spent from 1632 to 1644 in and around the colony. He was extremely critical of some policies of the W.I.C., and especially of Director Kieft. His notes were recorded as the *Korte Historiael, ende Journaels Aenteyckeninge van Verscheyden Voyagiens in de vier deelen des Wereldts-Ronde, als Europa, Africa, Asia, ende Amerika gedaen.* It was first published in Alkmaar in 1655.

[26] *Ibid.,* p. 260. The priest was Isaac Jogues, a Frenchman born at Orleans in 1607. A professor of theology for five years at Rouen, he entered the mission field in New France (Quebec) in 1636. In 1642 he was captured and tortured by the Iroquois, from whom he was rescued by the Dutch *predikant* Johannes Megapolensis at Rensselaerswijck. From Rensselaerswijck he journeyed down the Hudson to New Amsterdam, whence he departed for France.

[27] *Ibid.,* p. 392.

[28] *Church and State in the United States: Historical Development and*

American colonial times along "three independent though parallel lines: in Puritan New England, in Anglican Virginia and other Southern colonies, and in the . . . middle . . . provinces." In New England there developed, generally speaking, a theocratic Church-State which "expected the State to support public worship and suppress heresy." In Anglican Virginia there developed—again speaking generally—a State-Church along the same lines as in New England, but with one significant difference: "In Virginia the State controlled the Church; in Massachusetts the Church tended to control the State." In the Middle Colonies, however, "a practical type of liberalism prevailed in welcoming newcomers of various types." William Marnell, in a more recent book, re-emphasizes the importance of this tertium quid, the Middle Colonies.[29] Even granting the full impact of later eighteenth-century Enlightenment thinking, it is questionable whether the antithetical concepts of Church-State and State-Church represented by New England and Virginia could have been peacefully reconciled into a single nation without the moderating influence of the Middle Colony tradition of religious toleration and liberty. It did, after all, require a civil war to accomplish this in England.

What place has been given to New Netherland—later New York—within this broader rubric of Middle Colonies? Comparatively speaking, a small one. The reason does not seem to be difficult to find. For although New Netherland did achieve a practical type of religious pluralism and de facto toleration at a very early date, no Dutch name stands out boldly as a champion of that achievement. New Netherland boasted no Cecil Calvert, no William Penn, no Roger Williams. Religious pluralism and de facto toleration were in germ a Dutch importation. They were by-products of two things distinctively Dutch—the religious strug-

Contemporary Problems of Religious Freedom under the Constitution, 3 vols. (New York: Harper, 1950), 1, 151–171.

[29] *The First Amendment: The History of Religious Freedom in America* (Garden City, N.Y.: Doubleday, 1964), pp. 84–85.

gles of the Low Countries during the Eighty Years' War against Spain and the essentially commercial character of the Dutch colonial empire, Amsterdam, and the Netherlands itself.

In succeeding chapters, I will first discuss the nature of religious pluralism in the Netherlands during the late sixteenth and early seventeenth centuries and then trace the transport of this pattern of pluralism to New Netherland. It is necessary first to consider briefly two major attempts which previously have been made to chronicle New Netherland's religious history. One was written in Dutch and has never become available in English translation, and the other advances some ideas about the religious situation in New Netherland that I intend to debate.

Both books belong to the second decade of the twentieth century. The first, Albert Eekhof's *De Hervormde Kerk in Noord-Amerika,* *(1624–1664)*,[30] is a two-volume treatment of New Netherland's church history based on extensive archival research on both sides of the Atlantic. Eekhof, a professor of church history at the University of Leiden, was an extremely meticulous craftsman, and it is truly unfortunate that this comprehensive work has never been translated. The first volume opens with a description of his archival research and a catalog of materials available in each archive. This catalog is now very outdated, especially where Amsterdam materials are concerned, for almost all Amsterdam archival material from the seventeenth century has now been moved to one central location at the *Gemeente Archief*. The remainder of volume one is a more or less chronological treatment of the Reformed Church in New Netherland from the arrival of the *krankenbezoeker* (visitor of the sick) Bastiaen Janszoon Krol in 1624 until the surrender of the colony to the English in 1664. Special attention is given to the ministries of Jonas Michaëlius, Everardus Bogardus, Johannes Megapolensis, and Samuel Drisius, and the more important congregations in the colony—New Amsterdam, Rensselaerswijck, Esopus,

---

[30] (The Hague: Nijhoff, 1913).

New Amstel, and those on Long Island—all have their own chapters.

In the second volume Eekhof deserts his chronological schema and deals topically with the response of the Reformed Church to the challenges raised by Lutherans, Roman Catholics, Jews, Quakers, and other kinds of dissenters in the colony. There are also final chapters treating moral life in New Netherland and the effect of the English conquest on the Reformed Church. It is in this second volume that Eekhof's work makes its best contribution, and I have depended on it rather heavily at some points. For example, in his discussion of the Lutheran attempt to destroy the Reformed establishment in New Netherland, Eekhof makes very plain the ambiguous and sometimes downright devious role played by the W.I.C.

Beyond the obvious fact that the book is in Dutch, its major shortcoming for American readers is that it was written for a Dutch audience; Eekhof has assumed that most of his readers will understand that almost all the important decisions about New Netherland were made in Europe, not in America, and thus most of his narrative concerns New Netherland itself. This is, I think, a false assumption to incorporate into an American book for an American audience, still unaccustomed to seeing its own history as that of Europeans in America; I have tried to avoid making that assumption.

The second book, Frederick Zwierlein's *Religion in New Netherland,* cannot be so quickly reviewed, although it is inferior to Eekhof's as a piece of historiographical craftsmanship. It is a curious book because, although the author states in his preface that he will "present the results of his work in a positive and not in a polemic light," the entire work is posed in a polemical, not to say belligerent, mood. Zwierlein's thesis is that "there was . . . in all New Netherland, except the South River territory, an absolute prohibition of nonconforming religions outside of the Reformed family."[31] Thus formulated, his appraisal of the religious

31 *Religion in New Netherland: A History of the Development of the*

situation in New Netherland diverges basically from my interpretation. Was New Netherland, as Zwierlein argues, primarily a Reformed community from which other religious confessions were systematically excluded, or was it first and foremost a commercial enterprise to which the Reformed faith was appended as a godly afterthought?

Although Zwierlein's disclaimer of polemic is explicit, his book is in fact a refutation of earlier historical writing that had tended grossly to exaggerate the extent of religious toleration in New Netherland. He refers obliquely in the preface to "much error in many publications dealing with the beginnings of the State of New York." Eight years after the appearance of *Religion in New Netherland*, Zwierlein contributed an angry article to the *Catholic Historical Review* in which he cites a good example of the "error."[32] In 1915 the University of the State of New York had published a bulletin to the schools in which a certain Dr. Williams presented some ideas about religion in New Netherland "for the benefit of the teachers and children of the State." This is part of what Williams said: "New York was the only colony in which perfect religious liberty was to be had. . . . The New England Puritans came to this country to seek religious liberty for themselves, but not to allow it to others. The Dutch in New York granted it to everyone. They had it at home."[33] Williams's statement, Zwierlein argues, contained "more historical errors than there are sentences."

Zwierlein sets out to demonstrate, both in his book and in his later article, that "perfect religious liberty" was not to be had in New Netherland and that the Dutch did not grant it to everyone, because they had not "had it at home." To a very large extent Zwierlein was justified in exploding the myth of "popular liberty,"

Religious Conditions in the Province of New Netherland, 1623–1664 (Rochester, N.Y.: John P. Smith, 1910), pp. vi and 5.

[32] *Ibid.*, p. vi; Zwierlein, "New Netherland Intolerance," *Catholic Historical Review*, 4, no. 2 (1918), 186–216.

[33] Quoted in Zwierlein, "New Netherland Intolerance," p. 187.

created by nineteenth-century historians, that New Netherland was an island of toleration and freedom in a sea of Puritan and Catholic bigotry.[34] In the early seventeenth century things had simply not yet come that far. The explicit elaboration of the principal of religious liberty lay far ahead at the end of the eighteenth century, and only a few radical visionaries (e.g., Roger Williams, William of Orange, Dirck Coornhert) had yet glimpsed its potential. For the most part the medieval notion of an organic relationship between the state and the "state religion" was still assumed to be valid. According to this theory, religious heresy was regarded as political subversion, and the state had as much right to defend its religious integrity as its territorial boundaries. Early seventeenth-century Dutchmen thought these thoughts just as did their European contemporaries, Catholic or Protestant.

Once Zwierlein established his course, however, he pursued it with such single-minded determination that his book in turn became a caricature rather than an accurate description of religious conditions in New Netherland. In his great zeal to show the Dutch as they were—children of their time—he neglects to point out several features already present in seventeenth-century Dutch society that indicated the possibility and even probability of a new order. Thus, for example, Zwierlein emphasizes that "the Director-General Stuyvesant was under oath to maintain exclusively the Reformed worship,"[35] while he takes no special notice of the fact that in 1654 the Dutch West India Company itself welcomed entrance of twenty-three Jews to New Netherland. Both facts are true, but Zwierlein puts the emphasis in the wrong place. That Stuyvesant was sworn to uphold religious uniformity in the territory he governed was in that age not remarkable, but it was quite remarkable indeed that the financial underwriters of the colony should themselves sanction the arrival of a group of religious deviants. Viewed from the twentieth century, it is Stuyvesant's posi-

---

[34] See Condon, p. 37, for a discussion of these historians of "liberty and democracy."

[35] *Religion in New Netherland,* p. 5.

tion that appears unusual, but in seventeenth-century context it was the W.I.C. directors who were behaving peculiarly.[36]

This issue of the nature of religion and religious pluralism in New Netherland was handled both by Zwierlein and by those he was refuting in a simplistic manner, but the issue itself is extremely complex. New Netherland's religious history is neither the history of "tolerance" nor the history of "intolerance." It is both. When it comes to the matter of religion in New Netherland, the Dutch colony has a choice of pasts.

This is so because Dutch religious history itself was so exceedingly complex during this period of political, social, and economic revolution and religious reformation. Zwierlein recognized the necessity of understanding the religious situation in the homeland before attempting to understand any of its colonies, and he even devotes his first chapter to "the Dutch background."[37] But it is here that he fails to understand the true nature of the Dutch situation. Overwhelmed by the volume of civil and ecclesiastical legislation against religious dissent he discovered in Dutch archives, Zwierlein points out that not only had the great Synod of Dordrecht condemned the heretics in 1619 but that thirty years later the States-General of the United Provinces was reiterating the Synod's opinions. Although the States-General in 1651 refused to take the drastic measures demanded by Reformed *predikanten* against "popish idolatry, superstition and hierarchy, against the innumerable Jesuits, priests, curates and monks overrunning the land in thousands like locusts," nevertheless they did call for the retention of ordinances against Catholic worship and

---

[36] A third book, of relatively recent appearance, should also be mentioned here: John Webb Pratt, *Religion, Politics, and Diversity: The Church-State Theme in New York History* (Ithaca, N.Y.: Cornell University Press, 1967). Pratt devotes only his first chapter to New Netherland, but his contention (p. 24) that "Dutch New Netherland permitted a latitude in religion much broader than was the case in many other early American colonies" is very close to what I hope to demonstrate.

[37] "New Netherland Intolerance," p. 186; *Religion in New Netherland*, pp. 9–35.

the allowance of other sects "in all good order and quiet."[38] Is this not, asks Zwierlein, sufficient evidence of the consistent Dutch policy of repression of religious groups outside the Reformed family? Once again the facts are correct, but his interpretation is questionable. The most interesting feature of the States-General's deliberation in 1651 is not its reiteration of the legal ordinances against Catholics, but the apparent necessity the Reformed *predikanten* felt to petition that body to enforce the ordinances. The Catholics were expressly forbidden by law to worship, yet their priests swarmed through the land like locusts.

Zwierlein's view of New Netherland's religious situation as that of a consistently establishmentarian Reformed community is a caricature, because it is based upon a simplified notion of the seventeenth-century Dutch religious situation. As one reviewer commented in 1911: "Exception must be taken . . . to the first chapter, in which the author, in an effort to show that the policy of the colonial authorities to foster the Dutch Reformed religion and to repress all organized dissent was in line with the oppressive measures against Catholics and Arminians in the Dutch Republic, draws a picture of Religious persecution which is hardly in accordance with the facts."[39] Zwierlein failed to understand that the religious situation, both in the Netherlands and in New Netherland, was dependent on more than one factor. It is true that the religious climate in the Netherlands was partially determined by the doctrinal opinions of the Reformed clergy, but it was also influenced by the political and economic necessities of a small, new nation whose only livelihood, in the final analysis, was trade.

[38] *Religion in New Netherland,* pp. 33–34.
[39] *American Historical Review,* 17, no. 1 (1911), 192.

PART I

The Netherlands:
The Church's Point of View

2. Church and State in Calvin's Theology

Although the United Provinces officially became a Protestant nation only on July 22, 1581, the winds of religious reform by that time had been blowing in the Low Countries for over a century. And they had been varied winds. As early as 1477 a Dutch vernacular Bible had been printed at Delft, and pamphlet literature against indulgences may have been in circulation there well before All Saints' Day, 1517. The people of the Low Countries had been heavily influenced by the itinerant preaching of Gerhard Groote and his Brethren of the Common Life. By the time of Aleander's visit to Louvain in 1521 enroute to the Diet of Worms the papal nuncio was able to burn eighty heretical books, many of them Lutheran. And in the fall of the same year, on the basis of a proclamation made by Charles V to his subjects in the Netherlands, four hundred Lutheran books were burned in Antwerp—three hundred of which were confiscated from the booksellers' stalls in the public market.[1] The large numbers of north German grain and lumber merchants who were living in the trade towns of Amsterdam and Antwerp provided an active channel through which Lutheran influence reached the Netherlands. In 1525 four Amsterdam women, banned by the municipal government because of a riotous display of their Catholic sympathies, declared in Antwerp that "in Amsterdam there was

[1] T. M. Lindsay, *A History of the Reformation* (Edinburgh: T. and T. Clark, 1908), 2, 228, 229.

much Luther-ism, especially in the sacrament of the altar."[2]

Lutheranism was not, however, the only current of reform swirling through the Netherlands during the turbulent sixteenth century. Especially among the urban regent families, well-to-do and well educated, the ideals of humanistic reform preached by Erasmus of Rotterdam had made a deep and lasting impression. The town magistrates, inclined to be moderate, tolerant, and above all convinced and even jealous of the role the civil magistracy must play in the regulation of public religious life, were in some respects a much more formidable barrier to the realization of militant Calvinist hopes in the Netherlands than any Spanish army.

There were also the Anabaptists. The city magistracy of Amsterdam responded to an outbreak of Anabaptist disturbances in 1535 by publicly cutting out the hearts of a number of the offenders.[3] And in the same year an edict from Charles's imperial court made Anabaptist propagandizing punishable by death at the stake, while anyone having submitted himself to rebaptism would be favored with death by the sword—if he recanted.[4] Nevertheless, the Anabaptists not only maintained themselves but multiplied in the Netherlands. One contemporary source, for instance, estimated the Anabaptist strength in the province of Friesland in 1581 at one quarter of the entire population![5]

[2] R. B. Evenhuis, *Ook Dat Was Amsterdam,* 2 vols. (Amsterdam: ten Have, 1965), 1, 28. See also J. F. M. Sterck, *De Heilige Stede in de Geschiedenis van Amsterdam* (Amsterdam, 1928), p. 98. Sterck goes so far as to argue that a majority of the town council which banned the women was favorable to Lutheran teachings, undoubtedly an overstatement.

[3] Evenhuis, p. 46, and picture facing p. 48.

[4] G. Brandt, *Historie der Reformatie, en Andere Kerkelyke Geschiedenissen, in en ontrent de Nederlanden* (2nd printing, Amsterdam, 1677), 1, 123–124.

[5] E. van Reyd, *Historie der Nederlantsche Oorlogen Begin ende Voortganck* (1628), p. 70. Cited in H. A. E. van Gelder, *Vrijheid en Onvrijheid in de Republiek* (Haarlem, 1947), p. 150. A large portion of the populations of the Dutch towns of Monnikendam, Deventer, Zwolle, and Kampen was of Anabaptist sympathy as early as 1534. See Lindsay, 2, 234–240.

The future of the Dutch Reformation, however, lay with none of these three currents, but with a fourth—that emanating from Geneva. When Den Briel fell to William of Orange's victorious *geuzen* (beggars) on April 1, 1572, it was not the followers of Luther or of Erasmus or of Menno, but those of John Calvin who stood ready to move in and consolidate the military victory into a permanent gain for the Protestant cause. It was no accident that Den Briel and the other Holland and Zealand towns that fell to William's raggedy recruits shortly thereafter were quickly organized along the ecclesiastical lines of Geneva. The coup had been carefully planned at least four years in advance by the large number of Dutch Protestant zealots who had fled the homeland to escape the carnage wrought by Alva's inquisition. By 1570 the cities to the south and east of the Low Countries (Aachen, Cologne, Wesel, Emden) were swarming with exiled Dutch protestants. On March 21, 1570, the leaders of the diaspora, Caspar van der Heyden and Philip van Marnix van St. Aldegonde, wrote of the necessity of unity: "so that if God opens the land to us tomorrow or the day after (as he undoubtedly will if we remain true to him and thankful), the building-up of His churches will not suffer from lack of ministers . . . and so that we may fend off the wrath of God and prepare the way for our return to the fatherland, where the Word of God and the Kingdom of Jesus Christ will enjoy a speedy growth."[6] They agreed to work in conjunction with the Prince of Orange, then in exile on his German estates, in whose hands the military and political details of reconquest could safely be laid. The brethren of the small Synod of Bedtbur, for example, stated on July 4, 1571, that they had decided "unanimously concerning the call to his Princely Grace and the righteousness of war and weapons, etc."[7]

---

[6] J. van Toorenenbergen, *Marnix' Godsdienstige en Kerkelijke Geschriften*, 3, 8–9. Quoted in van Gelder, p. 64 [translation mine].

[7] H. Q. Jansen and J. J. van Toorenenbergen, eds., *Acten van Classicale en Synodale Vergaderingen der Verstrooide Gemeenten in het Land van*

The theology supporting this Protestant ecclesiastical underground came neither from Wittenberg nor Zurich but from Geneva. Many of the Dutch exiles had studied there and had become convinced not only of the profound correctness of the *ware religie* (true religion) as it was preached there but also of its practical value as a means for achieving the long-desired religious reform in the fatherland. Calvinism's tightly knit ecclesiastical structure of consistory, classis, and synod afforded a functional independence from the political power (and thus a freedom to work against a possibly hostile government) which neither Luther's nor Zwingli's doctrine of the church provided.[8] The ecclesiastical structure of Calvinism enabled the Dutch exiles to play well the role in which they found themselves cast—that of a "church under the cross."

Thus, in order to understand the ideals of the Calvinist *predikanten* for Dutch society, it is necessary to determine the outlines of Calvin's own ecclesiology. Calvin's ideals for church-state relations were never fully implemented even in Geneva; yet, as H. G. Koenigsberger points out, it was these ideals that were learned by Dutch and French refugees and then carried back to their respective countries to provide revolutionary ferment.[9] And thus they did have an important life of their own.

It is often argued that Calvin's theology established ideals for the relationship between church and civil authority that can be called "theocratic," in the sense that all worldly governments (whether monarchies, republics, or whatever) are viewed as no more and no less than instruments of the will of God. By casting the issue in such broad terms, however, one loses sight of the

Cleef, Sticht van Keulen en Aken, 1571–1589 (Utrecht: Kemink, 1882), p. 5 [translation mine].

[8] Lindsay, 2, 271.

[9] H. G. Koenigsberger, "The Organization of Revolutionary Parties in France and the Netherlands during the Sixteenth Century," *The Journal of Modern History,* vol. 27, no. 4 (December, 1955), pp. 335–351, reprinted in *Estates and Revolutions* (Ithaca. N.Y.: Cornell University Press, 1971), pp. 224–252.

distinctive characteristics of Calvin's theocratic ideal; for the view
that God is the world's ultimate ruler and that the worldly powers only serve His ends is not exclusively Calvin's but generally
Biblical and Christian. It is common to most of the medieval
Christian thought systems.[10]

To say, then, that the Dutch reformers after about 1572, since
they were heavily influenced by Geneva and Calvin, were nursing "theocratic" ideals for the Low Countries merely states the
problem rather than solving it. What was Calvin's concept of
the ideal relationship between the Christian church and civil
authority? This question implies two others: What was Calvin's
doctrine of the state, and What was his doctrine of the church?

Calvin rejects the Aristotelian notion that the essence of the
state is independent of the existence of its subjects and that the
state therefore has its own ends apart from those of its individual
members. He rejects equally emphatically the medieval concept
of the state as the *corpus mysticum*.[11] This Pauline term he is
willing to apply only to the invisible church. Calvin is inclined
to give the individual a place of far greater importance in the
state than he is given by either classical or scholastic philosophy,
but Calvin is not modern, if one sees the modern theory of the
state as related to Kant's statement that the parts of an organism
"assembled together, having their form as well as their connection in common, bring about the whole through their own cau-
sality."[12] Calvin simply does not grant this much freedom and
independence to the individual.

Calvin's ideal state thus belongs neither to a tyrannical government nor to the free individual subject. He rejects both ex-

[10] Josef Bohatec, *Calvins Lehre von Staat und Kirche* (Breslau: Marcus,
1937), p. 176. My interpretation of Calvin's doctrine of church and state
is heavily indebted to this exhaustive work. Bohatec reviews, pp. 581–596,
the medieval views of church-state as expressed both by the "papal party"
(e.g., Gelasius I, Gregory VII, Boniface VIII, and St. Thomas) and the
"state party" (e.g., Occam, Dante).

[11] *Ibid.*, p. 9; Aquinas, *Summa Theol.*, II, quest. 81, art. 1.

[12] Bohatec, p. 10.

tremes. Rather, the government and its subjects are bound together in a relationship of reciprocity; and both are responsible to the legal order, which holds the relationship together and makes it function. This common bond to the law insures both that the government will rule kindly and wisely, not despotically, and that the subjects will obey willfully and gladly, not slavishly. The law thus becomes the bond of fellowship between men (*ius fraternae coniunctionis*)[13] and gives the organism of the state an ethical as well as a legal dimension.

Governor and governed are both bound to the law. But the law is God's creation, as are also the stations in the legal order (i.e., governor, governed). The ruler enjoys no special privileges because of his station, as the subjects suffer no oppressions or deprivations because of theirs. Both parties know only services pledged (via the law to the other party) and the counterbalancing mutual pledge (via the law from the other party).[14] This leads Calvin to exalt the oath as one of God's most noble creations. Through the oath all contracts and covenants receive their highest consecration. They become contracts and covenants with God himself, and if a party to an oath breaks the trust he also breaks his covenant with God, which is tantamount to a declaration of war on the Almighty.

With these basic principles in mind, Calvin opts for an aristocracy or a mixture of aristocracy and democracy, as the ideal form of government. This form of government is best able to

[13] Guilielmus Baum, Eduardus Cunitz, Eduardus Reuss, eds., *Joannis Calvini Opera Quae Supersunt Omnia*, 59 vols. (Braunschweig: C. A. Schwetschke, 1863–1900), 24, 731. Hereafter cited as *Opera*.

[14] *Sermons on Deuteronomy*, *Opera*, 28, 286. Calvin explains the concept of *mutua obligatio* with an example of a private law contract: "If one party wants to present the other with a gift, he does so under the condition that the other party, the receiver, feels himself mutually obligated; the receiver receives the gift, and for his part obligates himself with respect to the giver, and the parties make respectively the following promises: 'I renounce all my rights and place them in the hands of another'; 'I take this gift under the condition that I will do what is desired from me' " [my translation].

restrict and limit freedom in such a way that freedom can enjoy
a long life in the state. In the first place—to consider the matter
purely from the standpoint of the government—it is far easier
for a government consisting of many men to resist the temptation
to tyrannize than it is for a single man.[15] While the monarch can
only with great difficulty bend his personal will to the demands
of justice, the members of an aristocratic governing collegium
can support, reprimand, and teach each other. But also—con-
sidering the matter from the standpoint of the whole state—an
aristocratic-democratic form is preferable to a monarchy because
the subjects have some degree of freedom in selecting their government. Calvin's ideal here is the time of the Old Testament
judges. He sees the roots of the Israelite judges' office in Mosaic
times, when the people selected seventy of their oldest and most
venerable men to "bear the burdens" of state along with Moses
(Num. 11:16–17). The people exercised a kind of popular suffrage in selecting their governors, but the choice was firmly controlled by the quality of the candidates, who had to be "elders
of the people," i.e., men respected for their wisdom and judgment.

Calvin's ideal form of government, then, restricts the freedom
of both ruler and ruled, so that that freedom may be preserved.
He goes to some length to define the nature of this restricted
political freedom as distinguished from the unbounded spiritual
freedom of the Christian life. Together with Luther, he argues
that the spiritual freedom of the inner man must not be confused
with an anarchistic disregard for the bounds of the God-given

[15] *Institutes of the Christian Religion* (1559), *Opera*, 2, 1098: "I will
not for a minute deny that neither an aristocracy nor a modification of
aristocracy can be far excelled by all other political states" [my transla-
tion]. *Institutes of the Christian Religion* (1536), *Opera*, 1, 1105: "I
freely admit that there is no form of government finer than this, when
liberty is constructed with that moderation which is fitting and duly
established for long life" [my translation]. *Commentaries on the Psalms,
Opera*, 32, 57: "It is a rare virtue that he who is able to do all things is so
self-contained that he permits himself no license" [my translation].

political order.[16] Here he is of course taking particular aim at the oath-refusing Anabaptists, the spiritualizers, and the rest of Luther's *Schwärmer*. But in addition Calvin still agrees with Aristotle that absolute arbitrary freedom on the part of the ruler or the ruled leads necessarily to the destruction of all political order.[17] Actually, he argues, the apparent tension between man's spiritual freedom in Christ and his inequality in the political order is not real, because both—spiritual equality and political inequality—are created by God.[18] Furthermore, as we have already seen, those chosen to rule in the political order have in fact no position of special privilege; they are bound to the law just as are the ruled. Their position of pre-eminence involves an equally increased responsibility.

Who is this aristocracy that rules Calvin's ideal state? For Calvin popular suffrage is limited by the demand that the chosen be of fit quality to rule. What characteristics comprise fitness? Here Calvin is partially influenced by the Greek philosophical ideal of a ruler with spiritual, intellectual, and physical attributes of heroic proportions. But with Calvin the ideal is reworked, because heroism is measured not in terms of human esteem and natural law but in terms of obedience to God's sovereignty. Personal worth is not fixed by human reckoning and not gained by winning human approval; it is determined by divine decree and received as a divine gift from God.[19] Thus the true company of the faithful always forms a sort of aristocracy of the spirit; and conversely the true aristocracy is always composed of believers

[16] *Institutes of the Christian Religion* (1559), *Opera*, 2, 1093: "Spiritual liberty is very well able to stand with political servitude" [my translation].

[17] Bohatec, pp. 145–146.

[18] *Sermons on Deuteronomy, Opera,* 26, 322: "This does not at all come from the fact that the one is better than the other; but it is for this that God has willed that those to whom he has given some preeminence may be held in honor—God has established a varied order" [my translation].

[19] *Institutes of the Christian Religion* (1559), *Opera,* 2, 691 and 693.

who wear Christ's yoke and whose spirits are modeled after his in purity, innocence, and simplicity. Furthermore, God never leaves his nobility idle; He imposes upon them a holy imperative to let the glory of His majesty stream forth through all of life by employing their energy in good works.[20] It is thus the "Christian hero" who is to occupy the seat of government in Calvin's ideal state, and his reign is to be characterized by mighty works for the Lord. The precise character of these heroic works the Christian magistrate is to perform for God becomes clearer in light of the nature of Calvin's church and its place in the ideal society.

His true church is a mystical body, with Christ as its head and the elect as its members. The foundation of this church is beyond the church itself; it is the elective grace of God which first rescues the chosen from the spiritual darkness, then adopts them as children of God, and finally plants them into the mystical body of Christ where eventually they receive the gifts of salvation and eternal life.[21] All members of the elect share a loyalty to the head of the mystical body—Christ. Thus, the church possesses a total unity. But Calvin rejects the Roman sacramental view that the unity of the church is achieved through Christ's magical imparting of his own substance to the members of the body. Rather, Christ rules his people through the psychological power of his spirit, and it is by means of this spiritual power that he shares his life with the members of the mystical body.[22] This

[20] Calvin uses the expression "noblesse" in describing the elect. *Sermons on Deuteronomy, Opera,* 28, 677.

[21] *Institutes of the Christian Religion* (1536), *Opera,* 1, 72: "Thus all the elect of God are united in Christ and joined together, so that as they depend on one head so they coalesce as if into one body; clinging to one another in this manner, by which they are members of the same body" [my translation]. Concerning the three-stage "order" in God's mercy, see *Commentary on the Gospel of John, Opera,* 47, 379. See also Bohatec, pp. 268–269.

[22] *Commentary on the Gospel of John, Opera,* 47, 387: "that we are one with Christ, not because he pours into us his own substance, but because by virtue of his spirit he shares with us his life and whatever good things he has received from the father" [my translation].

spiritual power of Christ is made efficacious through the proclamation of the Word, and since the church is the place where the
Word is both preached and heard and Christ's rule is thus established, the church is nothing less than the kingdom of God.[23]
This means that the church has an eternal character. As God's
kingdom, it was before the world was and will be after the world
has ceased to be. It is subject to none of the laws of creatureli-
ness and mortality. The church furthermore bestows this immortal
nature on each of its members.[24]

This true church is invisible. Its membership cannot be counted
by men, and its mystical body is not a thing which can be said to
rest in a certain place or to occupy space. The essence, existence,
and unity of the true church are always, from the human perspective, subjects of faith. Nevertheless, only this invisible church
is the true church; in comparison, the church organized and labeled by men is a mere hollow shell which may or may not contain members of the true church.[25]

The invisible true church, however, is no intellectual abstrac-
tion. It is not a pure idea. There exists between the members of
the mystical body real "communion," and this communion is
expressed externally as "communication." The very essence of
election is submission to God's will as expressed in Christ, and
God's will is that the elect share out of brotherly love their freely
received spiritual and material gifts. Thus the invisible church
will necessarily be characterized by visible acts of brotherly love,
and a temporal, spatial community will appear as the expression
of the mystical, eternal body.[26] This temporal community will be

---

[23] Bohatec, p. 272.

[24] *Institutes of the Christian Religion* (1559), *Opera*, 2, 363: "Its
nature is spiritual, whence its power and eternity is derived. . . . This
must be established in two ways: for the one pertains to the whole body
of the church, and the other pertains to each member" [my translation].

[25] Bohatec (p. 276) argues that Calvin's concept concerning the invisi-
bility of the true church never changed, although after 1539 he tended increasingly to be interested in the external manifestations of the invisible
church.

[26] Bohatec, pp. 281–282.

composed of individuals with a wide variety of gifts and talents, but such diversity in no way damages the internal unity of the fellowship. Calvin argues, in fact, that the fellowship cannot survive without a manifold symmetry of members—a symmetry established by God. Therefore, the community of the external church is not necessarily characterized by an equality of members but by an active spirit of charity among members whose occupations, talents, and stations may vary widely. In one vital respect, however, this external expression of the true church can tolerate no variety, and that is in respect to doctrine. The community of the faithful is not only an ethical community but also a religious community, and as a religious community it unites in acknowledging one head, Jesus Christ. Thus the members of the true church, diverse as they may be with regard to wealth or social and political position, will always unite spiritually and doctrinally in acknowledging Christ as their head.[27]

Where, then, is this external expression of the true church to be sought and how is it to be identified? The members of the true church, Calvin says, are known to God alone. But the two congregations, the true and the visible, do not manifest themselves separately. Only God knows his true children, but, taking compassion on the limited powers of human understanding, He has ordained that we should view as His children all those who hold to God and Christ through confession of faith, example of life, and participation in the sacraments. Thus, wherever the Word of God is preached and heard and the sacraments practiced as Christ instituted them, there is the "face" (*facies*) of the invisible

---

[27] *Commentary on I Corinthians, Opera,* 49, 503: "It shows that God has not recklessly given varied gifts to the members, but inasmuch as it was necessary for the preservation of the body: for there would be confused and dissipated chaos if such symmetry were removed" [my translation]. *Commentary on the Paternal Admonition of Pope Paul III to Emperor Charles V* (1545), *Opera,* 7, 264: "If, however, there is indeed to be true unity of the church, it will be when there is sincere truth of Christ, when there is integral consensus both of doctrine and of spirit in Christ among all the faithful" [my translation].

true church. It is true that the Word and the Sacrament are in the first place signs of the visible church. But they point at the same time to the presence of the invisible true church within the external fellowship.[28]

Wherever a local congregation gathers to hear the Word preached the invisible church is truly present. This means that each individual congregation, though it may contain but one or two members of the true church, enjoys autonomy and authority in matters pertaining to doctrine. Such autonomy of the local congregation, however, does not impinge in any way on the unity of the church universal, and the individual congregations must be very careful not to force any of their peculiar local usages or customs on other congregations as general ecclesiastical law.[29]

Even more dangerous than the attempt of one local congregation to gain ascendancy over the church universal on points of ecclesiastical usage or custom is the attempt to cause unrest or schism in the local congregation. This must be avoided at all costs because where a congregation has gathered to hear the Word preached there is also the true invisible church of God. One who causes schism in the local congregation is therefore destroying the unity of God's true church, which is tantamount to a criminal act committed against God himself. This is the point which, after 1539, Calvin brings constantly to bear against the Anabaptists and other spiritual enthusiasts, whom he believes are spiritual descendants of the schismatic Donatists, Novatians, and Cathari.[30] In so doing, however, Calvin is drawn to focus more and

---

[28] *Institutes of the Christian Religion* (1559), *Opera*, 2, 753 and 759: "God willed that in this external society of his church the communion be celebrated . . . that in the great multitude there be many truly sacred and innocent before the eyes of God" [my translation].

[29] *Ibid.*, 2, 754: "Thus we preserve unity for the universal church . . . nor do we deprive of their own authority legitimate gatherings, which are distributed according to local convenience" [my translation]. *Commentary on Galatians, Opera*, 50, 164: "Such an evil is a most dreadful plague: when we wish that the custom of a single church prevail as a universal law" [my translation].

[30] *Apology to the Illustrious James of Burgundy, Opera*, 10, Part I,

more on the visible local congregation as God's true church and
the invisible church of the elect fades constantly more into the
background of his thought and writing.

What, then, was Calvin's concept of the ideal relationship between the Christian church and the civil authority? Calvin conceives of humanity as a single organism, that is, as a unity embracing diversity. In this, he is simply continuing in the tradition
of medieval thought before him. Thomas Aquinas says that to
belong to the human race is to participate in the one unified
body of humanity, which can be thought of as one man.[31] Christ,
as the head of the church, is the head of this body of humanity.
Thus for Aquinas the human race and the mystical body of the
church are indistinguishable. His thinking, however, represents
only one side of the great medieval argument concerning the relationship of ecclesiastical and civil powers; he speaks for the
papal party. The other side of the medieval debate also utilizes
the concept of humanity's organic unity, but employs it to a
different end. William of Occam, who is as representative of the
imperial party as Thomas Aquinas is of the papal, sees humanity
as composed not only of faithful Christians but also of infidels,
but he argues that insofar as all mortals renounce evil and live
together in good order they may be viewed as an organic unity.[32]
In Occam's view, however, the organism has two heads—one
worldly and one spiritual.

Calvin also conceives of humanity as an organism; all hu-

289: "All the pious ought to preserve the unity of the church . . . and it
is a capital crime before God if they destroy this unity and institute their
own sects" [my translation]. *Commentaries on the Psalms, Opera,* 31, 143.
Calvin, along with Luther, rejects the possibility of a fully realized per-
fection within the visible church, which the Donatists, Novatians, Cathari,
and Anabaptists so often proclaimed. The visible church, said the two
reformers, is always at best a mixture of the elect and the hypocrites.

[31] *Summa Theol.,* II, quest. 81, art. 1.

[32] William of Occam, *Dialogues,* II, book 1, chap. 1: "As all mortals,
not just the faithful but also the infidels, renouncing the devil through
faith and love ought to adhere firmly to Christ, so all, if living in good
order, ought to be one body" [my translation from Bohatec, p. 589].

manity shares the common nature bestowed by God upon man, whom he created in his own image. At an important point, however, Calvin parts company with his medieval predecessors. Humanity, he argues, is not identical with the universal church; it is not identical with Christendom. To the true invisible church belong only the elect, chosen by God's grace; to the visible worldly church belong only those who confess God and Christ, who turn to faith in the son of God through baptism, and who preserve this faith through partaking of the sacraments and listening to the proclamation of the Word. Therefore, there must be a clear distinction drawn between Christendom (*corps de l' église*) on the one hand and humanity (*tous hommes en général*) on the other. Humanity in its present fallen state consists of two basic groups: Christendom and the infidels. Eschatologically, God will reunite humanity into an organic whole under the single headship of Christ, but that time is not yet. Neither the ecclesiastical nor the civil authority thus may hope to unite humanity in a single organic whole under its direction.[33]

Nevertheless, despite this fragmented situation God rules the whole world and not just that segment of faithful humanity called Christendom. Therefore he employs both the ecclesiastical and the civil regiments to carry out his rule. Through the church he cares for man's spiritual salvation; through the civil order he cares for his worldly welfare. Since God employs both orders in this complementary fashion, there must be between the two the closest imaginable connection and association. Ideally, this bond will be so tight that if either order is disrupted the other also suffers.[34] In practical terms this means that the church may be subjected to the state in some matters—and conversely in other

[33] *Sermons on Ephesians, Opera,* 51, 765ff.: "God has created us in such a way that we are like one mass. For just as there are many members and one human body, if there are many nerves that does not mean that all are not one" [my translation]. *Institutes of the Christian Religion* (1559), *Opera,* 2, 752ff. *Sermons on I Timothy, Opera,* 43, 135; quoted in Bohatec, p. 598.

[34] *Homily on I Samuel, Opera,* 29, 659; quoted in Bohatec, p. 612.

matters—without either order losing its independence and authority. But the rule of the church over the state in matters civil is a papist tyranny, while the rule of the state over the church in matters doctrinal is equally tyrannical. The ideal relationship between the civil and ecclesiastical powers is thus complementary and harmonious. From this idea there follow certain decisive characteristics of Calvinist theocracy.

First, the ruler will ideally use his power of the sword to defend the pure doctrine of the church and the glory of God from the threat of heresy.[35] Though most agreed with him, Calvin did face sharp criticism from certain of his contemporaries on this point. Castellio, in his plea for toleration issued after the burning of Servetus in Geneva, argued that this doctrine of Calvin's led the church backward into the time of the Inquisition. Calvin stood fast, however, for three reasons. First, the falsification of the pure doctrine is a violation of God's honor and glory, the greatest possible sin. Second, it endangers the salvation of men's souls by seducing them away from the eternal truth. Finally, even the heathen realize that a strong, unified religion is the key to maintaining a well-ordered state.[36] Thus, although Calvin is well aware that religious faith is neither originated nor perpetuated in the heart of man by armed force, he nevertheless argues that it is God's will that the faithful make use of his own ordained means (the state) to protect the purity of doctrine. The pure doctrine is threatened in different degrees from different sources. Those who have never heard the gospel proclaimed in its pure

[35] *Sermons on Deuteronomy, Opera,* 27, 247: "Our Lord wishes that the Princes and the Magistrates employ the power which has been given them to maintain his honor" [my translation].

[36] Bohatec, p. 621. This doctrine of Calvin's was to have enormous influence on the Reformed Church in the Netherlands. It was eloquently defended by Beza in 1554 in his tract "De Haereticis a Civile Magistratu Puniendis Libellus." This tract appeared in Dutch translation in Friesland in 1601, and its principles were echoed in pamphlets by Gomarus, Trigland, Grevinchoven, and Acronius, four of the more prominent Dutch Reformed *predikanten* of the time, as well as by countless anonymous pamphlet authors.

form constitute a relatively minor threat to the church and to the good order of society. Thus Jews, Turks, and Roman Catholics, being people who have never heard or confessed the pure doctrine, need not be actively persecuted by the state, though of course they may not be allowed the public exercise of their false religions. In contrast, most dangerous to the true church and to the Christian state are the "apostates," those people who have heard and confessed the Word and subsequently broken away from it, frequently taking other human souls with them into perdition.[37] These schismatics must be squelched at every opportunity by the civil authority, for, asks Calvin, "How can a religion exist, by what signs is the Church to be differentiated from other societies, what finally will become of Christ himself if the true doctrine of piety remains hanging uncertainly in the air?"[38]

A second consequence of Calvin's idea that the ecclesiastical and civil powers are intricately related is that if confusion breaks out in one realm it is bound to affect the other. The civil ruler is sworn to maintain the God-ordained political order, but if disruption and confusion reign in the church this will be impossible.[39] Unity in the church, in turn, depends upon unanimity with regard to doctrine, and it is therefore incumbent upon the civil magistracy to enforce with the worldly power the true doctrine of the true church.

Many of the Dutch reformers were directly or indirectly inspired by these ideals. They may not have understood themselves

---

[37] For "apostates" we may read the Anabaptists and spiritualizers in Calvin's own time and, later in Dutch history, the Arminians. *Defense of the Orthodox Faith of the Sacred Trinity against the Prodigious Errors of Michael Servetus* (1554), *Opera*, 8, 475: "For God does not subject to a just punishment all the promiscuous in equal measure, but more especially the apostates, who impiously alienate themselves from the way of truth and attempt to drag others away to a similar defection" [my translation].

[38] *Opera*, 8, 464. My translation from Bohatec, p. 623.

[39] *Ibid.*, 8, 474: "For neglect of ordered piety so dissipates that which is the proper end of politics—the conservation of legal order among men— that the life of men is brutal in that mutilated form of government in which religion is neglected." My translation from Bohatec, p. 624.

explicitly as "Calvinists" (the parlance of a later day), but they
had studied at Geneva or studied with men who had studied
there. Calvin's doctrine of church and state led these Dutch reformers to work relentlessly in the direction of three points. First,
since God employs both the political and spiritual realms in the
service of his will, the civil authority—be it royal, aristocratic,
or democratic—must be open to the theological and ecclesiastical
advice of the church, which of course means the Calvinist or
"true" church. The Dutch Calvinists turned unceasingly to the
local magistracies, the provincial magistracies, the States-General,
and the House of Orange and demanded of them mighty works
for the Lord. Secondly, the church on its own ground—i.e., that
of doctrine, ecclesiology, and morals—must be absolutely free
and independent of all interference from the state. The Dutch
Calvinists tolerated no tampering by the state in matters of doctrine, call and dismissal of ministers, or exercise of the ecclesiastical discipline. Two exciting episodes of the Dutch Reformation,
the struggle over the "church order" and the Arminian controversy, revolved around this point. Finally, wherever and when-
ever possible the state and the church must work harmoniously
together to promote and preserve the good order of society and
the unity of Christ's church. Since heresy and schism can only
lead to political chaos and thus to the disintegration of God's
overall plan of salvation, the state is required to take an active
role in warding off heresy by employing civil law in the defense
of the pure doctrine of the true church. Therefore, all religious
worship and belief except that of the "true" church must, at
least in its public expression, be banned as illegal.

To what extent did these Dutch Reformed *predikanten* suc-
ceed in establishing their Calvinist Zion in the Low Countries
after the fateful events of April 1, 1571, at Den Briel? It is to
that story that we now turn.

3. The Struggle over the Church Order and the Arminian Schism

William of Orange possessed a theological insight and vision far in advance of his time. On July 19, 1572, he made to the first postrevolutionary gathering of the States of Holland at Dordrecht a proposal that must surely rank him among the earliest forefathers of religious toleration. The proposal said, in part, that "there shall be maintained (in the conquered provinces) freedom of religion as well for the reformed as for the Roman religion, and . . . everyone of both religions shall enjoy this freedom both in public and in various churches or chapels (provided that this shall be ordained proper by the government), without anyone suffering hindrance or harm, while the [Roman] clergy shall remain untroubled in its present state."[1] Here is a spirit far removed from that outlined in the previous chapter. And this proposal shows in what way William's character differed from that of Calvin. William was never fully able to understand or accurately to evaluate the goals of the Calvinist revolutionaries with

[1] J. N. Bakhuizen van den Brink, W. F. Dankbaar, W. J. Kooiman, eds., *Documenta Reformatoria* (Kampen: J. H. Kok, 1960), 2, 155 [translation mine]. William's feelings on the subject of religious toleration had not changed since his years of German exile (1566–1572). In one of his manifestos during this period the prince declared his intention to "bring freedom for all, no matter what faith you may be," in order to restore in the Netherlands "the exercise of the true Christian religion." See Pieter Bor, *Oorsprongk, Begin ende Vervolgh der Nederlandsche Oorlogen, 1555–1600,* 4 vols. in folio (Amsterdam, 1679–1684), book 4, folio 138.

whom he had made common cause. Clearly, these Calvinist refugees when they spoke of "religious freedom" for their homeland had something in mind other than the concept William articulated before the States. William, and the States also insofar as they went along with him,[2] were of the opinion that the long sought-for religious freedom had been achieved now that the heavy political and spiritual yoke of Spain had been thrown off and God's Word could be freely and publicly preached. On the contrary, the Calvinist *predikanten* held that this was but the first step along the way that would lead to the ultimate and complete victory of the true church. They knew exactly *which* church was the only true church, exactly *how* God's Word must be interpreted, and exactly *what* was in conflict with the pure doctrine and therefore could not be permitted.[3]

Although William stood almost alone in his conviction that a free toleration of both Catholics and Reformed in the Low Countries was both necessary and desirable, a large number of the Dutch urban regent class shared his apprehension at the prospect of a new ecclesiastical power structure among the Reformed similar to the Roman organization that had just been overthrown. The reasons for this apprehension are not hard to find. The ashes of the Spanish heretic fires were still smoldering in the northern Netherlands at the time the new nation came into being. All kinds of Dutchmen, of high and low estate, shared vivid memories of the terrible religious persecutions of the previous decades. Furthermore, while the reuniting of the southern Netherlands

[2] The States of Holland initially heeded William's request and granted freedom of worship to Reformed and Catholic alike (July 20, 1572), but apparently reversed this decision and refused liberty to Catholics by the following spring (1573). When the States offered William the Stadholdership in Holland in 1575 one of the conditions was that he pledge to maintain the Reformed worship and suppress the Catholic. See J. Reitsma and J. Lindeboom, *Geschiedenis van de Hervorming en de Hervormde Kerk der Nederlanden* (The Hague: Nijhoff, 1949), pp. 114–115.

[3] H. A. Enno van Gelder, *Vrijheid en Onvrijheid in de Republiek: Geschiedenis der Vrijheid van Drukpers en Godsdienst van 1572 tot 1798* (Haarlem: Tjeenk Willink, 1947), p. 57.

with the Spanish Habsburg empire through the Union of Atrecht in 1579 had had a centralizing effect on that area with a subsequent loss of autonomy for the local town and city governments, in the newly formed republic in the northern provinces the effect of the Union of Utrecht (1579) was the opposite.[4] Here, the provisions of the union tended to rob the state of its authority and bestow it instead on the individual provinces. But more important still, within the provinces the real power lay with the "voting members"—in most cases, the nobility and the towns.[5] The latter usually enjoyed the upper hand. And the northern Dutch towns were ruled throughout the sixteenth and seventeenth centuries by aristocratic oligarchies, within which a relatively small number of families, and often only a few individuals, made all the important decisions. Thus, both the domestic and foreign policy of the new republic were often determined within the circle of these powerful urban regent families. These oligarchies were intensely jealous of their power and prestige, which they would not relinquish easily, and throughout the lifetime of the republic they felt threatened primarily from two sources: a powerful *Stadhouder* (Stadholder), and a powerful, well-organized Reformed clergy.

Thus the scene was set in the northern Netherlands for a showdown between the Calvinist zealots, who wished to establish a Dutch theocracy, and the politicians ("libertines" from the Calvinist viewpoint) who, although sympathetic to an official Reformed Church, were not at all prepared to submit indiscriminately to every desire of the Reformed clergy. Two years after the birth of the republic in 1581, the drama had begun. The first act concerned itself with the "church order," that is, the civil law defining the structure and function of the Reformed Church and its relationship to the state.

The politicians and the clergy were at odds over several points

[4] Johan E. Elias, *Geschiedenis van het Amsterdamsche Regentenpatriciaat*, 2 vols. (The Hague: Nijhoff, 1923), 1, pp. 2–3.

[5] *Ibid.*, 1, p. 2; the "stemhebbende leden."

in the church order, but certainly the most volatile was that of the procedure for the calling of ministers. The Reformed argued that the calling of a minister to the local congregation was strictly ecclesiastical business and must therefore be carried out under strictly ecclesiastical supervision. The civil authorities, on the other hand, demanded a voice in the selection of new ministers. Jealousy may have played a role in their viewpoint, but the position did have further validity. At this time the ministers were the leading demagogues in Dutch society; their influence on the masses was often enormous, and it was thus very much in the interest of the politicians to exercise some measure of control over what emanated from the local pulpit. Political order often hung in the balance.[6]

Already at the Convent of Wesel in 1568, the exiled but optimistic delegates had adopted an article concerning the procedure for calling a minister to the local congregation. A legal calling, they decided, should be constituted by the "ripe deliberation" of the elders of the local congregation, with consent and approval from the appropriate classis and synod. Until such time, however, as a functioning system of classes and synods should exist in the Netherlands, they advised that "the godly [local] governments should offer hand and help to the elders" in their deliberations, in order to prevent the "unruly whims of the people and the honor-seeking pleasure of the elders" from gaining the upper hand. This was an article in which the regents could take considerable satisfaction. But the Calvinists regarded this only as a provisional measure, until an ecclesiastical organization could take shape in the Netherlands, and the church's position was soon more strongly stated. At the Synod of Emden, which convened October 5, 1571 (six months after Den Briel had signaled the beginning of Reformed success in the northern provinces), there was nothing more to be heard of the civil magistracy's role

[6] W. P. C. Knuttel, "Kerk en Burgerlijke Overheid," in *Uit Onzen Bloeitijd: Schetsen van het Leven onzer Vaderen in de Zeventiende Eeuw* (Amsterdam, n.d.), p. 273.

in the calling of ministers. "The servants of the Word shall be chosen by the Consistory, with the consent and approval either of the classical gathering or of three ministers from neighboring churches," read Article 13 of the Emden church order.[7]

The progress of the Reformed Church was swift in Holland and Zealand after 1571. On November 26, 1574, it became for all practical purposes the official church in Holland when a resolution by the States of the province stipulated that henceforth "all teachers and servants of the Holy Word [i.e., the Reformed ministers], both in the towns and in the country of Holland, shall be paid out of the available incomes from the goods which formerly belonged to the Church in the towns and/or regions where they live."[8] In other words, the former ecclesiastical possessions of the Roman Church in Holland, confiscated by the civil authority, would now be used by the government to support the Reformed ministry.

The Reformed followed up this success by making new demands in the area of the church order. Already in June 1574 a provincial synod convening in Dordrecht, South Holland, agreed to abide by the provisions of Article 13 of the Emden church order in the calling of ministers.[9] The civil magistracy was thus not to be consulted. Four years later the first "national" synod, convening at Dordrecht on June 2 and adjourning June 18, 1578, went much further. A minister, stated Article 4, was to be called and examined exclusively by the local consistory, with the supervision and approval of the classis. A candidate called and approved by the consistory was then to be "presented" to the local civil magistracy, which could bring any complaints or dissatisfactions concerning the candidate before the consistory. The consistory in conjunction with the classis would then exercise final

---

[7] C. Hooijer, ed., *Oude Kerkordeningen der Nederlandsche Hervormde Gemeenten* (Zaltbommel, 1865), p. 36, 66–89 [my translation].

[8] *Resolutien Staten van Holland,* November 26, 1574. In the *Gemeente Archief* in Amsterdam [translation mine].

[9] Hooijer, p. 101.

judgment concerning the candidate. Furthermore, the synod served blunt notice that "those who serve the Word in any princedoms or in the territories of any nobility shall be called in an orderly and legal fashion, as the others." Finally, Article 9 declared, "Those appearing in the service of the Word without calling and outside the legal order of the Churches, whether this occur in a congregation where order is already established or whether they be called by private persons among whom there is no order, shall be warned by their neighboring ministers to follow the church order: and if, having been twice warned, they do not comply, the Classis shall meet and declare these persons splitters of the Churches and wanderers."[10]

One does not have to read far between the lines to sense that something was happening in the churches that the Reformed clergy found unacceptable. The civil magistracies in the towns of Holland and Zealand were not resting content with a subordinate role in the calling of ministers. In 1576 the States of Holland and Zealand in conjunction with William of Orange published a set of "ecclesiastical laws"[11] that made it clear that ministers in the employ of the state (and after 1574 the Reformed ministers were being paid from public funds) were expected to meet state specifications. Article 1 stated that "the magistracy of each major town shall, upon presentation of and consultation with its ministers [*predikanten*], choose ministers [*predikanten*] for her town and all the places of her jurisdiction." To the local consistory was granted at least the theoretical right of veto of a candidate, since they could examine him for "learning, adequate facility of expression, and upright good life" (doctrinal orthodoxy was significantly omitted). The magistracy had the final say, however, because before assuming his ecclesiastical office the candidate was to swear an oath, the first clause of which read: "I swear by God Almighty and our Lord Jesus Christ that I will be a true subject of the King of Spain, his *stadhouder* in these prov-

---

[10] *Ibid.*, pp. 145–147 [translation mine].
[11] "Kerkelijke wetten."

inces the Prince of Orange, and also this magistracy in everything not conflicting with the will of God and my office; and
that I, to the best of my ability, will labor to the end that also
the people should obey these authorities in quietness and good
order."[12]

Clearly, a wide gap was opening between church and state
over the issue of what constituted a legal call to the ministry. The
second "national" synod, meeting May 29 to June 21, 1581, in
Middelburg, Zealand, widened the gap.[13] Like the previous synods, Middelburg reiterated the demand that a minister be chosen
and finally approved by the local consistory in conference with
the classis. The local magistracy should be consulted but have no
final authority in the selection. Middelburg also added a new
demand: a candidate chosen by the consistory should be presented to the local magistracy "doing profession of the Reformed
Religion."[14] The unwritten but well-understood corollary of this
provision was that a magistracy, or any members of a magistracy,
not confessing the Reformed creed should be deprived even of
the right to consultation.

This was a very difficult situation. The provisions of the church
orders of Dordrecht (1578) and Middelburg (1581) were rejected by the States. The provisions of the ecclesiastical laws in
1576 and a new set of ecclesiastical laws in 1583, proposed by
the States, were rejected by the church. The third national synod,
meeting in The Hague in 1586, now had the fortune to receive
the political backing of Robert Dudley, Count of Leicester, self-
styled savior of the Reformed cause in the Low Countries, who
was at the zenith of his popularity in the province of Utrecht.[15]

---

[12] Hooijer, pp. 121–122 [translations mine].

[13] The United Provinces only officially renounced their Spanish allegiance on July 22, 1581. Thus, neither Dordrecht (1578) nor Middelburg
(1581) was a "national" synod in the precise political sense; rather, they
were "general" synods, representing all of the northern provinces where
the Reformed were gaining a foothold.

[14] Hooijer, p. 201 [translation mine].

[15] Leicester arrived in the Low Countries at Vlissingen, Zealand, on

The provisions for the ministerial call adopted by this synod were every bit as strict as those of Middelburg, and through Leicester's influence they were accepted by the States in Zealand, Utrecht, Gelderland, Overijssel, and provisionally in Holland.[16] The Reformed star seemed momentarily in ascendance, but it set just as quickly as it had risen when Leicester's enterprise in Utrecht failed and he left the country.

The individual provinces now reverted to their own church orders.[17] In Holland, the States called together, on February 1, 1591, a commission composed of eight ecclesiastics and eight politicians, charging them to do the impossible—create a church order acceptable to both parties. They failed, but they failed in an interesting way. On March 9, 1591, the commission submitted its proposal for church order to the States. On the subject of the ministerial call, the following compromise was proposed. A committee consisting of four members delegated by the magistrates and four delegated by the church would select and approve the candidate. His name would then be submitted to the magistracy

---

December 29, 1585. Commissioned by Queen Elizabeth to come to the United Provinces as head of all English troops fighting in the war against Spain, he was to have control over the war and internal affairs. He was an important leader of the Puritan cause in England during Elizabeth's reign.

[16] The procedure for ministerial call adopted in The Hague in 1586 was: (1) selection by the local consistory and deacons meeting in conjunction with the classis; (2) examination of the candidate's doctrine and morals by the consistory; (3) approval of the candidate's civil demeanor by the local magistracy. See Hooijer, p. 270; Reitsma and Lindeboom, pp. 158–159.

[17] This was entirely possible under the provisions of Article 13 of the Union of Utrecht: "Concerning the matter of religion, Holland and Zealand shall conduct themselves as they see fit, and the other provinces shall regulate themselves according to the content of the Peace of Religion already proposed by Archduke Mathias . . . and the States General, or according to such general or particular order as they shall find to be in the interests of the peace and welfare of the provinces." This clause, which time and again prevented the adoption of common regulations among the provinces in respect to religion, was a constant thorn in the flesh of the Calvinists, who wished to make the cause of the church a national cause.

for final official approval. Then the candidate would be examined by a professor in theology at the University of Leiden in conjunction with two ministerial examiners appointed annually by the provincial synod, two political examiners appointed annually by the States, and a number of examiners delegated by the local magistracy.[18] Surprisingly, it was the States who rejected the proposal, the towns of Delft, Rotterdam, Gouda, Hoorn, and Medemblik voting negative. The church accepted it, albeit not enthusiastically.

A church order regarded as valid and acceptable by both the church and the state was never achieved during the time of the Dutch republic—not even by the great national Synod of Dordrecht in 1618–1619. Although that gathering made several sizeable concessions to the demands of the States-General on the subject of the ministerial call,[19] the States-General, because of opposition from Holland, Zealand, and Friesland, never recognized the Dordrecht church order. The long-enduring and never-satisfied complaints of the Holland clergy on this point are to be found in the consistorial, classical, and synodal archives of the province.

The struggle between church and state over the church order concerned, of course, far more than the procedure for ministerial call. To see the battle in its broader scope, one must turn to several further incidents involving church polity and theology.

Between the years 1579 and 1582 a tense drama was played out in the city of Leiden. It has become so notorious in the annals of Dutch church history that it may be referred to simply as the "Coolhaes affair."[20] The issue at stake was only slightly different from the one already outlined: it concerned the right of the local

[18] Hooijer, pp. 339–341.

[19] Most notably concerning the right of selection, which was to belong to the consistory and deacons, but not to be exercised without "good correspondence with the local Christian government." See Hooijer, p. 449.

[20] See H. C. Rogge, *Caspar Janszoon Coolhaes*, 2 vols. (Amsterdam: H. W. Mooij, 1856); also Reitsma and Lindeboom, pp. 171–173; also Hooijer, pp. 188–192.

magistracy to appoint members of the consistory. Caspar Coolhaes, a member of the Leiden clergy, took up the cause of the
magistrates and thereby came under suspicion of heresy in the
eyes of his colleagues, who saw the church's freedom gravely
threatened by this civil incursion into ecclesiastical territory. In
the ensuing struggle, the Leiden magistracy dismissed from office
the entire local clergy and consistory, except for Coolhaes and the
one elder in agreement with their viewpoint. The following year,
however, Coolhaes submitted his case to the decision of a court
of eight persons—four representing the church and four the magistracy. This tribunal demanded from both Coolhaes and his
ecclesiastical opponents a "public confession of guilt before the
whole congregation in the St. Peter's Church." The confession
took place, and peace appeared restored. The matter might have
rested there, but the Synod of Middelburg (1581) demanded
in addition that Coolhaes publicly retract his previously written
theological defense as unorthodox doctrine. Coolhaes refused and
was therefore excommunicated the following year by the provincial synod meeting at Haarlem on March 25, 1582.

The Synod of Middelburg also renewed the demands of the
church over against the civil magistracy with regard to selection
of elders and ministers.[21] This called forth a thundering reply
from the Leiden magistracy. In their "Remonstrance" the magistrates asked the ecclesiastics pointedly:

With what authority do you proceed? We do not recognize that God
would have given you the right to rule over the government; neither
the States-General nor the States of Holland have given you that
right. . . . We are not vassals of the synod, and we cannot tolerate
that the magistracy, much less the magistracy "doing profession of
the Reformed Religion," should only be able to approve the calling
of ministers. What would the synod think then? Thereby only
creatures of the synod would be able to rule! Let others appoint and
pay such powerful "teachers"; for our part, we will not be
coerced![22]

[21] Hooijer, pp. 201–203.
[22] Pamphlet No. 621 in W. P. C. Knuttel, *Catalogus van de Pamfletten*

More mildly worded, but no less certain, came the "Antwoorde" of the ministers. The church, they said, wished only that

the ecclesiastical government, inasmuch as it is spiritual, remain in the hands of the shepherds and overseers of the church, and that the politicians who make it obvious that they are not of the Reformed Religion (indeed, that they are despisers of all external exercises of religion) may be prevented from an unsuitable jurisdiction and mastery over the Church. For indeed, this would be every bit as objectionable a thing to us as the papist tyranny, and we would rather revert once more to creeping around in secret, where we could more easily enjoy the freedom of our consciences, which is refused not even to the Anabaptists in their false religion.[23]

The Coolhaes affair was primarily concerned with church polity. Theology was involved, of course, but in a secondary way. In cases where orthodox doctrine was directly at stake, however, the church became even more sensitive about civil intervention. Two such minor cases, which occurred in the final years of the sixteenth century, deserve mention here as a prelude to the great Remonstrant–Counter-Remonstrant struggle that rocked the Reformed Church throughout the first half of the next century.

Herman Herbertszoon began his ecclesiastical career in the Cistercian cloister of Groot-Buurlo in Westphalia.[24] Converted

---

Verzameling Berustende in de Koninklijke Bibliotheek. The full title is: *Remonstrance of Vertooch by die van Leyden den Heeren Ritterschappen ende Steden representerende de Staten slants van Hollant, in Februario xvcLxxxii hare mede-litmaten gedaen, nopende tverhandelde der Predicanten, inden laetsvoorledenen zomer tot Middelburch in het Nationael Synodus (zo zijt noemen) vergadert geweest zijnde, met den gevolge van dien.* Excerpted and paraphrased in van Gelder, p. 78 [my translation from van Gelder].

[23] Knuttel, No. 622. *Antwoorde Der Dienaren des Woordts ende Ouderlingen der Kercken van Hollandt . . . onlancks vergadert gheweest zijnde tot Haerlem: Aen . . . de Staten desselven Landts: Op de Remonstrantie by de Overicheyt van Leyden, . . . aengaende t'verhandelde der Dienaren des Woordts end' Ouderlinghen der Nederlantsche Kercken in het Synodus tot Middelburch,* etc. Quoted in van Gelder, p. 79 [my translation from van Gelder].

[24] Reitsma and Lindeboom, pp. 174–175.

to the Reformed confession, he subsequently preached in the towns of Wesel and Dordrecht, arriving in 1582 in Gouda. Through sermons and pamphlets he made known his disagreement with several points of Reformed doctrine. An ecclesiastical investigation followed, with the result that he was suspended from the ministry in 1591. The Gouda magistracy, however, refused to abide by the synodal sentence and maintained Herbertszoon in his church with full salary. After long negotiations between the ecclesiastical and civil powers, Herbertszoon finally (1593) composed a "confession of faith" that, although not removing all suspicion, was regarded by his ecclesiastical colleagues as sufficiently orthodox to effect his reconciliation with the church. He was left further unhindered in his ministry, but his presence in Gouda did much to earn that town the title of "receptacle of the heretics."

Meanwhile, a similar incident was taking place in the North Holland town of Hoorn. Cornelis Wiggertszoon was called to the ministry there in 1590.[25] Soon complaints were heard of "unorthodoxy" concerning his theology, which actually did reject the cardinal Reformed doctrine of predestination. He rested his whole theological position on the covenants of God with Adam and Abraham, which, he argued, offered the promise of salvation to man in general and therefore made predestination an untenable doctrine. He was suspended from his office by the provincial synod meeting at Alkmaar on June 14, 1593, but, supported by two of his local ministerial colleagues and above all by the Hoorn magistracy, he remained in his pulpit. The church brought the matter before the provincial States who, in order to prevent a schism and civil unrest, physically barred Wiggertszoon from his pulpit. Nevertheless, still supported by the local government, he continued to preach before conventicles gathered in private homes. The States of Holland dismissed him formally from his ministry in July 1596. The provincial synod excommunicated him in 1598. Everything was in vain. Wiggertszoon preached for the conventicles in Hoorn until his death in 1624.

25 *Ibid.*, pp. 175–176.

Church polity, then, was one important area the Dutch Calvinist clergy sought to dominate and to defend against the civil authority. A second important, from Calvinist perspective even crucial, area, was that of doctrine. A short discussion of the events revolving around Jacob Arminius will illustrate the Dutch Reformed attitude on this issue.

Although the combined political-ecclesiastical commission, appointed in 1591 by the States of Holland to seek a modus vivendi with regard to the problem of the church order, failed in its ultimate purpose, the speed with which it was able to accomplish its appointed task of constructing a compromise[26] suggests that there may have been some ecclesiastics on the commission who were more disposed than the average Reformed *predikant* to listen to the magistrates' point of view. Among the eight clerical delegates to that commission there sat Jacob Arminius, minister in Amsterdam, and Johannes Uytenbogaert, court preacher of Prince Maurits in The Hague.[27]

This fact suggests an aspect of the great "Arminian debate" that is sometimes underplayed by church historians. Although the debate is of prime significance for the history of Christian doctrine, it is also one of the most exciting chapters in the history of church-state relations. For even though the theological point at issue was a crucial one for Calvinism, it is unthinkable that so much social, political, and religious uproar could have stemmed from an issue of purely theological significance. The debate must have involved a deep-rooted difference of principle concerning the essence of the church and religious life, and this was indeed the case.[28]

[26] The commission met for the first time on February 25, 1591, and submitted its proposed church order to the States on March 9.

[27] Knuttel, "Kerk en Burgerlijke Overheid," p. 277.

[28] A real appreciation of the breadth of Arminius's significance can be found in Carl Bangs, *Arminius: A Study in the Dutch Reformation* (Nashville, Tenn.: Abingdon, 1971). Bangs says in the preface: "Tranquillity, however, was not [Arminius's] lot in life, nor obscurity his lot in death. During his last six years he became the focal point of Dutch national life.

Given their theological dependence on Calvin, the Reformed ministers could only with great difficulty tolerate the meddling of the civil magistracy in affairs of ecclesiastical polity. This was *a fortiori* true when it came to doctrine, the domain that must at all costs be preserved for the community of the elect and maintained undefiled by the meddling of the civil authority. Within the true church the pure doctrine must prevail. Therefore, the ecclesiastical powers must be free to determine what doctrine could and could not be taught within the church. Furthermore, the church must be free to govern itself and exercise ecclesiastical discipline according to its own judgment in order to maintain doctrinal unity and weed out false (i.e., dissenting) dogma.[29]

By 1600 the fortunes of the war against Spain had quite firmly established the future of the United Provinces as an independent republic, and within most of the seven provinces the Reformed Church was now viewed as more or less official. This meant that the civil powers (the local magistracies, the provincial States, and the States-General) also had an interest in promoting unity and preventing schism in the church. But while "unity" for the ecclesiastics meant strict doctrinal consensus, "unity" for the politicians meant a church as broad and tolerant as possible to include as many different shades of generally "reformed" theological opinion as possible.[30] Thus the stage was set for still another showdown between ecclesiastics and politicians—this time in the area of doctrine.

Onto the stage stepped Jacob Arminius, pastor in Amsterdam and after 1603 professor of theology at Leiden. For the purposes of this story it is not important to explain exhaustively his theological position. Already in 1590, Wiggertszoon was contesting the Reformed doctrine of predestination, and it therefore seems

---

Around him raged not only the debates of the theologians but also the national issues of foreign policy, war and peace, world trade, and the relation of church and state."

[29] van Gelder, p. 160.
[30] *Ibid.*

likely that Arminius was less theologically original than has sometimes been supposed.[31] In any case, his interpretation of the doctrine of predestination was that it is a decree of God's good will
in Christ, whereby God from eternity has decided to justify those
to whom he has resolved to give the gift of faith and to adopt
them as children and endow them with eternal life. Reprobation,
he taught, is the decision of God made in eternity whereby he
has resolved to condemn to eternal death the infidels, who because of their own sinful obstinacy and God's righteous judgment
will never believe. Franciscus Gomarus, Arminius's colleague on
the Leiden faculty and his bitter theological enemy, argued that
the objects of predestination are the rational, subservient, dam-
nable creations of God's hand, which are, however, capable of
being saved. Out of these creations God has, by his own free will,
selected some for eternal life and presented them with the means
of salvation (i.e., doctrine, church, and so forth). The rest God
has doomed to eternal death and provided with the means thereto,
namely, their own sinful nature which God allowed by permitting the Fall.[32]

Arminius, thus, did not himself promote or defend the doctrine
of the generality of grace, although his followers later did. His
formulation of the doctrine of predestination placed more emphasis on the role of human faith than did that of his theological
opponent, but only slightly more. Faith, for Arminius, was still
entirely a divine gift. Therefore, he felt himself to be, and maintained to his death in 1609 that he was, a true confessor of the
Reformed doctrine.

It is this fact that is of great significance for our story, for it
meant that a challenge had arisen to the Reformed doctrine,
not from another church or sect but from within the Reformed

[31] According to Bangs (pp. 311–312), Arminius viewed not only Wiggertszoon but also Coolhaes and Herbertszoon as "kindred spirits."

[32] Reitsma and Lindeboom, pp. 197–198. See Bangs, chaps. 25 and 26,
where Arminius's doctrine of predestination is set forth within the context
of his whole theology.

Church itself. The true church must be characterized by pure doctrine, but which doctrine was now to be regarded as pure? Moreover, who was to decide which doctrine was pure—the church or the civil authority? The church demanded the right of decision for itself; the government could not risk the possibility of civil anarchy which the granting of such a right might entail.[33]

If the church were to judge its own case, a national synod would have to be called. This, however, could not happen without prior permission from the States-General. On March 15, 1606, permission was granted, but on condition that a provisional meeting be held first and report to the States-General the proposed agenda for the national gathering. The States of Utrecht, where there was a large amount of Arminian sympathy among the clergy, furthermore added that "revision of Confession, Catechism and the present church-order" was expected.[34]

The presynodal meeting of the Reformed clergy, held on May 26, 1607, resulted in a tumultuous altercation between the Arminian and Gomarian factions. It was now clear to the States-General that no reconciliation and union in the ecclesiastical realm could be expected from a national synod, but rather only strife and schism. They therefore resorted to drastic measures to curb the growing unrest in the church. Permission for a national synod was withdrawn, and the gathering of any provincial or even particular synods in North or South Holland was forbidden.

Arminius himself, in October 1608, had pleaded the case for doctrinal tolerance within the church in an impressive manner. On that occasion he declared, "I shall force my fellow men, who

---

[33] The affair was further complicated by the peace negotiations being carried on at the time with Spain and which resulted in the twelve-year truce in 1609. The Raad-Pensionaris of Holland, Johan van Oldenbarnevelt, was well aware that a strong, unified national church rallying around pure Calvinist doctrine would be a formidable opponent of his peace negotiations and could possibly bring them to ruin. See Bangs, pp. 225–226.

[34] Reitsma and Lindeboom, pp. 201–202.

see the issue differently, to believe no article, even though I may have demonstrated the truth of it with abundant arguments, unless I demonstrate clearly out of God's word—yes, just as clearly as I should have demonstrated the article's truth—that it is an article essential to salvation and that it is therefore held by every Christian."[35] This was patently a position with which the politicians could feel comfortable and make common cause. The States-General were thus inclined to lend a very sympathetic ear when, in 1610, the followers of Arminius composed and submitted their now famous "Remonstrance."

On January 14, 1610, this document appeared. About forty Reformed clergy who favored a review of the Belgic Confession and Heidelberg Catechism met secretly under the leadership of Uytenbogaert, probably in Gouda. They argued that there must be freedom within the church both to review and to alter the Confession and Catechism, and defined at length their interpretation of the predestination doctrine. Finally, they decided to rest their case in the hands of the States of Holland, to which they attributed authority in ecclesiastical as well as civil affairs.[36]

The States moved quickly in response to this action. On March 11, 1610, they sent an open letter to all the clergy of North and South Holland, concerning "the rest and peace of the Church." Their motive for this action, they explained, was the furtherance "of God's honor and glory, the advocacy and salvation of the true Christian religion, the destruction of all misunderstanding and difference, and the concern to promote common love and unity of doctrine among the ministers of the church." To this end, the ministers would have to "refrain in the future from expressing themselves in print on the issue of the authority of the government in churchly affairs, (and) on the doctrine of predes-

---

[35] G. Brandt, *Historie der Reformatie, en Andere Kerkelyke Geschiedenissen, in en ontrent de Nederlanden* (2nd printing, Amsterdam, 1677), 2, 86 [translation mine].

[36] Reitsma and Lindeboom, pp. 208–209.

tination with its related points" on pain of being punished for civil disobedience.[37]

How was it possible, asked the Counter-Remonstrant clergy, to proclaim God's word and maintain the true church in its pure doctrine if certain doctrinal points could not be discussed and if those points themselves were determined by such a "libertine" political regime? The States' proclamation of "rest and peace" in the church produced very little rest and less peace. Conflict burned everywhere. The Counter-Remonstrant ministers refused to avoid the contested doctrines. The States would not recall their proclamation. The inevitable head-on collision occurred.

The first skirmish was fought in Alkmaar.[38] There Adolph Venator, a very liberal and very vocal Arminian, was opposed by his ministerial colleague, the equally vocal Counter-Remonstrant Cornelis van Hille. Hille succeeded in 1608 in getting the Classis of Alkmaar to require of all clergy in its service the signing of both Confession and Catechism. Venator refused, offering to sign the Bible instead. He was therefore suspended by the classis, but, in a now familiar move, the local magistracy maintained him in his office. The States demanded that the classis reinstate Venator; the classis flatly refused the demand. The States thereupon intervened, suspending Hille from his office (December 1610) and barring him physically from the church. Hille took his congregation with him to the neighboring village of Koedijk for a time, returning later to form a dissenting church within the town of Alkmaar. Within the next four years a different variation of the same theme was played in a half-dozen towns in Holland and Utrecht.

[37] "Aanschryvinge aan alle Classen van Holland en Westvriesland, tot ruste en vreede der Kerke," in P. Scheltus, *Kerkelyk Placaatboek* (The Hague, 1735), 2, 218–219. This act was followed by a second, on June 25, 1610, which stipulated that candidates being examined for the ministry by the church classes could not be forced to take a stand on the "highly mysterious points which are currently being far too much debated in the Church." p. 221 [translations mine].

[38] Reitsma and Lindeboom, pp. 210–211.

Unrest and schism ruled the day. In January 1614, therefore, the States of Holland decided to issue still another proclamation that would silence the rabble-rousing doctrinal zealots and prescribe a moderate course for the whole church. In this manner, reasoned the States, the strife could be quieted. If both doctrinal positions, maintained in a moderate way, were allowed within the church, how could there be strife? "The Resolution for the Peace of the Churches" thus stated, "We [the States] do not intend that those who, with respect to [the doctrine of predestination], do not teach or believe higher than [there follows the five points of the Arminians' remonstrance] should be molested or coerced to teach or believe higher; we hold this same doctrine [i.e., that of the Remonstrants] to be sufficient for salvation and suitable for Christian piety."[39]

Unfortunately, the rub came just there. The Counter-Remonstrants regarded the Remonstrant doctrine to be neither sufficient for salvation, nor suitable for Christian piety, nor a pure doctrinal mark of the true church. What they held to be essential for salvation, piety, and orthodoxy was viewed by the States as "extreme." Thus, what the Arminians and the States regarded as a regulation insuring doctrinal freedom, the Calvinist zealots regarded as the worst possible sort of conscience-coercion and "inquisition" by a tyrannical political regime. In their view, the true church had become once again a church "under the cross."

The factors that gradually began to turn the tide in favor of the Counter-Remonstrant cause were partly religious, but mostly military, political, and economic. The Raad-Pensionaris of Holland, Johan van Oldenbarnevelt, had been from the beginning the architect of the States' policy in this theological dispute. At the same time, he had worked to achieve the negotiated truce with Spain in 1609, thereby incurring the wrath of Prince Maurits (whose military plans he had foiled), of the Amsterdam merchants (whose plans for vast profit privateering against Spanish

[39] "Resolutie tot vrede der Kerken," in Scheltus, 2, 272 [translation mine].

shipping he had ruined), and of the Calvinist zealots (who viewed the war against Spain as a holy war which must be fought to the finish for the honor and glory of God). These three frustrated elements in Dutch society now began to align themselves to undo their common foe, the Raad-Pensionaris.

Their efforts succeeded during the winter of 1618–1619. The preceding years had been characterized by increasingly sharp measures taken by the States of Holland and Utrecht to maintain peace in the church. Oldenbarnevelt proposed, in December 1616, to take four thousand militia into provincial service and to dispatch them wherever trouble broke out. This plan was rejected, but many Holland towns maintained their own militia to control the religious strife. In the province of Utrecht six hundred militia were hired for this purpose.[40] The day looked dark for the Counter-Remonstrants, but when Prince Maurits, who had long maintained a neutral posture in the dispute, decided on July 23, 1617, to adopt their cause,[41] the days of Oldenbarnevelt and his policies were suddenly numbered. Maurits began to use his influence in the States-General to achieve the calling of a national synod. He persuaded Zealand, Friesland, Gelderland, and Groningen to introduce such a resolution to the States-General. The States of Holland of course offered stiff opposition, but eventually, greatly weakened by the dissent of Amsterdam, they were forced to acquiesce in the prince's plans on October 4, 1617. Throughout the spring and summer of 1618, Maurits continued to consolidate the position of the Counter-Remonstrants. On July 31, 1618, he gave a clear indication of the new position of the central government in the religious dispute when he entered Utrecht and, as commander-in-chief of the national military, or-

---

[40] Reitsma and Lindeboom, pp. 229–230. See J. C. Naber, *Calvinist of Libertijnsch?* (Utrecht, 1884), pp. 108–114.

[41] This he did by ignoring the Sunday service conducted by his court preacher, the Remonstrant Uytenbogaert, and going to church with the dissenting Counter-Remonstrant congregation in The Hague. Reitsma and Lindeboom, p. 230.

dered the provincial militia to lay down their arms. The course thus embarked upon in Utrecht was carried out by the prince during the following months, as he journeyed through the towns of Holland personally dismissing enough "libertine" members of each town council to give the strong Calvinists a majority. The next time the States-General convened, the "libertine" faction had nearly disappeared from its midst. The two-act drama of the winter of 1618–1619 was merely the end product of this chain of events.[42] In act one, the national synod of the Reformed Church met in Dordrecht from November 13 to May 28—the first national synod since that in The Hague in 1586 and still regarded by many as the doctrinal birth certificate of the Dutch Reformed Church. In act two, the gray head of Johan van Oldenbarnevelt rolled from a block in The Hague. The triumph of the Counter-Remonstrants was for the moment complete.

In many respects, the Synod of Dordrecht *was* the birth certificate of the Dutch Reformed Church. Its decisions concerning Bible-translation, catechism, printing of "licentious" books, and doctrine were of lasting importance.[43] But all of these things were overshadowed by its handling of the Remonstrant clergy. Seeing themselves to be a majority within the church and that the power of the civil authority now lay with them, the Counter-Remonstrants felt it beneath their dignity to deal with the summoned Remonstrants as theological opponents. They viewed them rather as a guilty party and demanded that they should confess and acquiesce in the procedure and judgment of the synod. The Remonstrants, on the other hand, maintained that the synod was merely a "conference" without legal status—a debate where both theological viewpoints might be aired.[44]

As proceedings wore on, the intransigence of the Remonstrants became more and more obvious to the assembly. Clearly, the

---

[42] *Ibid.*, pp. 230–234.

[43] See H. Bouwman et al., *De Dordtsche Synode van 1618–1619* (Gereformeerde Traktaatgenootschap "Filippus," 1918).

[44] Reitsma and Lindeboom, p. 247.

only viable method of procedure against them was a legal cen-
sure and ban, but to make this effective the explicit support of
the States-General was essential. To gain this support, a delegation was sent to The Hague, on December 10, 1618. On January
2, 1619, the delegation returned with a resolution from the States,
which declared that they "approved the acts and decrees of the
synod, denounced the cited Remonstrants, and ordered the latter
to submit themselves to the acts and decrees of the synod."[45] The
way was now clear for the synod to declare the Remonstrant
clergy and their followers enemies of both the church and the
state. This occurred during the 57th session on January 14, 1619.
The president of the synod, Maurits's court preacher, Johannes
Bogerman, shaking with rage, cast the dissenters into the outer
darkness saying: "God, who is a protector of his church, who
knows all hearts, knows your tricks, your cunning, wherewith
you have tried to deceive the Synod. . . . But inasmuch as you
yourselves are the reason that the Synod can no longer deal with
you, you are cast out. . . . Dimittimini, exite!"[46]

The postsynodal history of the Remonstrants is as interesting
and important for our story as the presynodal. For although the
synod's decree of banishment was followed by strong resolutions
from the States-General on July 3, 1619, and February 1, 1620,
forbidding the holding of Remonstrant conventicles on pain of
heavy punishment,[47] the Remonstrants were gathering for worship quite regularly and freely again in the Netherlands by
1628.[48] Already upon the death of Maurits and the assumption
of the *stadhoudership* by Frederik Hendrik in 1626 the exiles,
including their acknowledged leader Uytenbogaert, had returned
from various parts of Europe.[49] The city council of Amsterdam

[45] *Ibid.*, p. 250.
[46] Bouwman et al., p. 48 [translation mine].
[47] Reitsma and Lindeboom, pp. 267–268.
[48] Witness the heavy storm of Reformed protest to be found in the
records of the Amsterdam consistory and classis for this year. In the Amsterdam *Gemeente Archief*.
[49] Reitsma and Lindeboom, pp. 276–277.

declared the resolutions of the States against the Remonstrants void in that city in September 1631,[50] but the volley of complaints emanating from the church consistory in Amsterdam indictates that the Remonstrants had been enjoying relatively free assembly there since about 1625.[51]

An item yielded by the Amsterdam Notarial Archives demonstrates very clearly the method by which the Remonstrants were reintegrated into Dutch church life.[52] On Sunday, May 27, 1629, about nine o'clock in the morning three apparently zealous young Calvinists spied out a Remonstrant conventicle being held in a private home on the Keizersgracht on the west side of town. They ran quickly across town to the Oude Kerk, where the sheriff was attending the Calvinist service piously wedged between two *burgemeesters* of the city, Abraham Boom and Andries Bicker, in a front pew. One of the young men entered the church and relayed the scandalous news to the sheriff, who "thereupon said nothing but waved him away with his hand." The young men returned to the Keizersgracht where about ten o'clock they saw the Remonstrant conventicle break up. About a half-hour later the sheriff arrived, entered the house, of course found nothing, and returned to the center of town.

This story illustrates very poignantly that in a second area, that of doctrine, the Synod of Dordrecht failed to achieve its intended goal—establishment of a uniform, national Calvinist church with

---

[50] *Ibid.*, pp. 278–279.

[51] The *Protocol* of the Amsterdam Consistory has this entry on October 2, 1625: "It was proposed that it would be advisable for us to observe the Arminians, so that we may be certain about their activities and their conventicles, which it is said they are very stubbornly holding in this city, and so that we may then bring the same to the attention of the magistracy and protest it." In the Amsterdam *Gemeente Archief.*

[52] *Verklaring Betreffende de houding van den Schout ten aanzien van een bijeenkomst van Remonstranten, waarvan hij verwittigd was,* in the Notarial Archives, No. 700, of Amsterdam. Reproduced in J. G. van Dillen, "Documenten Betreffende de Politieke en Kerkelijke Twisten te Amsterdam," *Bijdragen en Mededeelingen van het Historisch Genootschap,* 59, 244–246.

freedom over against the civil authority. We have already seen that in the area of church polity the church order proposed by Dordrecht was never accepted by the States-General. The Arminian debate, whatever its significance in the history of Christian doctrine, meant this in the history of Dutch church-state relations: despite the fond hopes and earnest efforts of zealous ministers there would be no Calvinist Zion established in the Republic of the United Netherlands. The Remonstrants, after the first four or five years of vigorous suppression,[53] returned to the Netherlands and became a permanent part of the Dutch religious scene. In 1630 they began building a church in Amsterdam, and in 1634 they opened in that city a seminary for training their own ministers,[54] an event that drew loud but vain complaints from the Amsterdam consistory for the next forty years.

[53] See Naber, pp. 169ff., for an account of the first strict measures taken against the Remonstrants.

[54] C. W. Roldanus, "Het Godsdienstig Leven in de Zeventiende Eeuw," in *Zeven Eeuwen Amsterdam,* ed. by A. E. d'Ailly (Amsterdam, 1946), 2, 230–232.

4. The Problem of Dissent

The Reformed interpreted a harmonious state to mean one in which magistracy and church worked together to preserve doctrinal and therefore civil unity. Conversely, they held that doctrinal diversity must necessarily lead to civil anarchy and disintegration of the state. The struggle over the church order and the Arminian debate showed, however, that although the Dutch regent oligarchs in the late sixteenth and early seventeenth centuries were open to the prospect of an official, generally "reformed" church for the new republic, their view of the form and authority of that church was on the whole very different from the view of the Calvinist ministers. The conflict over the church order and the Arminian controversy both ended in ways more palatable to the regents than to the *predikanten*. Such was also the case with respect to the problem of religious dissent.

Calvinism was far from the only current of religious reform that had swept the Low Countries in the sixteenth century. Among the common people Lutheranism and Anabaptism had made lasting impressions, while among the educated ruling families the teachings of Erasmus had been popular. Furthermore, Catholicism itself remained deeply and stubbornly rooted in many parts of the Netherlands—especially in the country, away from the urban intellectual market places. Taking all these things into consideration, one should not be too surprised at the testimony of Oldenbarnevelt who, years after the successful revolt in 1572, stated that certainly no more than 10 percent of the people of the province of Holland were Calvinists.[1] The Reformed Church became the official church of the revolting provinces through its zeal, dedication, and superb organization, *not* through numerical superiority.

A scanning of the minutes of consistories, classes, and synods of the early Dutch Reformed Church shows that the Calvinists used three basically different means to establish and perpetuate themselves as the true church over against the embarrassingly numerous "heretics."[2] The first means employed was simple refutation. In the first years after the revolt in 1572 the Reformed were still too few and too poorly organized to resort to stronger measures. The rather naive enthusiasm engendered by their initial victories probably also led to overconfidence. At the first provincial synod of South Holland at Dordrecht in 1574 the problem of the *wederdoopers*[3] was approached through the following resolution:

> The ministers shall advise and warn their magistracies that they should neither accept nor tolerate anyone who does not legally swear his obedience to the government, and that they should warn those already in residence to be obedient to the word of God, and bring their children to be baptised. The magistracy should summon anyone refusing this into the presence of the ministers and command him to explain and defend his religious opinions. It is furthermore found good that the ministers search out and attend their [i.e., the Anabaptists'] secret gatherings and demonstrate to them that their opinions are incorrect.[4]

This refutation approach to the problem of religious heterodoxy was one in which the civil authorities could acquiesce without endangering their own interests and authority. And in fact

[1] Van Gelder, *Vrijheid en Onvrijheid in de Republiek* (Haarlem: Tjeenk Willink, 1947), pp. 44–45.

[2] *Ibid.,* pp. 84–88.

[3] Anabaptists.

[4] J. Reitsma and S. D. van Veen, eds., *Acta der Provinciale en Particuliere Synoden Gehouden in de Noordelijke Nederlanden Gedurende de Jaren 1572–1620,* vol. 2 (Groningen: J. B. Wolters, 1893), 146 [translation mine].

they frequently employed it. In February 1583 the States of Holland decided to proceed against Dirck Coornhert, the famous Dutch advocate of religious toleration and an archenemy of the Reformed *predikanten*.[5] His *Preuve van de Nederlandsche Catechismus* had just been published in Haarlem, and the States reasoned in a notably political and nontheological way that "great uproar could be caused in the land by such writings."[6] Coornhert's books were turned over to the theology professors at Leiden, who were to examine them for that which was in conflict with scripture and to formulate the same in propositions. Coornhert was then asked if he persisted in the ideas expressed by these propositions. He did. He was then required "to demonstrate in writing the grounding of these propositions in Scripture," so that they could be refuted by the Reformed *predikanten* and theologians.

Coornhert's "trial" points up the obvious inadequacy of the "refutation approach" for achieving the Calvinist ideal of religious homogeneity. What better forum could Coornhert have asked for the propagation of his ideas than the compulsory written demonstration of the scripturality of his principles? Such an approach to the heretics was as likely to increase their number as decrease it, since it often offered to their theologies precisely the opportunity of public expression they sought.

Realizing this, the Calvinists soon turned to a second, more vigorous procedure against the heretics. As the Reformed gained organization and numerical strength, they began to work in many ways on both the local and provincial levels to make dissent either impossible or at least uncomfortable for citizens of the republic. This method, which might be called the "multiple obstruction approach," had several different manifestations. Already on March 31, 1573, the provincial synod of North Holland meeting at Alkmaar decided to combat the prospect of future heresy by making

[5] See van Gelder, p. 107.

[6] Scheltus, *Kerkelyk Placaatboek* (The Hague, 1735), 2, 40. Quoted in van Gelder, p. 107 [my translation from van Gelder].

Reformed doctrine an integral part of school instruction: "Each congregation with its minister shall strive to obtain schoolmasters who are pious and favorable in all respects to the true religion, who can also teach the children the Catechism, who can guide the children in all good morals and godly manners, who can give the children a good example in word and deed, and who, finally, can also teach reading and writing."[7]

If the Reformed thus seemed to show more regard for piety than for literacy, they also sometimes regarded orthodoxy as more important than marriage. The South Holland provincial synod at Dordrecht, June 15–28, 1574, put an enormous hurdle in the path of those faithful who might be inclined to marry with the heretics. In answer to the question whether a member of the Reformed congregation might be married to a Catholic, Anabaptist, or atheist by a Reformed *predikant,* the synod said: "He should first be warned and admonished, but if he persists in wanting to marry in spite of the admonition, that he should be married by the minister, inasmuch as public marriage is only civil." If, however, he refused to receive thoughtfully his pastor's admonition that he was endangering his salvation, then the consistory should proceed against him "either with public penance, or temporary exclusion from the sacraments, or with the steps for excommunication, according to its discretion."[8] Thus the best a member of the Reformed congregation could hope for if he married with a heretic was a marriage performed by, but not recognized by the church. At worst, he could expect to be excommunicated. Implicitly contained in this act of the synod, of course, was the church's view of marriage between two heretics completely outside the church. This was no marriage at all but perpetual adultery and therefore liable to possible civil interference and dissolution. One further expression of this multiple obstruction approach to heresy was uttered by the same Dordrecht synod. The local magistracy, it insisted, should demand from each resident

[7] Reitsma and van Veen, 1 (1892), 10 [translation mine].
[8] *Ibid.,* 2 (1893), 146–147 [translation mine].

a civil oath of obedience to the local government (which the Anabaptists almost always refused). Anyone refusing to swear his allegiance should be deprived of his right to practice a trade within the town walls.[9]

Even these obstructionary measures against the heretics, however, while more effective than the hopeless enterprise of theological refutation, were indirect and did not produce the immediate results hoped for by many a zealous Calvinist *predikant*.[10] Therefore, the church soon went over to the most direct of all possible approaches to the problem of heresy—the demand for civil suppression of heterodox worship. While Lutheranism, Anabaptism, Erasmianism, and other fresh, generally reformed currents drifted through the United Provinces and incited the indignation of the Reformed *predikanten,* the large stagnant pool of stubborn, persisting, unconverted Catholicism aroused their wrath. On May 10, 1588, the North Holland synod meeting at Haarlem viewed the Catholic problem this way:

Inasmuch as there is currently great insolence and audacity practiced by the superstitious papists and monks, in the public celebration of their hideous mass and other superstitions of baptism and marriage, and also in the propagation of their false doctrine—which is in direct contradiction with the evangelical truth, in the holding of public schools in which Jesuit and Roman superstitions are implanted in the tender youth: all of which tends to the dishonor of God's holy name, the betrayal of the pure doctrine of the holy gospel with which the Lord has blessed these provinces, and great partisanship and hate between the citizens—it is therefore regarded by this assembly as necessary . . . to appeal to our lords the States and to humbly beseech them that they attend to this problem by the most fitting means.[11]

[9] See van Gelder, p. 85.

[10] Such as, for example, the Reformed *predikant* Arnoldus in Delft who declared at the South Holland provincial synod in 1607 that he would "regard the Government as Christian only if and when it should ban from the land all sects, or those refusing to accept the Reformed Religion." In Brandt, *Historie der Reformatie* (2nd printing, Amsterdam, 1677), 2, 75 [translation mine].

[11] Reitsma and van Veen, 1 (1892), 147 [translation mine].

For the last four words of this resolution we may read "armed physical force." This was just the point—other more peaceful means had already been employed, but the heretics remained obdurate, maintained themselves, and even multiplied! What means short of direct civil intervention could now cleanse this Augean stable, asked the *predikanten* by 1588.

At first superficial glance, it would appear that the Calvinists won their point in the young republic and that the civil magistracy sided with the Reformed Church to establish a monolithic church-state in the United Provinces. William's dream of official religious toleration for both Catholics and reformed Christians was frustrated by the States of Holland and Zealand as early as 1573. Furthermore, when William was offered the *stadhouder-ship* of Holland in 1575, it was on condition that he support the Reformed religion and suppress the Catholic. The fact that Catholics were viewed, often justly, by the States as potentially subversive to the political struggle of the new republic against Spain led to a new edict by the States of Holland against them in 1581. All papist gatherings, "whereby unrest and uproar could easily arise, and secret collaboration with the Enemy be furthered,"[12] were forbidden on the pain of one hundred guilders fine for every participant. The assassination of the Prince of Orange at Delft in 1584 by a Catholic fanatic destroyed his dream of complete religious toleration for the United Provinces; a new outburst of hate and distrust of the followers of Rome occurred in Holland. The provincial States published a new edict in 1587 against Catholic pilgrimages and renewed the edict against papist conventicles in 1588, 1589, 1591, and 1594. The States-General, as late as 1641, restated the ban on Catholic gatherings on a national scale, and Holland published new edicts in 1653 and 1659.[13]

Not only the Catholics were affected by this civil extension of

[12] *Kerkelyk Placaatboek* (The Hague, 1735), 1, 516–518 [translation mine].

[13] *Ibid., passim;* see also van Gelder, pp. 93–94.

Reformed zeal. In Holland, edicts against the Lutherans and Anabaptists were never published, much to the chagrin of many Calvinist *predikanten*. But in Friesland, for example, the Anabaptists as well as Catholics were expressly forbidden to gather for worship by the ordinance published by the Prince of Orange as *stadhouder* of the province in 1581. Later, in 1598, the States of Friesland threatened with banishment from the province any householders shunning the marriage ceremony—a custom typical of the followers of Menno Simonsz. In Groningen it was proclaimed in 1594 that "within the town and province of Groningen no other religion shall be exercised than the Reformed, as it is at present publicly exercised in the United Provinces."[14]

Thus by 1600 and throughout the first half of the seventeenth century the Reformed *predikanten* had achieved their goal and either obliterated or severely restricted the freedom of all other religions within the United Provinces—on paper. In practice, however, almost nothing changed, because the official edicts were so casually and poorly enforced. This fact cannot be overemphasized. It provides the key to an otherwise enigmatic feature of the Dutch Reformation—the Reformed Church became the only official church of the United Provinces, and it was not a tolerant church, and yet Jews, Catholics, Lutherans, Anabaptists, Socinians, Quakers, and Brownists sought asylum within Dutch borders. The religious rejects of a whole continent began pouring into a tiny nation whose laws only promised them more repression and rejection. But, for a combination of reasons social, political, and economic, they were not rejected in fact, however much they may have been rejected on paper.

Sometimes the local magistracies blatantly refused to carry out the edicts of the States. So in 1582 Leiden's magistrates, already described as archenemies of the *predikanten* in the Coolhaes affair, defended a policy of almost complete religious toleration against the demands both of the national Synod of Middelburg and of the 1581 edict of the States of Holland against the Cath-

---

[14] van Gelder, pp. 150–154 [translation mine].

olics. "Our illness," lamented the Leiden government, "is doctrinal wrangling, and the danger is threatening that the unity with which we have won [against Spain] shall be destroyed."[15] If Leiden was willing to sacrifice the ideal religious unity of society for sorely needed political unity, the town council in Gouda, that "receptacle of heretics," went one step further and questioned the ideal of religious unity itself. In a resolution on September 23, 1583, they declared, "The deputies of this city . . . , although the Reformed religion is accepted provisionally, . . . nevertheless do not understand nor would they want to agree that anyone contrary of doctrine should be injured or hindered in his conscience because of his religious views, and they furthermore maintain that the city magistrates shall remain free to judge in such matters."[16]

Cases like Leiden and Gouda, however, were relatively rare. While the magistrates in those two towns formulated their principles and spoke them aloud, the magistrates in the vast majority of Dutch towns simply acted, or rather neglected to act, to preserve the dissenters from the Calvinist establishment in their freedoms. The evidence pointing to this fact comes from both the Calvinist side and the dissenters' side in quantities so great as to be almost boring. In the minutes of the synod of North Holland, the scandalous blasphemy of Mennonites, Catholics, "Ubiquitists," "Flaccians," and Socinians becomes a permanent item on the agenda by 1580 and remains so throughout the seventeenth century.[17] Scarcely a synodal meeting in all that time goes by without the indignant report by at least one classis of a new papist outrage in its district. To quote but one typical entry from all the thousands, there is the complaint of the classis of Hoorn in the provincial synod of 1605 at Alkmaar: "Since the brothers

---

[15] Quoted *ibid.*, p. 89 [translation mine].

[16] Quoted *ibid.*, p. 90 [translation mine].

[17] The North Holland synodal records from 1571 to 1619 may be consulted in Reitsma and van Veen, vols. 1 (1892) and 2 (1893). From 1619 on, the original manuscript records are found in the *Gemeente Archief* in Amsterdam.

from Hoorn have reported the great licentiousness of the Papists
—not only in the holding of conventicles, but also in celebrating
funerals, burning incense publicly, and lighting candles in the
churches, such as has occurred in Berckhout, Woggenum and
Grosthuysen—it is resolved that the brothers relay their knowledge of this affair to the deputies (of the States-General) so that
it may be remedied."[18]

The fact that this kind of entry continues unabated in the
synodal records throughout the seventeenth century serves once
again as a reminder that the great Synod of Dordrecht in 1618–
1619 fell far short of its goal—the establishment of a uniform,
national Calvinist church in the Netherlands. Glancing randomly
through the minutes of the North Holland synod of 1633, fourteen years after Dordrecht, one finds that the *predikanten* formulated a total of 53 resolutions, 10 of which—or 19 percent—
dealt directly with the problem of uncurbed dissent.[19] In some
North Holland synodal gatherings the percentage would have
been even higher. Furthermore, the interprovincial synodal correspondence for this same year reveals that the provincial synods
in South Holland, Utrecht, Friesland, and Overijssel were also
busy with such problems as "the insolence of the papists," "the
audacity of the Arminian faction," and "the appearance of Jesuits and strange Mennonite bishops."[20]

The Calvinists were by no means ignorant of the root of the
problem. The Classis of Amsterdam resolved on July 5, 1610:
"Since it is found that the conventicles of the papists still continue, and even increase daily; and since this is scarcely hindered—it is resolved that Rev. Plancius and Lucas Jansz. shall
protest this to the *burgemeesters* of Amsterdam, *along with the
laxity of the Sheriff Rodenburchs,* begging them to do all in their
power to remedy the situation [emphasis mine]."[21] Here indeed

---

[18] Reitsma and van Veen, 1 (1892), 381 [translation mine].

[19] *Gemeente Archief,* Amsterdam.

[20] *Ibid.* [translation mine].

[21] In vol. 2 of the manuscript records of the Amsterdam Classis, in the
Gemeente Archief, Amsterdam [translation mine].

lay the crux of the matter. The *predikanten* remonstrated against the dissenters. The provincial and general States legislated against the dissenters. But in the final and most important analysis almost nobody on the local level *acted* against the dissenters. And in this gap between word and deed, between law and practice, the Netherlands became a land of religious toleration. A most interesting document in the *Rijksarchief* in The Hague shows how the system worked. The document concerns Amelis van den Boekhorst, the Heer van Wimmenum, who in 1642 was sheriff of Rijnland. It follows in its entirety:

To Wimmenum is in 1642 (paid?) :
By van der Meer from Berendrecht in

payment for a cancelled intrusion . . .	400 guilders
From van der Meulen many thousands . . .	?
From van der Graef . . .	60 guilders
From the reporting of van der Graef . . .	120 guilders
From Berckel . . .	120 guilders
From Uterwaal . . .	120 guilders
From Gillis Teumen at Sevenhoven . . .	700 guilders

The Jesuits from The Hague who preach at
Voorburch settle separately with Wimmenum.[22]

This document relates in the first place the story of a sheriff who made a good deal of money, in the second place the story of a number of Roman Catholics under the very nose of the Dutch central government in The Hague who were not disturbed for their illegal religious services, and in the third place the story of the Dutch solution for the problem of religious diversity. For this document illustrates not an isolated case, but a national practice. The bribery and connivance of the local law-enforcement officers became such a systematic practice that when Roman Catholics finally won their official toleration in the Netherlands in 1787 sheriffs' salaries had to be raised across the board to compensate for the lost source of income.[23] "In vain," wrote an English ob-

[22] Cited in Knuttel, "Kerk en Burgerlijke Overheid," in *Uit Onzen Bloeitijd* (Amsterdam, n.d.), p. 301 [translation mine].

[23] Boxer, *Dutch Seaborne Empire* (New York: Alfred A. Knopf, 1965), p. 125.

server in 1728, "are penal laws whilst the city and village bailiffs remain the overseers and prosecutors of criminal affairs; for these will ever dispense with the practices of the priests for a sum of money, which they are always in a condition to furnish upon such an occasion."[24]

The Dutch *predikanten* visualized three essentials in their Calvinist Zion. These were ecclesiastical independence from the civil authority, doctrinal independence from the civil authority, and political support by the civil authority to the exclusion of all other religious confessions. But in each case the realization of the Calvinist ideal was frustrated by other interests in the young Dutch republic.

[24] Onslow Burrish, *Batavia Illustrata, Or a View of the Policy, and Commerce, of the United Provinces, Particularly of Holland* (London, 1728), p. 149. Quoted in Boxer, p. 125.

PART II

The Netherlands:
The Merchants' Point of View

5. Amsterdam: The Center of a Dutch World Enterprise

The tension between the Calvinist ideal for Dutch society and that of the civil authorities was nowhere greater in the seventeenth-century Netherlands than in Amsterdam. At the same time, Amsterdam was emerging as the hub of a burgeoning Dutch world enterprise. This enterprise had both ecclesiastical and economic aspects, and Amsterdam was central to both. On the ecclesiastical side, decisions concerning the colonies of both the East and West India companies were made before 1636 by the Amsterdam consistory and thereafter by the Amsterdam classis.[1] It was the Amsterdam *predikanten* who approved ministers and *ziekentroosters*[2] for the Dutch *handelskerken*,[3] recalled

[1] A. Eekhof, *De Hervormde Kerk in Noord-Amerika (1624–1664)*, 2 vols. (The Hague: Nijhoff, 1913), 1, 8.

[2] The *ziekentrooster* or *krankenbezoeker* (visitor of the sick) was a lay official in the Dutch Reformed Church of the sixteenth and seventeenth centuries whose duties were largely concerned with the cure of souls. In Amsterdam they were employed mainly in the hospitals. When the voyages of discovery opened up vast new territories to Dutch commerce and colonization at the beginning of the seventeenth century, the shortage of ordained clergy for these ventures was so great that the *ziekentroosters* were pressed into service on the merchant vessels and in the colonial churches. Their intellectual and spiritual qualifications often left much to be desired. Thus, Bastiaen Janszoon Krol, the first *ziekentrooster* in New Netherland, is known to have signed his marriage license with an X—he could not write. Jan Pieterszoon Coen, the great governor-general of the Dutch East Indies, described the *ziekentroosters* collectively in 1614 as "clownish, uncircumcised idiots."

[3] The *handelskerk* (literally: "commercial church") was a Reformed

77

inadequate or unsatisfactory men from the field, regulated ecclesiastical polity in the Dutch colonies, and generally pleaded the
cause of the Reformed religion with the Heren XVII and the
Heren XIX.[4] Therefore the position taken by the Amsterdam
clergy on matters of church and state had a direct bearing on
church-state relations in all the Dutch colonies, New Netherland
of course included.

Economically, Amsterdam's dominance was even more complete. The directorship of both the Dutch India companies was
heavily influenced, indeed, almost monopolized by the voices of
Amsterdam merchants. Out of the scramble to protect local and
provincial interests that preceded the organization of the East
India Company in 1602, Amsterdam, whose citizens contributed
by far the greatest amount of capital, emerged with the lion's
share of policy-making power.[5] The charter drawn up by the
States-General and approved on March 20, 1602, by all the
parties concerned stipulated that the directorship of the company
should be carried out by a college of seventeen men (the famous
Heren XVII), of whom eight were to be from the Amsterdam
chamber, four from Zealand, and one from each of the "little
chambers"—Delft, Rotterdam, Hoorn, and Enkhuizen. The
seventeenth man was to be chosen in turn by each of the chambers except Amsterdam, so that the latter could never have an
absolute majority. Amsterdam was also successful in resisting a

---

congregation living anywhere under the colonial authority of one of the
Dutch India companies. Its character was nearly always that of a state-
church, a fact which greatly outraged the Calvinist *predikanten* at home.

[4] The Heren XVII were the governing board of directors of the East
India Company. The Heren XIX were their counterparts in the West
India Company.

[5] A breakdown by chambers of the original capital strength of the
East India Company shows that Amsterdam more than earned her domi-
nant position: Amsterdam, f3,674,915; Zealand, f1,300,405; Delft, f469,400;
Rotterdam, f173,000; Hoorn, f266,868; Enkhuizen, f540,000; total, f6,424,-
588. J. G. van Dillen, *Het Oudste Aandeelhoudersregister van de Kamer
Amsterdam der Oost-Indische Compagnie* (The Hague: Nijhoff, 1958),
p. 35.

demand by Zealand that voting in the directing body be by chamber rather than by head so that the chambers would wield equal influence. The Heren met annually for six consecutive years in Amsterdam, followed by two consecutive years in Zealand. The "little" chambers never hosted a meeting.[6]

At the establishment of the West India Company in 1621 the situation remained essentially the same, although this time Amsterdam merchants contributed only 40 percent of the company's original capital while in 1602 they had contributed 57 percent.[7] Amsterdam named eight of the *bewindhebbers* (directors), Zealand four, and the other three chambers two each. The nineteenth *bewindhebber* was appointed directly by the States-General. As with the East India Company the directors met six consecutive years in Amsterdam followed by two years in Middelburg, and the voting was by heads rather than chambers. Thus, although it was probably the case that Amsterdam enjoyed somewhat less influence in the making of policy for the W.I.C. (West-Indische Compagnie) than for the V.O.C. (Vereenigde Oost-Indische Compagnie), in the final analysis no policy that Amsterdam did not support could prevail in either company.

It is impossible to study Dutch colonial church history, or Dutch colonial history in general, without repeatedly returning to the city on the Amstel as the source and root of Dutch colonial policy. Here the decisions were made that shaped the economic, political, and religious destinies of colonies and native populations around the globe from Brazil to Formosa. Who made these decisions? What kind of men were they? In a word, they were merchants. Carl Bangs has correctly noted that a city actually run

---

[6] *Ibid.*, pp. 15–17.

[7] A breakdown by chambers of the original capital strength of the West India Company: States-General, f500,000; Amsterdam, f2,846,582; Zealand, f1,379,775; The Maas (Rotterdam, Delft, Dordrecht), f1,039,202; Westfriesland (Hoorn, Enkhuizen), f505,627; Growingen and Friesland, f836,975; total, f7,108,161. J. G. van Dillen, "De West-Indische Compagnie, Het Calvinisme en De Politiek," *Tijdschrift voor Geschiedenis,* vol. 74 (Gromingen: Noordhoff, 1961), p. 151.

by merchants was an almost unique phenomenon in Europe at the turn of the seventeenth century.[8] Yet that was precisely Amsterdam's situation. The money and power of its city fathers derived not from hereditary landholdings but from trade. For one who has been enchanted by modern Amsterdam, which mirrors its seventeenth-century predecessor to a remarkable degree, the temptation to discuss this trade in detail is great. Nevertheless, that is unnecessary for the Dutch sources are excellent and the English sources have increased notably in recent years.[9] What follows is only the barest outline of one of the earliest manifestations of modern capitalism.

In 1585, the year in which Antwerp fell to the Spanish-Habsburg armies, Amsterdam's estimated population was 30,000; fifteen years later the 1600 census counted 50,000; the 1630 census showed 115,000.[10] In 45 years the city's population had increased nearly four-fold, which is even more noteworthy because urban death rates typically exceeded birth rates in Europe at the time.

Meanwhile, as population was booming so was business, of which there were essentially three types. Shipping was the base. After the fall of Antwerp, Amsterdam rose meteorically to become the center of the long-established Baltic-Iberian trade routes, earlier controlled by Antwerp and the German Hanse towns. Ancillary to her shipping supremacy, Amsterdam also

[8] Bangs, *Arminius* (Nashville, Tenn.: Abingdon, 1971), p. 176.

[9] In English, *the* source is Violet Barbour, *Capitalism in Amsterdam in the Seventeenth Century* (Baltimore: Johns Hopkins Press, 1950). Bangs also includes a good bit "between the lines." In Dutch, two very reliable discussions of Amsterdam's trade are J. G. van Dillen, "Amsterdam als Wereldstad," and J. C. Westermann, "Beschouwingen over de Opkomst en den Bloei des Handels in de Gouden Eeuw," both in A. E. d'Ailley, ed., *Zeven Eeuwen Amsterdam,* vol. 2 (Amsterdam, 1946). The second volume of A. Bredius et al., eds., *Amsterdam in de Zeventiende Eeuw* (The Hague: Van Stockum, 1901) is an exhaustive treatment of Amsterdam's trade.

[10] Van Dillen, "Amsterdam als Wereldstad," p. 14. Also Barbour, pp. 17–18.

seized the European lead in shipbuilding. Here she excelled not
only quantitatively but also qualitatively, for around the turn of
the century she began to manufacture the *fluit* (flute)—a cargo
ship of cheap construction and good sailing qualities first developed in Hoorn.[11]

That Dutch carriers were now beginning to haul most of the
Iberian salt, oil, and fruit to the Baltic and most of the Baltic
grain and timber to Spain led to a second facet of Amsterdam's
new commercial life. The city became a veritable stockpile of
trade commodities, and all along its new canal system (built in
1612) warehouses began to rise. These warehouses, loaded to
their gabled roofs with goods, could produce a cargo for an outgoing freighter on almost instant notice or buy up a whole fleet
load of produce, which only served to further enhance the city's
attractiveness from a shipping standpoint since the shipper assured of a quick return trip with a full load would charge lower
freight rates.

Banking was the third type of commercial activity that characterized seventeenth-century Amsterdam. It was, of course, an
economic superstructure built upon the solid wealth accrued to
Amsterdam shippers, shipbuilders, and merchants. Many Amsterdammers (and many Antwerp immigrants after 1585[12]) watched
their humble commercial beginnings turn into modest fortunes
through investment in the Amsterdam money market.

The subject of investment profits leads to the topic of the India
companies and their role in the life of Amsterdam capitalism.
In 1594 the Compagnie van Verre outfitted a fleet of four vessels and sent them around the Cape of Good Hope under the
leadership of Cornelis de Houtman. In nearly all respects the
expedition was a failure. Of the four outgoing vessels only three
returned; of the outgoing crew of 249 men, 89 returned. The
cargo of Oriental curiosities was just barely sufficient to meet the

[11] B. Hagedorn, *Die Entwicklung der Wichtigsten Schiffstypen Bis ins
19. Jahrhundert* (Berlin: Curtius, 1914), pp. 102ff.
[12] Barbour, pp. 23–24.

expenses of the venture.[13] Nevertheless, in the most important respect the voyage was an overwhelming success—the trail had been blazed. For the first time, Netherlanders had successfully navigated the round trip to the Indies, and no reprisals had been suffered at the hands of the Portuguese.

Holland and Zealand merchants wasted no time capitalizing on the implications of Houtman's successful return. In Amsterdam, another company, the Old Company, was immediately formed, with a capital of f768,466. A fleet of six ships and two yachts was outfitted and sailed under Admiral Jacob van Neck, on May 1, 1598, from the island of Texel. When the eighth ship had finally returned to Amsterdam and the investors were able to total their returns, the profit was reckoned at roughly 400 percent.[14] Understandably, this news woke a feverish interest in the new India traffic, and all over Holland and Zealand new companies were hastily assembled and ships outfitted. By the end of 1601, fifteen fleets, a total of 65 ships, had sailed from the Netherlands for the Indies.[15] Approximately half of them had sailed out of Amsterdam.

It soon became clear, however, that continued free competition in the Indies trade would eventually render that trade unprofitable. With countless small companies scrambling to reap the enormous profits, buying competition in the Indies sent prices upward while selling competition in the Netherlands sent prices down. As early as 1598 the shrewd Oldenbarnevelt recognized that the trade, if left to itself, would wither as quickly as it had blossomed. Only an amalgamation of the companies, the formation of a monopoly or cartel, could save the trade, perpetuate the Dutch presence in the Indies, and break the back of Luso-Hispanic power there. For four stormy years Oldenbarnevelt, working through the States of Holland and the States-General, fought

[13] Van Dillen, *Het Oudste Aandeelhoudersregister,* pp. 5–6.
[14] *Ibid.,* p. 7.
[15] Bredius, et al., II, 23.

to achieve a single united East India Company, and in March 1602 he finally succeeded.[16]

From 1602 the East India Company (Vereenigde Oost-Indische Compagnie) played a major role in the economic life of Amsterdam. In fact, contemporary observers were wont to associate the Indies trade almost exclusively with the city on the Amstel. Pieter de la Court, for example, in his *True Interest of Holland*, states that "after that the Antwerp Trade was added to their Eastern [Baltic] trade and Fishing, the Amsterdammers then got by their Sword the whole East-India Trade, at least the Monopoly of all the richest spices, and a great Trade to the West Indies."[17] The company declared no dividend whatsoever during its first eight years, but the return of a 75 percent dividend in 1610 followed by a second of 50 percent later the same year must have caused rejoicing among heavy investors. Only in 1625 did dividends begin to be declared with any regularity, but from that time forward an annual dividend was paid, and beginning in 1632 shareholders were guaranteed a 12.5 percent annual return on their investments. In only one year of its entire existence did the company fail this guarantee, and it often tripled it. Since Amsterdam merchants and burghers subscribed over half the company's original capital, the greater part of the dividends came to Amsterdam. The great merchants profited most from the years of bumper dividends, and Amsterdam archives show that some possessed as much as f27,800 worth of shares in the East India Company. But the same records show shareholders subscribed for anywhere from 3 to 700 guilders, meaning that the general welfare produced by the company did not totally by-pass the lower classes.[18]

[16] van Dillen, *Het Oudste Aandeelhoudersregister*, pp. 5–20.

[17] *The True Interest and Political Maxims of the Republic of Holland and West Friesland* (London, 1702), pp. 56–57. This is the first English edition of a work published anonymously in Dutch in 1662 as *Interest van Holland ofte Gronden van Hollands Welvaren*.

[18] Bredius, et al., 2, 107–108.

The East India Company also bolstered Amsterdam's economy in other ways. The laboring class, who for the most part could not save the extra capital for investment, nevertheless benefitted by the tremendous demand for labor the V.O.C. brought to the city. After the earliest years approximately six giant East Indiamen departed from the island of Texel annually, carrying crews of about 300 each. Estimating half (probably conservative) of each crew to be Amsterdammers the V.O.C. would already be regarded as a major employer for the city. But this was only the beginning. The Indiamen were too large to deposit or take on cargo in Amsterdam's harbor on the Ij; rather, they anchored off Texel at the top of the Zuider Zee and were relieved of their loads by lighter freight vessels, which could navigate the narrows and shallows of the Zuider Zee without difficulty. Scores of laborers were necessary for the loading and unloading involved in this process. In addition, building and outfitting Indiamen was a constant job that kept about 1,200 Amsterdammers steadily employed. And finally, there was the job of provisioning each ship for the outward voyage. The fact that the V.O.C. maintained its own slaughterhouse where approximately 1,000 oxen were slaughtered and salted annually provides some idea of the scope of this task.[19]

All that has been said of the influence of the East India Company on Amsterdam's economic life can be repeated in the case of the West India Company, albeit with less emphasis. Approximately half the original capital of the W.I.C. was contributed by Amsterdam, and thus much of the dividend profit came to rest there. As time passed, however, and the company failed in its attack on the fabled Spanish treasure-land of Peru (1623), lost its rights of privateering against Spanish shipping (Treaty of Münster, 1648), and saw Brazil revert to Portuguese domination (1654), it gradually became clear that the W.I.C. would never know the unqualified, stable success of her older sister company.

[19] *Ibid.*, 2, 108.

Nevertheless, during the "good years" (about 1623-1628) the company's stock soared spectacularly, even threatening at first to eclipse the profits of the older V.O.C. Between 1623 and 1636 the W.I.C. sent more than 800 ships into the Atlantic and, besides making colonial beginnings in Guinea, Brazil, North America, and the West Indies, reaped more than 40 million guilders profit in booty from privateering.[20] The zenith of this activity was reached in 1628 when Vice-Admiral Piet Heyn, on September 8, successfully surprised the annual Spanish silver fleet in Havana Bay. The prize on this occasion was worth approximately f11,000,000, and the following year a dividend of 50 percent was declared.

J. C. Westermann has correctly cautioned against overestimating the extent to which the economy of seventeenth-century Amsterdam depended on the glamorous Indies trade.[21] The older Baltic-Iberian trade always remained the basic lynch pin in Amsterdam's commercial success. It remains true, however, that Amsterdam more than any other single Dutch province or town was intimately related to Dutch colonizing and trading in the East and West Indies, and it was the social and political patterns influencing the shape of religion in Amsterdam that were exported to a Dutch world empire. These patterns were reflected in what could be termed Amsterdam's "business ethic."

In this city that spawned the first of a type come to be known in the modern world as the "big businessman," an intangible but very real ethical attitude appeared. It was an attitude difficult to define with precision, but it might be referred to as an attitude of "business first."[22]

Both Dutch and American historians have noted this attitude. The eminent Dutch economic historian J. G. van Dillen has said

[20] *Ibid.*, 2, 144.

[21] Westermann, p. 79.

[22] This nomenclature is definitely not intended to be pejorative. There were important reasons why the Seven Provinces, and especially Amsterdam, tended to place such a high priority on trade.

concerning the merchant directors of the Amsterdam chamber of the W.I.C.: "It is well-known that the directors as well as the chief stockholders were scarcely exemplars of a Calvinistic style of life. With several exceptions—as, among others, the learned Johannes de Laet—they were typical moneyhounds [*geldwolven*], who repeatedly promoted their own financial interests at the expense of the Company in a grotesque manner."[23] Less scathing but no less poignant is Violet Barbour's observation concerning Amsterdam capitalists in general: "The cosmopolitan spirit and geographical dispersion of certain merchant families whose business headquarters were in Amsterdam, interestingly foreshadowed the international histories of later capitalist families. The international capitalist from his earliest to his latest appearance has generally been, where business was concerned, a Man without a Country, and the seventeenth-century Amsterdammer, though by no means a man without a city, was strikingly uninhibited by abstract considerations of patriotism or by theories of economic nationalism."[24]

This tendency of the great Amsterdam *heren* to place business interests above religion, country, and just about everything else did not go unnoticed by their contemporaries, both those who applauded the worship of business and those who heaped scorn upon it. The placing of business before religion was especially conspicuous. Pieter de la Court rejoiced that "freedom or toleration in the matter of religious services is the most powerful means to preserve many inhabitants in Holland and to allure foreigners to dwell among us."[25] The Puritan poet Andrew Marvell, in his satirical "Character of Holland," laid the blame for Amsterdam's abominable religious diversity directly at the feet of the blind acquisitiveness of the merchants:

[23] "De West-Indische Compagnie," p. 157.

[24] P. 130.

[25] Pieter de la Court, *Aanwysing der Heilsame Politike Gronden en Maximen van de Republike van Holland en West-Vriesland* (Leiden: Hakkens, 1669), p. 59. Quoted in Boxer, *Dutch Seaborne Empire* (New York: Alfred Knopf, 1965), p. 131 [translation mine].

Hence Amsterdam, Turk, Christian, Pagan, Jew,
Staple of sects and mint of schism grew:
That bank of conscience, where not one so strange
Opinion but finds credit and exchange.[26]

In the same vein was the indignant tone of the Reformed *predikant* at Delft who complained in 1650 concerning the wealthy merchants of the Amsterdam city council that they "have greatly caressed the Papists, and Bicker [Amsterdam's most powerful merchant and burgomaster at this time, Andries Bicker] has set himself up as their patron to favor their requests and abuse the Reformed, managing through his henchmen to obstruct all resolutions and actions against the increasing obstinacy of the Papists."[27] And perhaps most illustrative of the point here under discussion was the reception accorded a Dutch diplomat by Charles X of Sweden. The Dutchman was extolling the freedom of religion enjoyed by his countrymen, whereupon Charles pulled a coin from his pocket and said, "There is your religion! You worship only your idol, which is commerce."[28]

Extreme caution must, however, be exercised in appraising this priority of business as it appeared in seventeenth-century Amsterdam. It is far too easy to wax cynical and fall back upon epithets such as *geldwolven* to describe the great *heren*. While incidents illustrating the grossest kind of selfish privateering are not lacking among the careers of Amsterdam merchants, there were other factors besides pure greed operative in the ethic of "business first." As far as the supposed lack of patriotism on the part of Amsterdam merchants is concerned, it has already been noted that, after the formation of the Union of Utrecht and the successful withdrawal of the northern provinces from the Spanish sphere of con-

[26] In A. B. Grosart, ed., *The Complete Works of Andrew Marvell* (New York: AMS Press, 1966), 1, 245. Quoted in Boxer, p. 131.

[27] Cited in W. P. C. Knuttel, *De Toestand der Nederlandsche Katholieken ten Tijde der Republiek,* 2 vols. (The Hague: Nijhoff, 1892–1894), 1, 298–299 [translation mine].

[28] E. Wrangel, *De Betrekkingen tusschen Zweden en de Nederlanden* (Leiden: E. J. Brill, 1901), pp. 8–9. Cited in Boxer, p. 115.

trol and influence, political allegiance within these provinces became highly localized.[29] Each province was a sovereign state, and the States-General, which consisted simply of delegates from each of the provinces, could act on matters that affected the "generality" only by unanimous vote. All of the provincial delegates protected their own respective provincial interests jealously, and, since each province chose its delegates from the various quasi-sovereign municipalities within that province, even municipal interests were often defended at The Hague at the expense of the general good of the United Provinces. Thus, the term "United Provinces" is more than slightly misleading, and something like "affiliated provinces" would be closer to the truth. In any case, to castigate Amsterdam merchants for placing local business interests above patriotic duty is a judgment historically unsound. "National loyalty" was a concept unknown to the age, and Amsterdam merchants protected the interests of the political entity to which they were loyal—their city.

Furthermore, international shipping and trade was the very lifeblood of the two maritime provinces—Holland and Zealand—and especially of Amsterdam. The trade of the maritime provinces, spearheaded by that of Amsterdam, was the *sine qua non* of the very existence of the Dutch republic and of the smooth operation of its war machine. Already in 1548 the States of Holland submitted to Charles V a petition in which they pointed out,

Holland contains many dunes, bogs, and lakes which grow daily more extensive, as well as other barren districts, unfit for crops or pasture. Wherefore the inhabitants of the said country in order to make a living for their wives, children and families, must maintain themselves by handicrafts and trades, in such wise that they fetch raw materials from foreign lands and re-export the finished products, including diverse sorts of cloth and draperies, to many places, such as the kingdoms of Spain, Portugal, Germany, Scotland, and especially to Denmark, the Baltic, Norway, and other like regions, whence they return with goods and merchandise from those parts,

[29] Elias, *Geschiedenis van het Amsterdamsche Regentenpatriciaat*, 2 vols. (The Hague: Nijhoff, 1923), 1, p. 2.

notably wheat and other grains. Consequently, the main business of
the country must needs be in shipping and related trades, from which
a great many people earn their living, like merchants, skippers,
masters, pilots, sailors, shipwrights and all those connected therewith.[30]

What was true of Holland in a general way was particularly true
of Amsterdam. Jan Wagenaar, the eighteenth-century historian
of the city, poses this question at the very beginning of the fore-
word of his massive four-volume work: "One longs to know," he
says, "by what special confluence of circumstances the poor Am-
stel-area was expanded into a world metropolis, and the low fish-
ermen's huts transformed into stately palaces." Discussing Amsterdam's trade and industry in Volume II, Wagenaar provides
his own answer. "We turn now," he begins, "to a general sketch
of the commerce of the city, the principal cause of her growth
and greatness."[31]

Commerce was the very heart of seventeenth-century Amsterdam's existence. The style of life and system of values evolved by
the city's merchant bourgeoisie were based squarely on this reality. Unfortunately, the average Dutch merchant of the time was a
man of affairs rather than—or at least before he was—a man of
learning, and he did not leave in writing a great deal of explicit
economic ideology.[32] Cornelis Pieterszoon Hooft, however, provides a happy exception.[33] A learned and articulate man who was
nevertheless first and foremost a merchant, Hooft was driven
from his native city as a refugee in 1569 for his Protestant sympathies. Returning to Holland in 1574 and to Amsterdam in
1578, he founded a commercial firm with his brother Willem in

---

[30] Cited in Boxer, p. 5.

[31] *Amsterdam* (Amsterdam: Isaak Tirion, 1760–1767), 1, i; 2, 413.

[32] Thus, one is confronted with a problem familiar to the intellectual
historian—the capriciousness of the sources. The theologians and *predikanten* leave almost too many documents; the merchants leave almost none.

[33] A fine intellectual biography of Hooft is H. A. E. van Gelder, *De
Levensbeschouwing van Cornelis Pieterszoon Hooft* (Amsterdam: A. H.
Kruyt, 1918).

1584, dealing in herring, grain, and oil. Also in 1584 he was named to the Amsterdam city council, and beginning in 1588 he was chosen burgomaster twelve times, for the last time in 1610.[34] Hooft's "Memoriën en Adviezen," his memoirs, provides a candid glimpse of the "business first" ethic. First, says Hooft, "our greatest power and welfare derives from the *Imperium maris,* and from foreign commerce." For this reason "the nature of these lands, and especially of this city (existing, by God's grace, mostly by shipping and commerce) most urgently demands familiar amiability between men."[35] Hooft is thus thoroughly impatient with the doctrinal strictness and theocratic tendencies of the Reformed *predikanten* and their synods. The welfare of the land—which patently rests upon continuous commercial traffic involving all sorts and conditions of men—demands mutual understanding and toleration of political and religious differences. But the *predikanten,* with their interminable theological wrangling and their rigid demands for the political combatting of heresy, encourage exactly the opposite—schism and bad blood between men of differing convictions. Numberless are the pages in his memoirs where he registers utter disgust and indignation at the pretensions of the Reformed clergy:

Contrary to manifold examples and places in the scripture they [the *predikanten*] wish to allow no knowledge of ecclesiastical affairs not only to the common man but also to the government of the lands and the cities. In this vein they do not scruple to accuse such fine governments as those of England, Scotland, the Palatinate and others of unjust usurpations of the privileges which the *predikanten,* in the opinion of a number of learned Reformed theologians, have exercised for many years and still continue to exercise. With this kind of audacity and sorry discretion, they label every opinion heretical which cannot accept their reasoning. They exhort the gov-

[34] *Ibid.,* pp. 8–9.
[35] "Memoriën en Adviezen," published in two parts in *Werken van het Historisch Genootschap Gevestigd te Utrecht,* New Series nos. 15 and 16, Third Series nos. 48 and 49, (Utrecht: Kemink, 1871 and 1925). Quotes from New Series nos. 15 and 16, p. 236, and p. 30.

ernment to proceed against these heresies as against the Canaanites and the priests of Baal, and they say that the thing must be done with a heavy foot and without the slightest regard for person. For the execution of the magistracy they pray to God that he will give us men who will pursue this course with the sword, and they pray also that the matter must be handled with zeal, even though all the trade of the land should be thereby lost. Sitting solemnly at table, they greet the new magistrates at the beginning of their terms of office with printed petitions to drive out the "heretics" with their children as if they were plagues and base men.

But I pray that the magistrates may consider with due deliberation what the outcome of this action would necessarily be. It is still well within the memory of the natives and naturalized citizens of our land (or else they have heard it from their parents) what great dangers it cost us to escape the tyranny of the Spaniards; accordingly, I believe that there is no evidence that these people would allow themselves to be used for this purpose (unless some should be depraved and degenerated), since any heresy proceedings would concern their own old acquaintances, relatives, or at least good naturalized citizens of the land; whom they would be forced to execute not as Judges, but without being able to gain any knowledge of the matter and solely on the knowledge and judgment of clergy, they themselves being nothing more than judicial assistants and beadles, as Dr. Pareus says. In this way, they [the *predikanten*] would be able to exercise, contrary to the law of the land, foreign jurisdiction over the people (since it would be strange and unfamiliar to them) without any pity or compassion. And so, in my opinion, the last error would be greater than the first.[36]

In Hooft are echoes of the voice of the Leiden magistracy. Like the Leiden city fathers, Hooft is concerned that civil power be retained in the hands of the regent class rather than falling into the hands of the "foreign jurisdiction" of the *predikanten*. To this extent, Hooft's argument is simply a reiteration of the regent class's intention to consolidate and perpetuate its recently won political supremacy in the United Provinces. But there is something more in Hooft's statement that betokens a peculiarly mercantile point of view. For him it is not just that the *predikan-*

[36] *Ibid.*, pp. 95–97 [translation mine].

ten overstep the theoretical boundaries of their power in enlisting the civil magistracy to hunt heretics. What really concerns Hooft is what he feels will be the practical consequence of the enactment of this clerical program. These zealots pray publicly that heresy must be uprooted "even though all the trade of the land should be thereby lost."

6. Amsterdam's Attitude toward Religious Dissent

The *predikanten* envisioned the United Provinces as an organic community, covenanted around and dedicated to a religious metaphysic to be supplied and interpreted by them. The merchants, though they articulated it less frequently, held a quite contrary vision for the new Dutch society. Their vision was one in which trade rather than religion would form the center of gravity and provide society's basic values. Oftentimes (usually under fire from the *predikanten*) the merchants would protest that they still operated within the framework of the old values. And an occasional shrewd operator like the enigmatic Petrus Plancius could actually purvey one set of values in public life while profiting from the other privately. But overall there was a shift in fundamental human values occurring among Dutchmen during the seventeenth century—an important chapter in the history of that process so imperfectly understood and so inadequately called "secularization." One good index of which interpretation of societal reality was prevailing in Amsterdam was the rapid growth of religious dissent and pluralism.

R. B. Evenhuis, the Dutch historian, begins his discussion of religious dissent in Amsterdam during the Golden Age with the following remark: "Amsterdam was, from an external viewpoint, a Reformed city, governed by Reformed Burgomasters, where only the Reformed religion might be publicly practiced. Nevertheless, there was no city in Holland where more dissenters lived.

Jews and Roman Catholics, Anabaptists and Lutherans, Brownists and heretics of all shades formed for a long time the majority of the population and in the beginning even a large majority."[1] This statement reveals two things: first, Amsterdam's internal religious life was not what it appeared from the outside; second, more than one strange species of plant was growing in this supposedly Calvinist Eden.

Emanuel Rodriguez Vega was the first Jew known to have become an Amsterdam citizen, having purchased that right in 1597 from the city magistrates.[2] Vega and the other Portuguese Maranos who quickly followed him to Amsterdam were theological and ecclesiastical orphans. Their Roman Catholicism was of course only external, but they had also become estranged from their Jewish heritage under the constant and persuasive pressure of the Inquisition. In Amsterdam they sought in the first place not religious toleration but business opportunity and relief from the Inquisition's oppression. When Vega swore the oath upon which his citizenship depended, it was made clear to him by the city fathers that only the Reformed religion might be practiced within the city. This apparently disturbed Vega not a whit, and nothing was heard of Jewish religious life in Amsterdam for several more years, although the community was continually growing.

This changed rather suddenly, however, in 1602 with the arrival of Urie Ha-levy. A learned man, the restless Ha-levy remained in Amsterdam only slightly over a year, but the Torah lessons he gave the apostate Maranos really formed the "birthrite" of the Jewish faith in that city. Presently two synagogues were built, both in the neighborhood of the present-day Waterlooplein on the city's east side—an area that was within the city

[1] Evenhuis, *Ook Dat Was Amsterdam* (Amsterdam: ten Have, 1965 and 1967), 2, 167.

[2] In what real sense Vega was a Jew in 1597 is not clear, and was probably not clear even to him. He was a Marano—one who had renounced Judaism and accepted Catholicism under the pressure of the Inquisition.

walls but far enough from the center of town not to be conspicuous to the watchful eyes of the Reformed consistory. Menasseh ben Israel, the rabbi of Newe Shalom synagogue became world-famous as a child prodigy, the master of ten languages who composed a Hebrew grammar at the age of sixteen, the author and publisher of sixty books in Hebrew, Latin, Portuguese, Spanish, and English, and the friend of de Groot and Rembrandt.[3] In addition to the two synagogues, there soon appeared another manifestation of Jewish religious life, the society Talmud Torah. The society founded a press that produced mainly devotional literature, as well as a school that taught the children Hebrew and the adults Old Testament and Talmud exegesis. This school achieved a European reputation during the seventeenth century and attracted such outstanding teachers as Saul Levi Morteira, the teacher of Spinoza. Scholarships provided by the society Talmud Torah opened the school to promising students of all economic stations. It was a model school, far ahead of its time in many respects.

The growth and bloom of Jewish culture in seventeenth-century Amsterdam is a fascinating phenomenon and highly important for the subsequent history of Judaism in Europe and the New World.[4] There can be no disputing that by 1640 the Jewish community at Amsterdam enjoyed a more favorable situation than did Jews in any other part of Europe.[5] But while the city magistracy was making the Amsterdam Maranos (and later the German and Polish Ashkenazim) feel heartily welcome in their adopted city, the Reformed consistory took quite another view of the situation.

What most outraged the consistory, the city's self-appointed religious and moral watchdog, was the prospect of a public syna-

---

[3] Evenhuis, 2, 178.

[4] See for additional information, H. Brugmans and A. Franck, *Geschiedenis der Joden in Nederland* (Amsterdam, 1940); and H. I. Bloom, *The Economic Activities of the Jews in Amsterdam in the Seventeenth and Eighteenth Centuries* (Williamsport, Pa.: Bayard Press, 1937).

[5] Evenhuis, 2, 172.

gogue. In 1612 the Jewish congregations, which until that time had met in closed gatherings in private homes or warehouses, began construction of a synagogue. Permission from the city magistrates was never asked, probably in order not to wake sleeping dogs. But the consistory was not asleep, and on March 22, 1612, it declared that "inasmuch as it is held to be certain that the building of the Jews by Vrooienburch is intended as a synagogue, it is resolved that Domine Hallius, Domine Rolandus and Frederick Jansson shall confer with the Honorable Burgomasters about this."[6] Three weeks later Domine Hallius was able to report favorably in consistory that the construction of the synagogue had been called to the attention of the burgomasters and that the latter had replied "that they had not permitted this and would see to the matter immediately."[7] The construction work was indeed stopped, and the foundation piles, which had already been driven, had to be pulled out of the ground. This was, however, only a temporary victory for the consistory; it turned to defeat in 1619, when the States-General ruled, on December 13, that each city should be free to decide for itself the policy to follow with regard to Jews. On January 16, 1620, the consistory resolved to appeal to the burgomasters to maintain their ban on a Jewish synagogue, since "the States-General have decided that each city shall be free to deal with the Jews as it shall see fittest."[8] But the burgomasters had a different idea about what was fittest; the ban was lifted, and the synagogue rose according to the original plan of 1612. When a new synagogue was begun in 1639 all the consistory could do was admonish the Reformed laity not to go and stare.[9] Upon its completion in 1642 it was visited by Prince Frederik Hendrik; his son, the future Prince Willem II; and Queen

[6] "Protocol of the Amsterdam Consistory," March 22, 1612. In the Amsterdam *Gemeente Archief*.

[7] *Ibid.*, April 12, 1612.

[8] I. H. van Eeghen, "De Gereformeerde Kerkeraad en de Joden te Amsterdam," in *Amstelodamum*, 47 (1960), 170.

[9] *Ibid.*

Henrietta Maria, the widow of Charles I of England. Frederik Hendrik received a gift of f2000 from the congregation and Menasseh ben Israel gave the speech—facts that speak for themselves.

In many other ways the Amsterdam magistracy favored the Jewish community to the great sorrow of the consistory. In 1605 the burgomasters declared that "the Jews also may clothe themselves according to their wishes just as the Christians, without wearing any external token to distinguish them from Christians and without being interrogated or molested." The Jews were not restricted in residence to one part of the city, and no ghetto developed. They were not required to do military service if they paid for a replacement; they were excused from appearing in court on Saturdays and had only to swear an Old Testament oath that they would not give false testimony. Marriage performed within a Jewish congregation by a rabbi was legally recognized if registered at the city hall.[10]

Nevertheless, the magistracy did pass a restrictive ordinance against the Jews in 1616, very probably—though not certainly—at the instigation of the consistory. On November 8, 1616, it was forbidden to Amsterdam Jews to speak or write "to the scorn of our Christian religion," "to attempt to entice away from our Christian religion or circumcise any Christian person," and to "associate and traffic with the women and daughters of this land." The final part of the ordinance is perhaps the most interesting. It specified that Jewish men were to have no sexual association whatsoever with Christian women, whether married, unmarried, or whores.[11] That it was effective in preventing interreligious courtship or marriage is highly doubtful. As late as 1663 the consistory, apparently despairing of the law's having any effect, agreed that "servant girls who are members of the congregation and who live with the Jews should be sought out by the brothers [predikanten] in their own neighborhoods, warned of

[10] Evenhuis, 2, pp. 172–173.
[11] Ibid., passim.

the danger to their souls, and advised to leave such houses and live with the Christians."[12] The first part of the ordinance meant that Jews must refrain from making public remarks about Jesus Christ, Mary, and other items of Christian faith as particularly scandalized the Reformed clergy. Petrus Plancius, the Amsterdam *predikant* renowned both as geographer and arch heretic-hunter, complained in 1610 that the Jews "have accustomed themselves to stating terrible blasphemies about our saviour Jesus Christ." And a Jew is supposed to have said in 1611 that Mary could not have remained a virgin and that she was not of the house of David.[13] As far as the second part of the ordinance was concerned, it was virtually impossible to prevent some conversion of Christians to Judaism. The primary force contributing thereto was mixed marriages resulting from the forbidden interreligious courtship.

Although the Amsterdam Jewish community was excluded from certain trades and made to bear a second-class citizenship in other various small ways, after 1619 it enjoyed virtual freedom of religion in all essential respects. This was the work of the city magistrates. If the Reformed consistory had had its way things would have been different, but as the minutes of the provincial Synod of Hoorn in 1641 so tersely put it: "The church at Amsterdam could not achieve its goal with the magistracy."[14]

This was also the reason that Roman Catholicism flourished in Amsterdam.[15] As was only natural, the Reformed consistory was even more outraged by the impunity with which the "papists" went about their business than by the relatively greater

[12] "Protocol of the Amsterdam Consistory," November 11, 1663, in the Amsterdam *Gemeente Archief*.

[13] Cited in Evenhuis, 2, 174.

[14] Cited in van Eeghen, p. 174.

[15] See W. P. C. Knuttel, *De Toestand der Nederlandsche Katholieken ten Tijde der Republiek,* vol. 1 (The Hague: Nijhoff, 1892); L. J. Rogier, *Geschiedenis van het Katholicisme in Noord-Nederland in de Zestiende en Zeventiende Eeuw* (Amsterdam, 1945), vol. 2; and I. H. van Eeghen, "De Eigendom van de Katholieke Kerken in Amsterdam ten tijde van de Republiek," *Bijdragen Bisdom Haarlem,* 1957, pp. 217–277.

freedom of the Jews. Again the consistory failed, but failure certainly was not owing to neglect of the problem. Scarcely a page in the minutes of the consistory's meetings in the seventeenth century fails to yield at least one item of Reformed indignation at the "papist audacities." All kinds of things form the grounds for complaint: Catholic church-goers who carry their superstitious papist books in a shamelessly visible way, Catholic ikons displayed in private homes so as to be visible from the street, carriages waiting in front of hidden Catholic churches (*schuilkerken*), audible singing of papist songs, children sitting on the front steps learning their papist catechisms, and many more.[16]

At first things did not go so well in Amsterdam for the Catholics. The *"handelsstad"* (trade city) held out longer than any other major Holland town against the revolutionary reformation of William's *geuzen,* but when the official shift to Protestantism finally occurred (May 25, 1578)[17] a strong reaction took place against the people loyal to Rome. In April 1580 a strict city ordinance was passed against Catholics in agreement with the similar decree of the States-General in that same year following the defection of Rennenburg in Groningen. In 1589 this ordinance was renewed, with the provision, however, that the local sheriffs should be free to moderate the punishments prescribed by the States. In 1591 an even sharper ordinance was passed; attendance at a forbidden papist conventicle was punishable by a f200 fine and banishment, while a priest saying mass received the same or "a year on beer and bread."[18]

Between 1578 and 1630 or thereabouts, when the picture began to change favorably for Catholics, Amsterdam civil authorities did enforce these strong ordinances against papist conventicles. It was, however, never impossible for the conventicles to continue. The Dutch historian Knuttel relates an interesting story

[16] Rogier, 1, 449.
[17] Elias, *Geschiedenis van het Amsterdamsche Regentenpatriciaat,* 2 vols. (The Hague: Nijhoff, 1923), 1, p. 18.
[18] Evenhuis, 2, 184.

from 1617 which illustrates both points. On the evening of Good
Friday 200 papists had gathered for mass. It was betrayed to the
sheriff, however, and he and his men surrounded the house. Escape appeared impossible, so the woman of the house, who was
expecting, pretended that her hour had come. Her groaning and
howling reached the street outside, and the sheriff called in to
ask what was the matter. The husband then came to the door
and answered in indignant fashion that he had need of no civil
servant but rather of a midwife. What did the sheriff mean by
banging on his door in the middle of the night, perhaps killing
both his wife and child from fright? Meanwhile, neighbors came
scurrying to the aid of the woman. The sheriff and his men, convinced that a mistake had indeed been made, departed.[19]

For the first fifty years after the Reformation in Holland the
Amsterdam Catholics thus held themselves to a quiet and cir-
cumspect (though patently illegal) performance of their religious
services. Around 1629, however, the political constellation in
Amsterdam began to change in connection with the greater freedom allowed to Remonstrants, and this worked greatly to the
advantage of Catholics. The period designated by the historian
Fruin as a "regeneration" (wederopluiking) of Dutch Catholicism was characterized in Amsterdam by a great increase in the
size of Roman gatherings and a much more open acknowledgment of faith on the part of many Catholics.[20] The changing
climate is illustrated by another story, this one dating from the
year 1629.[21] On December 26, a Roman priest, Leonardus Marius, was saying mass before a Catholic conventicle in a private
home. The sheriff executed a surprise raid but Marius was able
to change clothes hastily and make good his escape. The sheriff,
however, found a portion of Marius's vestments which had been

[19] Knuttel, De Toestand der Nederlandsche Katholieken, 1, 92.
[20] R. Fruin, "De Wederopluiking van het Katholicisme in Noord-Nederland omstreeks den Aanvang der XVIIde Eeuw," in Verspreide Geschriften (The Hague, 1900), vol. 3.
[21] Cited in Evenhuis, 2, 189.

left behind. He reported the incident to the magistrates, in the expectation that they would issue a warrant for Marius's arrest. On the contrary, they strongly reprimanded the sheriff and instructed him henceforth to leave the priest in peace.

This increased freedom and audacity on the part of Catholics spurred the consistory to action. Of the several resolutions passed by the clergy about this time, the following one, dating from April 30, 1629, is a good example: "It is brought to the attention of the gathering of the [consistory] that the Papists, in a bold manner, daily exercise their superstitions and idolatry, and that the Arminians have also held conventicles and preached on the Nieuwe Syts Achterburgwal by the Sea Cruycken next to the Spycker of the Mennonites; also that much murmuring of the citizenry has occurred in that neighborhood. The gathering has resolved that the Honorable Lords Burgomasters be petitioned concerning both the boldness of the Papists and the conventicles of the Arminians."[22]

After about 1630 the Catholics also developed an institution that became characteristic of seventeenth-century Amsterdam's religious life—the *schuilkerk,* or hidden church. There were two types of *schuilkerken:* those concealed in attics (*zolderkerken*) and those concealed on the ground floor (*huiskerken*). As the "papist boldness" increased, the *schuilkerken* became larger and more elaborately furnished. The closely built (usually contiguous) canal houses of the city were ideal for the purpose of expansion. The watchful consistory reported that "some of the *schuilkerken* have two or three attics attached together, with the entrances scattered around at various places."[23] The various routes of entrance and exit were to facilitate quick escape in time of emergency. Again, the consistory noted on April 4, 1641, that there was a Catholic *schuilkerk* on the Gelderse Kade "where

---

[22] "Protocol of the Amsterdam Consistory," in the Amsterdam *Gemeente Archief* [translation mine].
[23] In Evenhuis, 2, 196.

some seven houses are joined together."[24] The visitor to modern Amsterdam can see, on the Oudezijds Voorburgwal on the east side of town, one of these original seventeenth-century *schuilkerken* in a nearly perfect state of preservation—*Onze Lieve Heer op Zolder,* or Our Blessed Lord in the Attic. By midcentury the *schuilkerk* had become the chief solution to the problem of religious pluralism in Amsterdam. In 1656 the consistory decided to conduct an investigation of the *schuilkerken* in order better to document its frequent protests to the city magistracy. Each *predikant* was commissioned to report on papist activities in his neighborhood. The final figures showed 62 "solemn-gathering places, decorated with altars and all kinds of papist ornaments." To these *schuilkerken* came, all week long in clear daylight, hundreds of papists "singing and playing on organs, violins and other instruments" so that it was audible from the street and neighboring houses."[25]

"Papist audacity" was anathema to the consistory but acceptable to, and to a certain extent protected by, the merchant-magistrates. On March 31, 1644, the consistory presented a lengthy memorandum to the burgomasters. The main line of the argument was as follows. As soon as idolatry enters a land God abandons that land, for idolatry is spiritual whoredom. For this reason God commanded Israel, upon its entry into Canaan, to root out all idolatry. This is also the only way of salvation for Amsterdam. The city's policy must be "rather die than, as a dog, return to its own vomit." But, at city hall, "the zeal has grown cold," and the magistrates have grown lukewarm and almost "frozen." The streets teem with nuns and monks, "a crafty invention of the Devil." The papists are called to church by church bells, and they act like lords and masters of the city. They incite the crowd by insinuating that every step toward a Reformed church is a step

[24] "Protocol of the Amsterdam Consistory," in the Amsterdam *Gemeente Archief* [translation mine].
[25] Evenhuis, 2, 203.

toward Hell. In short, everything calls for a new reformation, and the sooner the better, for it is "dangerous to walk on hot coals and sharp swords, perilous to let wolves into the sheep pen, and unfitting to kiss the feet of the Antichrist."[26]

The magistrates refused to listen. Confronted by a delegation from the consistory on March 18, 1638, demanding curbs on papist worship, the burgomasters replied that they "would handle the matter as the situation of the land should demand."[27] In other words, their action would be determined by political and economic expediency. Still clearer was the response of the burgomasters on February 21, 1641: "concerning the abundance of priests and nuns, if they perform their services quietly there are no ordinances against them."[28] Thus for the magistrates there could be no question of repressing the "papists" in accordance with Reformed demands. Evenhuis is completely correct when he says that "in practice the Roman Catholics had total religious freedom in Amsterdam after 1630, in spite of the fact that they could build no churches with towers on the public streets."[29]

The third strange plant, after Judaism and Catholicism, that grew in the nominally Reformed Eden of Amsterdam was the Remonstrant brotherhood. This stock, genetically and genealogically so closely related to the Reformed themselves, was perhaps because of this very resemblance particularly anathema to the Calvinist *predikanten*. No other series of incidents illustrates so well as the struggle surrounding the Remonstrant conventicles the following two points: (1) that the Reformed *predikanten* strove to create a Calvinist theocracy in Amsterdam, and (2) that the city magistracy, while working within the bounds of a legal Reformed establishment, thwarted the *predikanten* for reasons primarily economic and political.

[26] "Protocol of the Amsterdam Consistory," March 31, 1644, in the Amsterdam *Gemeente Archief* [translation mine].
[27] *Ibid.*, July 22, 1638.
[28] *Ibid.*, February 21, 1641.
[29] 2, 196.

Until this point the Amsterdam magistracy has been considered as a more or less homogeneous group ideologically. Events in the city between about 1612 and 1630, connected with the question of the Remonstrants, however, give the lie to that generalization. When it came to the question of religious dissent—and especially Remonstrant dissent—there were different kinds of magistrates.

The course pursued by the Advocate of Holland, Oldenbarnevelt, with respect to the Remonstrants has been outlined previously. Oldenbarnevelt's policy was to prevent theological and religious dispute by civil intervention in the doctrinal and practical life of the church. From 1612 onward, however, Amsterdam opposed the Advocate's policy bitterly. Three explanations are generally given for Amsterdam's position in the matter—economic, political, and religious. In the first place the plans forwarded since 1602 by Willem Usselincx for a West India Company to plunder and capture Spain's American possessions were dear to the Amsterdam merchants, who saw in them a chance to win enormous profits. Oldenbarnevelt's engineering of the truce in 1609 temporarily dashed the plans for a W.I.C., and many Amsterdam merchants never forgave him.[30] In the second place, Amsterdam opposed Oldenbarnevelt politically because his policy in working for the truce was designed largely to benefit the United Provinces as a whole, which were desperately weary from a nearly forty-year war. Amsterdam, however, paid little or no attention to the union. Amsterdam leaders thought about Amsterdam first, Amsterdam second, and the union third, and Amsterdam found the war economically profitable despite the havoc it might be wreaking on the other provinces. Both of these factors, economic and political, tended to throw Amsterdam into a position vis à vis Oldenbarnevelt shared by the Calvinist *predikanten* for reasons wholly religious. The practical result of all this was that in the burgomaster elections of 1612 the Counter-

[30] Elias, p. 46.

Remonstrant party[31] achieved success with the election of Reynier Pauw, a merchant of ardent Calvinist complexion. Under Pauw's able and dynamic leadership the Amsterdam civil magistracy gradually became more sympathetic to the demands of the Reformed consistory regarding the Remonstrants. This process was speeded by Maurits's visit to the city in 1618 at the height of the religious tensions. Exercising his power arbitrarily, the prince removed from the city council all those men who could be regarded as dangerous to the Counter-Remonstrant cause, including Cornelis Pieterszoon Hooft, some of whose opinions concerning the Reformed clergy have been quoted above.[32] The situation in 1619 is best indicated by the magistracy's reply in that year to a request from the Amsterdam Remonstrants for religious toleration shortly after the Synod of Dordrecht. They should be allowed, said the Remonstrants, "no less freedom than was permitted to other Christians in the land; and also to the Jews in Amsterdam, for no other reason than the business advantages thereby gained." The burgomasters, in conjunction with the now-Counter-Remonstrant States of Holland, flatly refused the request on June 24, 1619.[33] By 1620 the Remonstrant cause had reached its nadir in Amsterdam. The burgomaster posts in that year were held by Pauw, Frederick de Vrij, Gerrit Jacob Witsen, and Jacob Gerritszoon Honig—each of whom had served the Reformed congregation either as elder or deacon.[34]

If this political group had managed to perpetuate itself, the story of Remonstrant dissent, and indeed of *religious* dissent, in seventeenth-century Amsterdam would have been completely

[31] By "the Counter-Remonstrant party" I mean simply those magistrates agreeing theologically with the Calvinist *predikanten* who opposed Arminius and agreeing politically with those who opposed Oldenbarnevelt. There were no organized political "parties," as we know them, in Amsterdam at this time.

[32] Elias, p. 59.

[33] Wagenaar, *Amsterdam* (Amsterdam: Isaak Tirion, 1760–1767), 1, 473.

[34] Evenhuis, 1, 282.

different. But, as soon as the immediate objective of Oldenbarne-velt's removal had been accomplished (May 13, 1619), the Amsterdam merchants began to look askance at their too insistent *ad hoc* allies—the *predikanten*. Even more quickly than it had been formed, Pauw's coalition disintegrated. In the burgomaster elections of 1622, Pauw was defeated, and four men of completely different character took office. The new burgomasters were: Frans Jacobszoon Oetgens, a nominal Calvinist but in reality an unscrupulous political and economic opportunist whose primary motive was greed;[35] Jacob van Neck, the hero of the second trip to the East Indies and a very respectable man, but no Calvinist;[36] Dirck Bas, who was a Remonstrant sympathizer and whose children were baptized Remonstrant;[37] and Jacob Poppen, who was suspected of Catholic leanings. Furthermore, in the same year Andries Bicker and Gerrit Dirkszoon van Beuningen, who would virtually control Amsterdam politics from about 1625 to 1650, made their political debuts by being elected to the *vroedschap* (city council). For the *predikanten* these were truly catastrophic events. Wagenaar says that several of the Reformed clergy "did not hesitate to say that the entire *vroedschap* had now become Arminian."[38] Domine Adrian Smout, one of the Calvinists' most outspoken heroes, grieved in the pulpit "how sorrowful it is that the choosing of public officials has been sloppily done, without once consulting the word of the Lord."[39]

The worst fears of the *predikanten* were realized. In the years between 1622 and 1626 the increasing frequency of the consistory's complaints about *Arminiaensche vergaderinghen* (Arminian conventicles) became monotonous. One example from the consistory minutes will suffice to demonstrate both the mounting

[35] Elias, p. 87.
[36] Evenhuis, 1, 284.
[37] *Doopboek van de Remonstrantsche Gemeente te Amsterdam.* Located in the Amsterdam *Gemeente Archief.*
[38] 1, 481.
[39] *Ibid.*, pp. 481–482. Not clear whether quoted or paraphrased.

indignation of the *predikanten* over the impunity with which Remonstrants gathered and the determination of the magistrates to steer a course for Amsterdam independent of Reformed demands. Throughout 1625 the Remonstrant conventicles had increased in openness and frequency. Finally on May 15, 1626, the consistory said:

It is resolved immediately to petition the Lords Burgomasters again over this issue, and, in order to clear our consciences, roundly to state our opinion and aforesaid objections: the alarm which we perceive in the congregation, and the danger which our persons and our services suffer from being accused as Remonstrant [sympathizers]. And we must also state that, on the contrary, we excuse ourselves from, and justify ourselves in the face of these charges; and we must declare that we do not in the least approve of the sedition [the conventicles] but regard it as evil and shameful and this petition shall be carried out by Domine Cloppenburg, D. Smoutius, Hans Janszoon, and Jan Willemszoon Bogaert. This having been done immediately, the Burgomasters have answered that it is the office of the Schepens to administer justice, concerning which office, they have sworn their oaths, and in which office the Burgomasters should scruple to interfere since it is not their office. The Burgomasters have also said that it is not the office of *predikanten* or the consistory to interfere with the conscience of the Schepens and to use confessional arguments against it.[40]

The situation was destined to grow worse before it improved. The *predikanten* did not stop at banging on the door of the burgomasters. From the pulpit they encouraged the laity to rise up and do the Lord's work with their own hands. And they were powerful demagogues. On Palm Sunday, 1626, the fiery Domine Smout preached on the entrance of Jesus into Jerusalem. An excerpt from his sermon: "If the Lords burgomasters do not improve in the rooting out of heresies to the honor of God and Christ, then shall the children, yes the stones of the street serve the Lord."[41] One week later, on April 13, 1626, the stones of

---

[40] "Protocol of the Amsterdam Consistory," May 15, 1626, in the Amsterdam *Gemeente Archief* [translation mine].

[41] Quoted in Evenhuis, 1, 291.

the street served the Lord. A Remonstrant conventicle was surrounded and dispersed by an irate mob which then proceeded
utterly to demolish the house. The sheriff and his militia were
only with difficulty able to restore order—after two of the mob
had been shot dead. Disorders of this sort continued and even
increased during the year 1627. In the elections of that year
Reynier Pauw, again running for burgomaster, was defeated, and
the four new burgomasters were Andries Bicker, Gerrit Dirckszoon van Beuningen, Dirk Bas, and Antony Oetgens, son of the
notorious Frans.[42] The positions of church and state in Amsterdam were moving farther and farther apart.

A visit to the city by Frederik Hendrik in 1628 calmed the situation momentarily but not permanently.[43] The Remonstrant
conventicles continued, for the most part undisturbed by the
magistrates. By mid-1629 the *predikanten* were on the attack
again, led by the redoubtable Domine Smout. On August 1,
1629, the valiant warrior pulled out all the stops. With the burgomasters seated piously in the front pew of the Oude Kerk,
Smout reached the climax of his sulphorous sermon and turned
to address himself specifically to them:

Who is the cause of this ordeal? Who are the disturbers of Israel?
You are the cause, with your procedures, that God Almighty has put
the enemy in the Veluwe. You regard us [the *predikanten*] as too
small and insignificant that you should hold council with us. We are
regarded as naughty boys. You would rather listen to a bunch of
"poets, orators, jurists and politicians" than to us. That is wrong.
They obtain their principles from the speeches and books of the
heathen. But we say to you: thus saith the Lord. We have God's
Word; hear therefore what we say to you. We are your shepherds,
we shall tell you nothing but the truth. Restore, then, those who have
been true to us and whom you have banished. Follow not in the
footsteps of Rehoboam, who valued the counsel of the younger above
that of the elder.[44]

[42] Wagenaar, 1, 492–493.

[43] For narratives of the prince's visit to the troubled city see Wagenaar,
1, 496–497, and Elias, pp. 95–96.

[44] The reference to the Veluwe is to the fact that Spanish troops had

This was the last straw. The magistrates acted swiftly. Smout was summoned to city hall and ordered to present a copy of the sermon in writing so that the magistrates could study it. Smout disobeyed on the advice of the consistory. The burgomasters and *vroedschap* waited until January 1630 for the consistory to comply, but when that failed to happen they met on January 7, 1630, and reviewed all their attempts to hold Smout "within the bounds of his calling and to make him desist from his seditious preaching." Burgomasters and *vroedschap* agreed: now was the time to act. The same day Smout received a note at home: "The Burgomasters and rulers of the city of Amsterdam order D. Adriaen Smout, for reasons [well-known], to leave the city and the freedom thereof tomorrow before the setting of the sun and not to return, on pain (should he not leave before this time) of being escorted out by the lord sheriff. Enacted the seventh of January 1630."[45] The banning of Smout had dire consequences for the *predikanten*. To avoid such embarrassing cases in the future, the magistrates determined to nip the problem in the bud, that is, in the consistory. From then on, they decided, delegates from the magistracy should sit in each meeting of the consistory to be sure that only ecclesiastical, and *purely* ecclesiastical, business was discussed. The consistory screamed in protest and turned to the provincial synod and the States-General for support. Throughout the year of 1631 the battle raged, and the States-General took the side of the consistory. But the Amsterdam magistracy bowed to the wishes of no one, not even the States-General. On May 6, 1632, the burgomasters prevailed and the magistracy's delegates sat in the consistory meeting for the first time. The delegates were

---

penetrated the Veluwe during the summer of 1629 and Amsterdam residents were fearful of a Spanish attack on North Holland and possibly even on the city itself. Those "whom you have banished" is a reference to the magistracy's banishment, in 1629, of Domine Cloppenburg, Smout's staunchly Counterremonstrant colleague in the Amsterdam ministry. Wagenaar, 1, 510–511 [translation mine].

[45] *Ibid.,* pp. 511, 513.

Andries Bicker and Gerrit Dirckszoon van Beuningen—a fact that spoke for itself.[46]

Meanwhile, the cause of the Remonstrants advanced in proportion to the decline of that of the Reformed zealots. Remonstrant conventicles gathered with increasingly less danger of being disturbed. On September 8, 1630, the Remonstrant congregation even dedicated its own church building, though it was a *schuilkerk* and hidden from public view by other buildings. Episcopius, a learned Amsterdam Remonstrant, dedicated the sanctuary with a sermon based on I Corinthians 7.23: "You were bought with a price."[47] Furthermore, in 1634 the congregation opened a Remonstrant seminary, with Episcopius as first teacher. The Amsterdam Remonstrant congregation was now the largest and most important in the United Provinces. Mindful of the role played by the merchant-magistrates in their struggle for toleration, the Remonstrants could gratefully join in the refrain sung by the poet Vondel in 1630:

God, God, says the Amsterdam gentleman, shall search each conscience:
Let freedom go its way and fly in and out of the Ij,
In full sail: thus is our fortress built:
Thus dips the merchant into gold up to his elbow.[48]

To describe thoroughly all the remaining streams and rivulets of dissent that ran through Amsterdam would be to depart too far from the central point. Lutherans, Anabaptists, Brownists, English Baptists, followers of the mystic Jacob Boehme and the rationalist René Descartes all sought and found room in Amsterdam, but the plot is so similar in each case that it grows monotonous. The dissenters gather in conventicles, the consistory protests, the burgomasters stall and connive, and in the end the presence of the new group is accepted as a *fait accompli.*

What makes the evaluation of seventeenth-century Amster-

[46] Evenhuis, 1, 317, 318.
[47] *Ibid.,* 1, 181.
[48] Cited in Wagenaar, 1, 514–515 [translation mine].

dam's religious pluralism so difficult is that the de facto toleration of this pluralism is about 150 years ahead of its philosophical
justification and legal articulation. Amsterdam's religious toleration is, as it were, a fact in search of an idea. Separation of
church and state is a concept that would not be born until the
French and American revolutions. In the seventeenth century the
solution of church-state friction was generally sought in subjuga-
tion of the church to the state, or the converse. Not only the
Reformed consistory but the magistrates as well accepted and
employed as a first principle the idea that state and church had
something to do with each other.

This unity between church and state had, in the Netherlands,
a more than casual rooting in history. The United Provinces and
the Dutch Reformed Church had been born together, then had
fought together, and together had gained independence from
Spanish inquisitorial domination. Recalling the 1566–1582 Reformed diaspora in the lands of Cologne, Aachen, Cleves, Emden, and the Palatinate, it might even be said that the Reformed
Church spawned the United Provinces. Groen van Prinsterer saw
it this way: "The Reformed Church was the middle point and
the kernel of the Commonwealth. Elsewhere the Church was
taken up into the State; here, the Republic was not only united
with the Church but also born out of the confession of the
Church."[49] In theory, such a close association of the ecclesiastical
and civil powers was acknowledged by both sides. At the Union
of Utrecht the States of Holland had reserved for themselves the
privilege of prohibiting public exercise of all other religions but
the Reformed, and the other provincial States soon followed. As
late as 1651 the States-General reiterated that "the States of the
respective Provinces have declared that they shall each hold fast
and maintain the true Christian, Reformed Religion."[50] And the

[49] G. Groen van Prinsterer, *Handboek der Geschiedenis van het Vader-
land* (Leiden: S. and J. Luchtmans, 1841), p. 205.
[50] Quoted in Evenhuis, 1, 276–277.

Reformed clergy described the relationship between church and state this way in Article 36 of the Belgic Confession:

> We believe that our gracious God, because of the depravity of mankind, hath ordained kings, princes and magistrates, willing that the world should be governed by certain laws and policies: to the end that the dissoluteness of men might be restrained and all things carried on among them with good order and decency. For this purpose He hath invested the magistracy with the sword, for the punishment of evil doers and for the praise of them that do well (Rom. 13:4). And their office is, not only to have regard unto and watch for the welfare of the civil state, but also that they protect the sacred ministry; and thus may remove and prevent all idolatry and false worship, that the kingdom of antichrist may be thus destroyed, and the Kingdom of Christ promoted. They must, therefore, countenance the preaching of the word of the Gospel everywhere, that God may be honored and worshipped by everyone as he commands in his word.[51]

The Amsterdam magistracy was, theoretically, in full agreement with this definition of the government's function. Externally viewed, Amsterdam was a Reformed city. It is remarkable how these opportunists (Bas, Oetgens, Bicker, and others) appeared every Sunday in prominent pews in the Reformed Church.

But the exegesis of this article in the Dutch confession of faith formed a shibboleth of enormous subtlety. The magistracy had to maintain the true Christian religion and root out idolatry and false religion. This the burgomasters agreed to in principle, but what was idolatry and false religion? Without a doubt Socinianism fitted in this category, and the magistrates were consistent in the zeal with which they set these heretics out of the city. But what of the Catholics, the Remonstrants, the Lutherans, the Anabaptists, the Brownists, and countless other sects—were they all categorically idolaters? And if they were, then how were these false religions to be rooted out? By inquisition? But Article 36

---

[51] Leroy Nixon, ed., *Reformed Standards of Unity* (Grand Rapids: Society for Reformed Publications, 1952). Article 36 of the *Confessio Belgica*, pp. 91–92.

spoke of rooting out *heresies*—not *heretics*. And if the rooting out of heresies involved legal restrictions against non-Reformed religious services, what kind of services must be restrained—all non-Reformed gatherings or only the public ones? Could the *schuilkerken* be left alone? Finally, what if the magistracy's maintenance of the "Divine Service" did not restrain man's dissoluteness and promote good order but rather encouraged that dissoluteness and disrupted that order? All these fine nuances and questions of interpretation of Article 36 in the confession provided potential chinks in the armor of Amsterdam, the Reformed city. And it was through these chinks that the dissenters penetrated Amsterdam's religious life.

The *schuilkerk* became symbolic of Amsterdam's solution for the problem of her religious pluralism. The *schuilkerk* was hidden from public view. Officially it did not exist, nor did the dissent that spawned it. Not until 1795—the beginning of *de Franse tijd* (the French period) and the end of the republic—was religious freedom as such to become part of the social landscape of the Netherlands. Yet the *schuilkerk* was indeed a church if the criteria are architectural or liturgical. The *schuilkerken,* complained the consistory, are "solemn gathering-places, decorated with altars and all kinds of papist ornaments," frequented by hundreds of papists "singing and playing on organs, violins and other instruments." And the *schuilkerken* were the chief reason that W. P. C. Knuttel closes his two-volume work on Catholics in the republic with the following: "For complete freedom of religion there was as little place here [in the Netherlands] between 1581 and 1795 as elsewhere. But, as was already observed in the Introduction of the first part of this work, compared with what Protestants had to endure in Catholic lands in that time, the lot of the Catholics in the Republic of the United Netherlands was in general very bearable."[52]

---

[52] Knuttel, *De Toestand der Nederlandsche Katholieken,* 2, 270 [translation mine].

7. Church and State in Dutch Colonial Policy

The general thrust of the argument so far has been that, religiously speaking, two widely divergent groups grappled for control of Dutch society in the Golden Age. Calvinist *predikant* and merchant-magistrate waged a genuine *Kulturkampf* to determine the nature and extent of Reformed influence on the economic, political, social, and religious life of the United Provinces, and this *Kulturkampf* in the homeland was transported overseas into Dutch colonial territories.

Following the lead of historian Jacob Burckhardt, we will look at several random examples of church-state relations in the colonies of the East and West India companies, "taking transverse sections of history in as many directions as possible."[1] This method serves the double purpose of demonstrating on the one hand that the church-state conflicts of the homeland were exported overseas, and on the other, that the soon-to-be-narrated conflicts in New Netherland were not isolated or unique but part of a larger pattern of church-state conflict in the Dutch colonial empire.

No mention whatsoever was made of religion in the original charter of the Dutch East India Company in 1602. Although this omission must be taken in context (at that early date not much serious thought had been given to the necessities and re-

[1] Jacob Burckhardt, *Force and Freedom* (New York: Pantheon, 1943), p. 80.

sponsibilities of the colonial task), it at least indicates where the V.O.C.'s priorities lay. In the second charter of 1623 this omission was remedied, and the V.O.C. certainly may not be accused of failing to provide for the propagation of the Reformed faith. During the two centuries of the company's existence it sent out about 900 *predikanten* to its colonial holdings and spent millions of guilders supporting these clergy and building churches.[2] The V.O.C. was, however, a rather strange guardian of Reformed interests. And, on numerous occasions, this self-appointed guardianship annoyed the Reformed clergy almost beyond endurance. Any number of incidents might be related as documentation, but only three will be mentioned here because they most aptly illustrate, in colonial context, the two points emphasized previously concerning the homeland: (1) the merchant-magistrates, who in the context of this chapter appear as directors (*bewindhebbers*) of the V.O.C., were adamant that the ecclesiastical power be subordinate to the civil power in the total picture of society; and (2) the merchant-magistrates held that religious dissent, while officially prohibited, might be permitted by "connivance" or "winking" where political and especially economic interests indicated its expediency. In the case of the V.O.C. (and W.I.C.), the overlap of economic and political interests that prevailed in Amsterdam (where many men appeared as both merchants and magistrates) now had become total congruence. The directors established colonial law and administered colonial justice—but they also held shares and collected dividends.

In 1607, just five years after the young company had begun to establish its grip on the archipelago that is today Indonesia, Admiral Matelieff de Jonge closed a treaty with the Muslim sultan of the island of Ternate. Article 13 of the treaty stipulated that all deserters from the Dutch garrison must be deliv-

---

[2] See C. W. Th. Baron van Boetzelaer van Asperen en Dubbeldam, *De Protestantsche Kerk in Nederlandsch-Indië* (The Hague: Nijhoff, 1947), pp. 4–6.

ered up by the natives, while the Dutch would reciprocate in the case of runaway natives. This article in itself was not particularly remarkable, but in 1609 Vice-Admiral Wittert interpreted it to apply to the conversion of Dutchmen to Islam and of Ternatese to Christianity. Wittert's reading of the clause made Reformed mission work on the island virtually impossible, and the Sultan of Ternate tried, on the basis of Wittert's interpretation, to ban even a Reformed *predikant* for the Dutch garrison. The Reformed clergy in the Netherlands were alarmed, and protested indignantly to the Heren XVII about this "abominable treaty" (*gruwelijk contract*). As a consequence, the Heren instructed the governor-general to "review" Article 13 of the treaty and to abandon Wittert's interpretation of it as not congruent with the article's original intent. The Dutch interpretation of the article was subsequently changed to appease the wrath of the *predikanten*. What the Sultan of Ternate thought about all this Dutch pettifogging has not been recorded and must be left to the imagination.[3]

Thus, from the very early years of its career, the V.O.C., as Boetzelaer van Asperen en Dubbeldam puts it, "found that it was not simple in the East Indies to hold the interests of the shareholders in view and act simultaneously as a Christian government."[4] Conversely, the Reformed Church found it no easy task to span the gap between authentic witness and mission as the Church of God and partnership with the politico-economic interests of Dutch colonial rule. The previous incident was a victory of sorts for the *predikanten* in their struggle to preserve the sacred and missionary character of Dutch colonial expansion. The next tale illustrates in piquant fashion the character and strength of the forces that opposed the Reformed clergy.

In about 1640, various provincial synods in the Netherlands began to discuss a "Japanese placard"—a set of regulations which, so it was rumored, the V.O.C. had imposed upon its

---

[3] *Ibid.*, p. 15.
[4] *Ibid.*, pp. 15–16 [translation mine].

employees sailing to Japan in order to conceal from the intolerant Japanese emperor the fact that the Dutch were Christians. Deputations from the synods of North and South Holland were repeatedly sent to the Heren XVII to find out about this placard, but the directors declined to dispense any information whatsoever on the subject—an attitude the *predikanten* correctly interpreted as a sign that the rumor contained more than a little truth. When the directors remained obdurate in their refusal to discuss the placard, the clergy was finally able to secure a copy of the text from underground sources. The text is interesting enough to bear quoting in full:

Greetings to all those who will see this and hear it read. Be each and every person warned against, and by this placard forbidden from— if life and welfare are dear to him—selling and exchanging with the Japanese or with any other nations which trade here any Christian ornaments such as psalmbooks or other spiritual authors. Furthermore, let everyone keep his eyes from such or similar texts when among the Japanese or other nations here present, and let him refrain from using such texts as long as he is in Japan. Similarly, let every person be hereby warned that henceforth he may celebrate no Sundays or other feast-days, but must, as on ordinary work-days, do the tasks of the day, as is the custom in Japan. Item. Be everyone advised that, so long as he is in Japan, he may attend no public gathering, prayers before or after meals, or any similar Christian exercise, such as is employed by the Portuguese. And, although it will be difficult for a Christian conscience to observe all this, nevertheless, as long as we are in Japan we must attempt it in order, as much as possible, to avoid all the difficulty which would otherwise ensue for the Company's rich capital, ships, and personnel. Meanwhile, let everyone attempt to serve his God with pious inner thoughts. Finally, be everyone advised—if his life and the welfare of his masters are dear to him—that he should take this warning to heart in such a way that he remain innocent of the aforesaid mischief. Apprehended violators must be turned over, without connivance, to the Japanese authorities for punishment.[5]

There is no other original text in the history of Dutch colonial

---

[5] Quoted *ibid.*, pp. 59–60 [translation mine].

enterprise that illustrates so starkly the hiatus between merchant and clerical purpose in colonization or that reveals with such clarity the crassness of the mercantile motive. Of course the document must be viewed in context of the extreme circumstances in Japan. In less desperate situations the company not only tolerated the Reformed Church but underwrote it at considerable expense. On the other hand, the height of the stakes in Japan revealed vividly the company's priorities. When a choice was ineluctable, business did indeed come first.

The *predikanten* in the homeland were furious. They repeatedly demanded from the Heren XVII that the placard be abolished, and now that the matter was in the open the directors could no longer ignore their demands. They promised to investigate the matter and to correspond with the authorities in Batavia about it. Later, the directors reported that the placard had been modified and the offensive parts deleted, but, in spite of repeated requests from the Amsterdam consistory to see a copy of the modified placard, the directors refused. In the end it appeared that the directors had deleted the third and fourth sentences—doubtless the most offensive—of the original placard but had left it further unmodified. The incident thus ended in compromise, though one heavily favoring the company. If the Heren XVII had been allowed to pursue unmolested their course in Japan, not only the missionary thrust but also the worshipping life of the Dutch colony would have been destroyed. The *predikanten* managed, through their persistent efforts, to salvage a subdued Reformed worship for the colony, but of a Dutch Reformed "mission" to the Japanese there was not the slightest trace under the V.O.C.

So the company would tamper with ecclesiastical business where the latter threatened to interfere with commerce. A third incident from the history of the V.O.C. illustrates that, where civil authority was concerned, the company guarded and exercised its prerogatives even more jealously.

In 1653, the V.O.C.'s governor-general at Batavia prescribed

a general thanksgiving and fast day to commemorate several recent Dutch victories over rebellious natives in Amboina. The Batavia *kerkeraad* (consistory), however, criticised this resolution.
pointing out that the Amboina "rebellion" had been the result
of the company's own repressive policies toward the Amboinese
(as in fact it had). The governor-general responded to this ecclesiastical criticism by labeling the *kerkeraad* "highly unpatri-
otic" and accusing it of "giving a bad impression of the Company's righteous trade." Furthermore, when this news reached
the Heren XVII they sent out a directive that any *predikanten*
registering such dissent in the future should be dismissed immediately and sent home on the first departing ship.[6] As C. R. Boxer
remarks with characteristic dryness: "The Company experienced
no further criticism from the ministers of the Dutch Reformed
Church concerning its wars, whether just or unjust, for the remainder of its existence."[7]

So much, then, for relations between church and company—
between God and Mammon—in the seventeenth-century preserve of the V.O.C. The company's primarily commercial purpose in the East Indies was accurately epitomized in the words
of company official Pieter Nuyts, who declared that he had "not
come out to Asia to eat hay."[8] And the low regard in which
company officials held ecclesiastical personnel, especially when
the latter interfered with company designs, is summarized in Jan
Pieterszoon Coen's evaluation of the *krankenbezoekers:* "clumsy
uncircumcised idiots" (*plompe onbesneden idioten*) was his ver-
dict.[9]

The question, then, is whether the general picture of church-

6 See J. A. van der Chijs, *Nederlandsch-Indisch Plakaatboek, 1602–
1799,* 12 vols. (Batavia, 1885–1894), 2, 185–186; and Pieter van Dam,
Beschryvinge van de Oostindische Compagnie, 4 books in 6 vols. (The
Hague, 1927–1954), book 4, p. 60.

7 Boxer, *The Dutch Seaborne Empire,* (New York: Alfred Knopf,
1965), p. 138.

8 Quoted *ibid.,* p. 52.

9 Quoted *ibid.,* p. 137.

company relations quickly sketched for the V.O.C. fits equally
well to the contemporary activities of the W.I.C., a question vigorously discussed by Dutch historians. While some have tended
to see the W.I.C. as, in a general way, more "Calvinistic" than
the V.O.C., others have contended that the two great joint-stock
companies were essentially the same, both economically and ideologically. The question is extremely complex, owing to factors
of religion, politics, and war which were unquestionably different
in the Netherlands in 1621 (founding of W.I.C.) from what
they had been in 1602 (V.O.C.).[10] The most recent round of
the historiographical argument was fought in 1960–1962 (in
rather polemic fashion) between W. J. van Hoboken, Director
of the Amsterdam Municipal Archives, and the economic historian J. G. van Dillen. Hoboken argued in 1960 that he could
show on the basis of Amsterdam archival materials that 50 percent of the original twenty Amsterdam directors of the W.I.C.
were of South Netherlands origin.[11] Following the eighteenth-
century Amsterdam historian Wagenaar, who called the Brabanter immigrant segment of the city's population "hard Reformed,"
Hoboken, along with the German historian Asher[12] before him,
thus concluded that Reformed ideology was very influential
among the founders of the W.I.C. Furthermore, he argued, it

[10] For general accounts of the religious, economic, and political factors
surrounding the creation of the W.I.C. see: W. R. Menkman, *De Geschiedenis van de West-Indische Compagnie* (Amsterdam: Van Kampen,
1947); P. J. Blok, *History of the People of the Netherlands,* 4 vols. (New
York: G. Putnam, 1900–1907), esp. vols. 2 and 3; J. Franklin Jameson,
"Willem Usselinx," *American Historical Association Papers,* vol. 2, no. 3
(1887); and J. G. van Dillen, "De West-Indische Compagnie, Het Calvinisme en De Politiek," *Tijdschrift voor Geschiedenis,* vol. 74 (Groningen:
Noordhoff, 1961).

[11] W. J. van Hoboken, "The Dutch West-India Company: The Political
Background of Its Rise and Decline," in *Britain and the Netherlands,* ed.
by J. S. Bromley and E. H. Kossmann (London: Chatto and Windus,
1960), 1, 51.

[12] G. M. Asher, *Bibliographical and Historical Essay on the Dutch Books
and Pamphlets Relating to New Netherland and to the Dutch West India
Company* (Amsterdam: F. Muller, 1854–1867).

was highly likely that of the first 66 directors of the Amsterdam chamber of the company between 1622 and 1636,[13] 33 were of Brabant origin while another 10 were Hollanders of Calvinist sympathy, 3 were Remonstrants, and 20 of unknown leaning. So, he maintained, the Amsterdam chamber possessed, at least in its first years, a markedly Calvinist character. Furthermore, during the extremely tumultuous Remonstrant difficulties in Amsterdam in 1628 (above, Chapter 6) the chief participants of the W.I.C. actually took open sides in the religious dispute. When Frederik Hendrik arrived in the city they addressed a petition to him asking that the Remonstrant conventicles be suppressed. They presented themselves to the prince as "mostly professors of the true Reformed religion" whose principal motives in subscribing capital to the company had been (in this order), "first the Honor of God, second the true Reformed religion and its spread to other lands, third the welfare of the Provinces and especially of Amsterdam, and fourth the defeat of the general enemy."[14] In sum, concluded Hoboken, the West India Company was "a stronghold of Calvinism."[15]

Dillen responded to Hoboken's argument in 1961. His article acknowledged the importance of the facts brought forth by Hoboken but questioned his evaluation of them. He showed that approximately the same percentage of directors of the V.O.C. were Brabanters or "hard Reformed" at the time of its founding.[16] Yet, he argued, no one would want to characterize the V.O.C. as specifically "South Netherlandish" or "Calvinistic."

[13] The Amsterdam directors from 1621 through 1636 are listed in J. de Laet, *Jaerlyck Verhael van de Verrichtingen der Geoctroyeerde West-Indische Compagnie* (The Hague: Nijhoff, 1937), vol. 1, introduction.

[14] Pamphlet 3813 in W. P. C. Knuttel, *Catalogus van Pamfletten Berustende in de Koninklijke Bibliotheek*. The pamphlet was entitled *Requeste vande West-Indische Compagnie overgelevert aen sijnen Vorstelijcke Genade, Prince Frederick Hendrick van Nassouwen, Prince van Oraignien*, 1628.

[15] P. 53.

[16] J. G. van Dillen, "De West-Indische Compagnie," p. 153.

Furthermore, although the petition to Frederik Hendrik in 1628 must be regarded as an important indication that Calvinist feeling did indeed run high among the W.I.C. shareholders and directors, the directors' analysis of their own motives for capital subscription cannot be accepted at face value. In fact, the Remonstrant leader Johannes Uytenbogaert perspicaciously suggested in a pamphlet published shortly after the directors' petition in 1628 that "God, who knows all hearts, knows whether [the directors'] first and principal motive is the honor of God and religion, together with the spreading of that in other lands. Many motives frequently operate in the same affair. God knows which horse pulls strongest. We will leave at that the question of how it goes at the present with the spread of religion in the West."[17] Willem Usselincx, chief architect of the W.I.C. and himself a convinced Calvinist and a Brabanter to boot, was more honest about motives for subscribing capital to the India companies than the directors were in their petition. Admitting that some subscribers would have idealistic motives, he added, "but the principal and most powerful motive will be the profit that each shall be able to reap for himself."[18] Dillen was willing to concede that Hoboken's characterization of the W.I.C. as "a stronghold of Calvinism" contained "a kernel of truth." But, with an eye on the insights of Uytenbogaert and Usselincx, he found Hoboken's position to be "very onesided." For it needed to be asked, Dillen argued, in what sense these supposedly "Calvinist" directors conducted the company's business affairs as "Calvinists." If the directors' actions rather than their words were allowed to speak, then "the directors as well as the participants were scarcely exemplars of a Calvinistic style of life." The ex-

[17] Pamphlet 3814 in Knuttel, *Catalogus*. The title is *Ondersoeck der Amsterdamsche requesten, tot verdedigingh der onschuldighe ende onderrechtingh der misleyde,* 1638. Uytenbogaert's authorship of this pamphlet is not certain [translation mine].

[18] Cited in O. van Rees, *Geschiedenis der Staathuishoudkunde in Nederland tot het Einde der Achttiende Eeuw* (Utrecht: Kemink, 1865–1868), 2, 418.

ample he chose was Samuel Bloemaert, who, said Dillen, "was one of the foremost and most influential directors . . . of Antwerp origin . . . whose correspondence with Swedish statesmen has been published by G. W. Kernkamp. In his letters he appears as a man of very spacious conscience, who for a large salary, is employed as adviser for the founding of a Swedish-American company, which will establish a colony on the Delaware River to compete with New Netherland—all of which he is trying to keep secret from his fellow-directors."[19] On the basis of this and several other incidents like it, Dillen felt justified in concluding that the W.I.C. directors were, "with several exceptions . . . typical moneyhounds [geldwolven], who repeatedly promoted their own financial interests at the expense of the Company in a grotesque manner."

Although in the main dissenting from Hoboken's claim that the W.I.C. was "a stronghold of Calvinism," Dillen did agree that the W.I.C.'s Calvinistic posture was occasionally expressed through "the opposition of the directors to the granting of religious freedom to Catholics and Jews [in W.I.C. territories]."[20] This was a concession Dillen need not have made, and the facts in the W.I.C.'s greatest colonial undertaking, Brazil, do not bear him out very well.

The first Dutch foothold in Brazil was established in May 1624 with the fall of the Portuguese coastal settlement of Bahia. Between 1624 and 1630 the Dutch gradually consolidated their position there and began to set their sights on the rich sugar crop of the province of Pernambuco, with its port settlements of Olinda and Recife.[21] In connection with this establishment of W.I.C. control in Brazil two very interesting items appear in the protocol of the Amsterdam consistory. The first is in the minutes for the meeting of November 28, 1624, and reads as follows:

[19] Van Dillen, "De West-Indische Compagnie," p. 157.
[20] Ibid., p. 158.
[21] C. R. Boxer, The Dutch in Brazil (Oxford: Clarendon Press, 1957), pp. 14–66.

There was read a certain letter from the Zealand [synod's] deputies
for Indian affairs, in which they make known their fears for the city
of Salvador in Brazil, namely that (since it is understood that the
Portuguese will not enter the city unless some practice of their
Papist superstitions be allowed them) something may be decided by
the nineteen to accommodate the Portuguese out of political motives
and worldly considerations. The Consistory was requested to oppose
and hinder this matter in the gathering of the nineteen (where
Brazilian policy on the matter is presently being discussed), in order
that no decision should be reached conflicting with the word of God
and that good order should be used in the takeover of cities and
towns.[22]

Where the Zealand *predikanten* got their information we are not
told: it was probably from some anonymous source such as finally
supplied the *predikanten* with a copy of the V.O.C.'s "Japanese
placard." In any case, what is so interesting about this brief
memorandum is that the Zealand brethren clearly distrust the
Heren XIX. Their attitude seems to be that, unless the Amsterdam consistory can intervene effectively, the Portuguese papists
will almost certainly be accommodated by the directors for reasons "political and worldly."

The second item, dating from the consistory meeting of December 5, 1624, is equally interesting: "The Brothers delegated
to Indian affairs, who were commissioned to the gathering of the
nineteen, report that they were not able to perform their task because the gathering had already adjourned. But they understood
that there were several proposals made concerning the granting
of free exercise of their religion to the Portuguese, and that these
proposals were rejected. They will further investigate the opinion of the gathering."[23] The Heren XIX avoided a direct con-
frontation with the *predikanten* in 1624 on the crucial issue of
the Portuguese Catholics. Doing their best to assure the Reformed

---

[22] *Protocol of the Amsterdam Consistory*. In the Amsterdam *Gemeente
Archief* [translation mine].

[23] *Ibid.* [translation mine].

that all was well, they proceeded to keep their own counsel on the matter of Catholic dissent in Brazil. Without doubt, they hoped to achieve a Reformed establishment there, provided it proved compatible with an economically vigorous and politically stable colony. As time wore on, however, it became evident that Brazil, and especially the rich sugar plantations of Pernambuco, could not be unified under Dutch rule except by substantial concessions in the area of religion. Just how far the Heren XIX were willing to go in this direction is most clearly illustrated in Article 1 of the "Capitulations" offered by the W.I.C. to the Portuguese inhabitants of Paraibo in Pernambuco in December 1635: "We [the W.I.C.] shall let them [the Portuguese] live in the freedom of their consciences in such manner as they have lived until now, using their Churches and Godly Masses in accordance with their laws and ordinances; we shall neither despoil their churches nor let them be despoiled, and we shall molest neither their images nor their priests, during the Mass or at any other time."[24]

On the whole, the position of the W.I.C. with regard to religion in its colonies did not differ greatly from the position taken by her sister company. A Reformed establishment was considered the "normal" state of religious affairs, but when the claims of the *predikanten* threatened the civil authority of the company, the political stability of a colony, or—most important of all—a colony's economic productivity, religion was invariably subordinated. This is the same principle we have seen again and again in the life of seventeenth-century Amsterdam with its bustling *beurs* (market) and its *schuilkerken,* and it is this principle that determined church-state relations in New Netherland.

Although the *Kulturkampf* between *predikanten* and merchants for control of Dutch society was active both at home and in the colonies, there was another, strictly colonial, aspect of this struggle—the institution of slavery and the slave trade. Slavery

[24] J. de Laet, 4, 132–134 [translation mine].

was not legal in the Netherlands in the sixteenth and seventeenth centuries.[25] Therefore, as the Dutch began and expanded their colonial enterprise they brought to it no catalog of legal precedent supporting the institution of slavery. Why, then, did they so quickly resort to slavery as a scheme of social and economic organization within the colonies? It was the most expedient answer to the problem of labor shortage that plagued all of the Dutch colonies. Free Dutchmen had little reason to leave the Netherlands; the economy was booming and, as shown previously, there was less actual pressure toward religious conformity than anywhere else in Europe. And in any case no Dutch colonist would work for board and room as would a slave. So the directors of the V.O.C. and W.I.C., tightfisted and pragmatic, took the path of least resistance to the solution of the colonial labor problem and that path was slavery.

What resistance to the institution of slavery did the *predikanten* in fact supply? On balance, the answer to this question must be "very little." There would seem to be at least three levels of explanation (not exculpation!) for the silence of the clergy on this issue. In the first place, while *predikanten* in the Dutch colonies were under the ecclesiastical jurisdiction of the Classis of Amsterdam they were in the financial employ of the India companies themselves, which meant that their salaries were in part made possible by profits from the slave trade. Neither the V.O.C. nor the W.I.C. tolerated very graciously criticism from its own employees, as we have already noted in the affair of the Amboinese rebellion in 1653. Company autocracy, however, cannot in itself explain the silence of the *predikanten*. The Calvinist *predikant,* after all, was typically a hard militant about those things that mattered to him crucially. For the sake of the *ware religie* he would endure political exile, preach impassioned sermons, lead street mobs to the barricades, and pay insistent visits to the chambers of government and commerce. Yet, on the ques-

[25] Edgar J. McManus, *A History of Negro Slavery in New York* (Syracuse, N.Y.: Syracuse University Press, 1966), p. 15.

tion of slavery the ecclesiastical records are mostly silent, and when the silence is broken it is more often for the purpose of condonation than condemnation.[26] Reverend Jacobus Hondius published a severe critique of the slave trade in 1679, but his fellow minister Godfried Udemans in 1640 argued that the system of slavery was acceptable and that the duty of a Christian was simply to treat slaves mercifully and labor to convert them.[27] Furthermore, by 1742 there is the interesting case of Jacobus Elisa Capitein, a black slave from West Africa who was brought back to the Netherlands by his master, where he automatically received manumission. Some wealthy friends of his former master paid for his education at the University of Leiden, and he graduated with a dissertation that "proved" the legality of slavery from the Bible. Shortly after his graduation he was ordained by the Reformed Church and sent back to West Africa as a missionary.[28] In brief, then, although there were scattered exceptions the majority of the Reformed clergy saw no theological or ethical incompatibility between Christian faith and the institution of slavery. Finally, there was a third reason why the *predikanten* were so nearly silent about an institution that any seventeenth-century Dutchman would have regarded as an outrage if applied to himself or any of his fellow countrymen, and that was "racism." The *predikanten* did not introduce slavery into the Dutch colonial enterprise; they did not even theorize about it until after it was established as an expedient, working system. And yet, deeply imbedded in the psychological construct of the typical *predikant* (is this not true of all white Euro-Americans?) was the idea that slavery was not an inappropriate social condition

[26] An excellent recent article on the attitude of the Reformed Church toward slavery, both in New Netherland and generally, is Gerald F. DeJong, "The Dutch Reformed Church and Negro Slavery in Colonial America," *Church History*, 40, no. 4 (December, 1971), 423–436.

[27] *Ibid.*, p. 424.

[28] *Ibid.*, pp. 424–425. On the story of Capitein see also Boxer, *Dutch Seaborne Empire*, pp. 152–153.

for the inferior black race. In 1628 Reverend Jonas Michaëlius wrote from New Netherland to a friend in the homeland that "the Angola slave women are thievish, lazy, and useless trash." In 1695 a committee from the Reformed churches of Long Island wrote the Classis of Amsterdam that if a minister were not sent to them soon the people, for lack of hearing the gospel preached, "may be turned into negroes, and become black and polluted."[29]

For economic, theological, and psychological reasons, then, the Reformed Church failed to raise an effective voice against a practice in the Dutch colonies that would never have been tolerated within Dutch society itself. Against the hard economic pragmatism that authored slavery, however, the *predikanten* frequently did protest, particularly when it interfered with the work of building a godly (i.e., Calvinist) society.

[29] *Ibid.*, p. 427.

PART III

New Netherland, 1609–1647:
Frustrations

8. Intentions and Frustrations

The Dutch came to New Netherland with not one but two distinct views on the subject of church-state relations. The Reformed *predikanten* held that the church must be autonomous in the areas of doctrine and ecclesiastical polity. Furthermore, they argued that the magistrates should be open to clerical advice on even the most purely civil matters, for the civil and ecclesiastical realms were inextricably and organically bound together. Finally, the *predikanten* maintained that church and state must work harmoniously together to preserve society's good order. The church must preach and teach allegiance to the state, while the state, as the Dutch confession of faith put it, must "remove and prevent all idolatry and false worship."

On their side, the merchant-magistrates of the Netherlands, and especially Amsterdam, retained an unshaken conviction that commerce must outweigh all other considerations in the determination of civil policy. Many prominent Dutch merchants held religious sympathies that were not Reformed at all but Catholic, Remonstrant, Lutheran, or even Anabaptist. Moreover, even in the case where a merchant's personal religious sympathies were Reformed, he was not likely to support a Reformed establishment to the extent of suppressing religious dissent. For physical coercion meant that those threatened with suppression would sooner or later leave in search of a more congenial situation, and from this the interests of business could only suffer.

So Dutchmen came to the New World, to that section of Atlantic coast stretching from 34½ to 41½ degrees north latitude. Already in 1598 some intrepid Dutch sailors may have spent the winter months on the banks of the North (later Hudson) River in a rude fort constructed for shelter and protection from the natives.[1] Henry Hudson "discovered" the area again in 1609 and Adriaen Block for a third time in 1611.[2] Gradually the Dutch began to come and permeate the area. But why did they come? Did they hope to trade, or build a colonial stronghold, or establish a Reformed community?

Almost every historian who has dealt with New Netherland in any depth has realized that although the colony's Dutch history was short it was complex. During the approximately forty years (1623–1664) that the Dutch were interested in that part of North America, change was the most consistently present aspect of the colony's physical, social, political, economic, and religious existence. For the historian, change raises the problem of periodization.

Various historians have approached this problem in different ways. Though Washington Irving's *Knickerbocker's History of New York*[3] was obviously a burlesque rather than a history of New Netherland, he was one of the first writers to employ the careers of the colony's governors as guides for separating the various epochs of the colony's history. Diedrich Knickerbocker saw the reign of Wouter "The Doubter" van Twiller as the colony's

---

[1] This statement occurs in "Report of the Board of Accounts on New Netherland," delivered to the W.I.C. directors on December 15, 1644. Located in E. B. O'Callaghan, ed., *Documents Relative to the Colonial History of the State of New York* (Albany: Weed, Parsons, 1856), 1, 149. This piece cannot be taken as positive evidence that the Dutch were in New Netherland by 1598, because the Dutch were always attempting to discredit the English claim to the area by demonstrating their own prior occupancy of it. The *Documents* are hereafter cited as *Col. Doc.*

[2] Adriaen Block was an energetic and fearless ship captain who made at least three voyages to New Netherland between the years 1611 and 1613 for an Amsterdam mercantile combination headed by Lambert van Tweenhuysen.

[3] (New York: G. P. Putnam's Sons, revised from 1848 ed.).

"golden age." The province fell from its days of dreaming innocence under the impulsive rule of Willem "The Testy" Kieft,
and its further decline and ultimate downfall occurred under the
administration of Peter "The Headstrong" Stuyvesant. The first
attempt at a serious and responsible history of New Netherland
was undertaken in about 1840 by E. B. O'Callaghan, and his
two-volume *History of New Netherland*[4] which appeared in
1845–1848 employed essentially the same periodization. Volume
one dealt with the colony's history from Hudson's discovery
through the reign of Governor Kieft. Volume two then began
with the appointment of Stuyvesant as director-general and extended to the loss of the colony to the English in 1664. The next
history of New Netherland appeared five years later, in 1853, as
volume one in J. R. Brodhead's projected four-volume *History
of the State of New York*,[5] and utilized essentially the same for-
mat. Brodhead separated the colony's history into four periods—
the administrations of Governors Minuit, van Twiller, Kieft, and
Stuyvesant.

Interestingly enough, two of the more recent histories of New
Netherland that employ Irving's periodization reject his work
on the grounds that it is historiographically irresponsible. M. G.
van Rensselaer's two-volume *History of the City of New York
in the Seventeenth Century*,[6] which appeared in 1909, devoted
the first volume to New Amsterdam. In her preface the author
criticized Diedrich Knickerbocker for "not merely distorting his
ideas about this fact or that, this personage or another, but per-
verting his general mental and emotional attitude toward the
place, the times, and the people in question."[7] Nevertheless, Mrs.
van Rensselaer herself employed the careers of New Netherland's
governors for grouping together the events of New Amsterdam's

---

[4] 2 vols. (New York: D. Appleton, 1848).
[5] *History of the State of New York: First Period, 1609–1664* (New
York: Harper, 1853).
[6] 2 vols. (New York: Macmillan, 1909).
[7] *Ibid.*, p. xvii.

history. Finally, the appearance in 1959 of a book entitled *Peter Stuyvesant and His New York*[8] has provided thoroughly modern testimony to the influence of Irving's periodization over subsequent historians. Though the authors allude to *Knickerbocker* in their preface as "a triumph of art over matter,"[9] the very title of the book implies (perhaps correctly) that New Netherland's history can best be understood in terms of what occurred during Stuyvesant's administration—all else being seen as prelude and epilogue.

There are, however, several schemes of periodization that do not rely upon the careers of the colony's governors. Frederick Zwierlein believed that three periods could be distinguished in the colony's religious history. The first extended from the beginnings of Dutch permeation to the beginnings of organized colonization in about 1624. During this period, no formal religious institutions were established. The second period, said Zwierlein, extended from 1624 to approximately 1654 and was characterized by a de facto, though unchallenged, establishment of the Dutch Reformed Church. The third period extended from 1654 to 1664 and witnessed both the rise of organized religious dissent within the colony and the legislative and physical repression of that dissent by the colonial authorities.[10]

As Zwierlein focused on the colony's religious history, so Thomas Condon, in his recent study of New York's commercial origins, has concentrated on the mercantile aspects of the colony's existence, which has led to another periodization of the colony's history. From 1609 until 1623, Condon says, New Netherland was simply exploited for its peltry by a number of private Dutch merchants. During this period the idea of permanent colonization was never even seriously entertained. From 1623 until 1629, the second period of the colony's history, the West India Com-

[8] H. H. Kessler and E. Rachlis (New York: Random House, 1959).
[9] *Ibid.*, p. v.
[10] *Religion in New Netherland* (Rochester, N.Y.: John P. Smith, 1910), p. 1.

pany underwrote and supervised the New Netherland venture, but they also envisioned no permanent colonization of the area. Only in 1629, when it finally became obvious that no consistent long-range return could be expected from the fur trade in New Netherland, did the W.I.C. make a preliminary move toward colonizing by granting its charter of "Freedoms and Exemptions for the Patroons, Masters, or Private Persons Who Will Plant Any Colonies in, and Send Cattle to New Netherland," the beginning of the patroon system. From 1629 till 1639, then, the company tried to induce immigrants to the province with this scheme but without any marked success. The fourth and most prosperous period of the colony's history began when, in 1639, the W.I.C. abandoned its monopoly of the lucrative fur trade and opened the trade to private individuals. Population of the colony steadily increased from this point onward and was estimated at approximately 10,000 at the time of the English takeover in 1664.[11]

The periodization that I propose as most apt for the purposes of this study differs from all of the schemes presented above, though it resembles most closely that suggested by Condon. For of all the historians who have dealt with New Netherland, Condon alone has recognized the tremendous importance that must be attached to the fact that New Netherland was, in the eyes of its proprietors, first, last, and always a commercial venture. Even after the W.I.C. in 1639 abandoned the idea of direct trade and began actively promoting colonization, the basic motive of profit remained the same. Colonization was simply a way of making the investment pay, since trade had patently failed to do so.

Sidney Mead has proposed that much of America's colonial religious history can be understood in terms of two themes: intention and frustration. What kinds of societies did the ecclesiastical bodies that came to North America intend to construct, Mead asks, and how were their intentions frustrated in the Amer-

[11] Condon, *New York Beginnings* (New York: New York University Press, 1968), *passim*.

ican wilderness? For the most part, Mead argues, the original intention of the ecclesiastical bodies was to perpetuate the ideal of religious uniformity that had dominated medieval Europe, and only gradually was this intention frustrated by a number of factors on the American scene.[12] I shall borrow Mead's categories of intention and frustration for the purpose of interpreting New Netherland's church-state history, but in doing so I shall complicate their sequence slightly.

There are two major periods in the church-state history of New Netherland. The first extends from the earliest Dutch arrival until approximately 1645–1647. During this time both church and state[13] failed to make explicit their intentions for the colony, though they failed for very different reasons. At the most basic level the intentions both of the early private merchants who traded to New Netherland and of the W.I.C., which later inherited the colony, were clear: essentially, all of these commercial agents wanted to make the venture pay. But the specifics of how to make New Netherland profitable only very gradually became clear. At first both the private merchants and the W.I.C. were determined to cash in on the quick and direct profits afforded by the peltry trade. As time went on, however, it was obvious that this trade, for a variety of reasons, could not be expected to turn a profit on a long-range basis. So the W.I.C. began to cast about for a scheme to adequately populate the province. Such a scheme, however, was hard to come by, because the leading inducement of the area to colonists was the fur trade and the W.I.C. insisted jealously upon reserving that trade for itself. Even after the company surrendered its monopoly on the peltry trade in 1639 the colony continued to languish because of a combination of administrative mismanagement in the colony itself and

---

[12] Sidney E. Mead, *The Lively Experiment* (New York: Harper and Row, 1963), p. 20.

[13] The "state" in New Netherland was, of course, always a commercial enterprise. During most of the province's history, civil authority was wielded by the West India Company.

the preoccupation of the W.I.C. directors with Brazil and other of its more lucrative ventures.

The church in New Netherland, meanwhile, was itself failing to make any very explicit statement about the form the colonial society should assume. Though the Reformed *predikanten,* as we have seen, had very definite ideas on this subject, the church in New Netherland was severely hampered during this first period of the colony's history by its own lack of manpower and the W.I.C.'s lack of interest in or even overt antagonism toward its ideals. Jonas Michaëlius, the first *predikant* to arrive in the colony, complained upon his arrival that he now lived among a "for the most part quite rough and dissolute people."[14] He furthermore expressed outrage that the W.I.C., instead of supplying him a salary, had granted him some land for his support; for there were scarcely any livestock in the settlement and no laborers to be hired.[15] Michaëlius eventually fell into a dispute with Director-General Minuit and returned to the fatherland. His successor, Everardus Bogardus, experienced similar difficulties with Directors-General van Twiller and Kieft.

The years 1647–1654 represent a short pivotal period. During this time a series of events caused a fundamental shift in attitude on the part of the W.I.C. toward her North American colony, while personnel changes and population increase within the colony itself ushered in new problems in the area of church-state relations.

Each of the factors involved here will be considered in more detail farther on, so that they need now be only briefly indicated. First, the Treaty of Münster which ended the Eighty Years' War in 1648 raised serious questions about the continued existence of the W.I.C. Originally designed and brought into being partially with the intention of preying on Spanish shipping in the

---

[14] A. Eekhof, *Jonas Michaëlius, Founder of the Church in New Netherland* (Leiden: A. W. Sijthoff, 1926), p. 129.

[15] A. Eekhof, *De Hervormde Kerk in Noord-Amerika* (1624–1664) (The Hague: Nijhoff, 1913), 2, vii of the Appendix.

west, the company now saw one of its chief justifications and sources of profit disappear. It turned increased attention toward colonization and particularly the growth of its American colonial holdings in Brazil, Surinam, the West Indies, and New Netherland. Second, the recapture of Brazil by the Portuguese in 1654 dealt a crushing—and, as it turned out, devastating—blow to the financial position of the company.[16] The immediate reaction of the directors to this disaster was to turn more attention and capital toward New Netherland and the company's other colonial holdings. Third, the increased interest in colonization on the part of the W.I.C. brought to New Netherland a population more heterogeneous in ethnic background and more heterodox in religious belief. Fourth, although the directors of the highly important Amsterdam chamber of the W.I.C. were almost exclusively Counter-Remonstrant during the early years of the company's existence, by 1650 a significant number of merchants of Remonstrant or Lutheran sympathies were serving or had served as directors.[17] This explains in part the increasingly tolerant attitude of the company toward religious dissent in the colonies. Fifth, during the course of the 1650's the W.I.C. became heavily indebted to the city of Amsterdam and attempted partially to reimburse the city by granting it a certain sphere of control in New Netherland. Amsterdam was by this time well-known for religious toleration and made its influence felt in this direction in New Netherland, particularly in its own colony of New Amstel on the

[16] See W. J. van Hoboken, "De West-Indische Compagnie en de Vrede van Münster," *Tijdschrift voor Geschiedenis,* vol. 70 (Groningen: P. Noordhoff, 1957), pp. 359–368.

[17] Here I rely upon the *Doopboek* (Baptismal Register) *van de Remonstrantsche Gemeente te Amsterdam* and the *Kasboek* (Financial Register) *van de Lutersche Gemeente te Amsterdam,* both of which are located in the Amsterdam Municipal Archives. Among the W.I.C. directors who held Remonstrant sympathies were Hans Bontemantel, Dr. Albert Bas, Albert Dirckszoon Pater, and Cornelis Cloeck. Some of those who were members of the Lutheran Church in Amsterdam were Jean Gras, Henry Gras, Abraham de Visscher, and Paulus Timmerman.

Delaware River. Finally, and from the standpoint of New Netherland itself probably most important, the appointment of Peter Stuyvesant as director-general in 1647 meant that for the first time since the colony's establishment a man of real competence was guiding the colonial government.

What each of these factors, and all of them taken collectively, meant was that New Netherland was changing from a casually founded and lackadaisically maintained trading outpost to a bona-fide colonial experiment. The W.I.C. was now beginning to speak clearly its intention for the colony. Several of the ordinances from the early years of Stuyvesant's administration illustrate this new seriousness of purpose. In 1647 the sale of beer and liquor on the Sabbath was made illegal; in 1650 measures were taken for the better organization and maintenance of New Amsterdam's streets; in 1653 construction was begun of a protective wall on the north side of the city.[18] Political, moral, and physical order was beginning to prevail. Even more significant, the colony began to grow. Estimated at about 1,000 in 1646,[19] the population of New Netherland was close to 10,000 by 1664.

As immigration increased, however, the Reformed *predikanten* also began to state more explicitly their intention for the colony. Previous to the period of 1650 the church, though it had its difficulties with the W.I.C. and particularly with the directors-general, felt its position as custodian of the colony's religious life to be essentially sound and unchallenged. Though the New Netherland venture was scarcely a scintillating example of the advancement of the gospel, it was in any case Reformed and safely within the fold of orthodoxy. Now, however, the W.I.C.'s intention to populate New Netherland at all costs raised a difficult new problem for the Reformed Church. Could it stand quietly by and watch the company import, or at least allow, all sorts of

[18] J. Paulding, *Affairs and Men of New Amsterdam in the Time of Peter Stuyvesant* (New York: Casper C. Childs, 1843), pp. 7, 32–33.
[19] O'Callaghan, *History of New Netherland*, 1, 386.

religious deviants into the colony? What place did these Lutherans, Jews, Quakers, Mennonites have in a Reformed society? What was New Netherland about? If it was in the first place a commercial venture, should not its ecclesiastical life at least be kept pure so that God's glory would not be defiled? By 1654 the Lutherans in New Netherland were agitating for freedom of worship, and in the same year the W.I.C. transported to Manhattan a boatload of Jews left to the company's charge when Brazil was lost to the Portuguese. In 1657 Quakers began appearing in the colony and performing their disruptive public antics. To all of this the colonial clergy, led by Johannes Megapolensis, replied vigorously. And the Classis of Amsterdam gave them ample support in the homeland by appealing frequently and insistently to the directors of the W.I.C.

Thus, the periodization of New Netherland's church-state history can be accomplished as follows. The first period of the colony's history extended from 1609 to 1647 and was characterized by the frustration of the ideals for the colony of both the W.I.C. and the Reformed *predikanten*. While the company kept casting about for some way to make the colony pay, the *predikanten* engaged in repeated clashes with the colonial administration on issues as diverse as salary and Indian war. Neither company nor church made during this first period a clear statement of its intention for the colony of New Netherland. The company was able but not yet willing to do so, while the church was willing but not able. Events from 1647 to 1654 led the colony into the second period of its church-state history. While the first period had been characterized by frustration, both church and state now began to state explicitly their intentions, but unfortunately the company's intentions diverged from those of the church at some important points. Viewed by the *predikanten* as a neat Reformed establishment, the colony was enlarged by the most divers religious types which were sometimes sent there by the company itself. Thus the Dutch experienced a second, and ultimately more bitter, frustration in New Netherland—the frustration of internal dispute. How this dispute would have developed in the long run is a question about which the historian can only speculate, for the events of 1664 brought Dutch rule in the province to an abrupt close.

9. The Merchants

The tiny Dutch republic, engaged in a life-and-death struggle with powerful Spain for its very right to exist, was a nation that had to trade to live. Hemmed in on two sides by the sea and on two sides by the Spanish-Habsburg empire, the Dutch chose the sea as the path of less resistance. Already in the sixteenth century the Dutch had been respected as European traders, and by 1600 they were expanding this trade to the farthest corners of the earth. The venture undertaken on the North American coast by these sailors and traders was only one small part of the total seventeenth-century Dutch colonial drama. In fact, New Netherland was not even the most important enterprise of the W.I.C., and that company itself comprised but a small part of the Dutch mercantile panorama.

It was with extreme casualness that Dutchmen first drifted to North American shores. For them North America was not in the first place a land of ideological or theological promise; it was not (as it was later to be for John Winthrop) a place where God's holy city could at last be set upon its proper hill for all to see. For the first Dutchmen who ever set eyes upon North America, this continent was no more than a place to spend the winter. A report given to the directors of the W.I.C. in 1644 stated that in the winter of 1598 some sailors in the employ of the Greenland Company had spent the coldest months in two temporary forts they erected on the South (Delaware) and North (Hudson) rivers.[1]

Once the Dutch had looked over this area of the North American coast, its prospects for fur trading appeared lucrative to them. The Dutch ship *Witte Leeuw* in 1606 entered the St. Lawrence, traded with the natives for furs in defiance of the French monopoly, captured two French ships, and took prizes of whale oil, guns, and codfish from Spanish and Portuguese vessels. This maverick privateering drew a loud protest from the French king to the States-General.[2] In 1607 Dutch ships were probing the St. Lawrence in search of peltries and, by the account of one author, were dealing treacherously with the Indians there; the avarice of these Hollanders was so great that they had opened Indian graves and taken the beaver skins in which the corpses had been buried.[3] Furthermore, the attention of learned Dutchmen as well as other learned Europeans continued to be fixed on the possibility, or even probability, of finding a short route to the Orient by following one of the North American rivers to its source. Although many leading European geographers still believed in 1609 that a short cut to the East most likely lay somewhere in the frozen Artic regions, there is good reason to believe that Henry Hudson doubted that hypothesis.

Hudson had twice, in the employ of the London Muscovy Company, sought a short route to the Orient via the Arctic and failed. It is quite possible that even as he accepted his instructions from the Amsterdam chamber of the Dutch East India Company on January 8, 1609, he intended to disregard them.[4] On April 4, 1609, Hudson, with his Dutch commission that ex-

[1] *Col. Doc.*, 1, 149.

[2] Simon Hart, *The Prehistory of the New Netherland Company* (Amsterdam: City of Amsterdam Press, 1959), pp. 13–15.

[3] O'Callaghan, *History of New Netherland* (New York: Appleton, 1848), 1, 32.

[4] Kessler and Rachlis, *Peter Stuyvesant and His New York* (New York: Random House, 1959), p. 29.

plicitly enjoined him "to think of discovering no other routes or passages," sailed out of Amsterdam to "search for a passage by the north, around the north side of Novaya Zemlya, and to continue thus along the parallel until he shall be able to sail southward." Precisely what happened to turn Hudson's path west instead of east will never be known. Probably the most trustworthy account is that of the contemporary Dutch historian Emanuel van Meteren, who wrote in 1611 that Hudson "found the sea as full of ice as he had found it in the preceding year, so that they lost the hope of effecting anything during the season. This circumstance, and the cold, which some of his men, who had been in the East Indies, could not bear, caused quarrels among the crew."[5] However it came to pass, the *Half Moon* was sailing west by May 19, and on July 12, 1609, it sighted the south coast of Nova Scotia. On August 3 the ship arrived at the north shore of Cape Cod, and on September 3 the crew went ashore at Sandy Hook Harbor, slightly to the south of what is now named Staten Island. Proceeding into Upper New York Bay on September 6, the *Half Moon* sailed cautiously up what ship's officer Robert Juet[6] called "the river" (later to be named for Hudson) until the head of navigation was reached on September 22. Regardless of what dealings the Dutch had previously had with this area, Hudson's voyage soon came to be considered by the Netherlanders as their legitimate claim to New Netherland. Adriaen van der Donck, in his *Remonstrance of New Netherland* published in 1649, cited Hudson as the basis for Dutch pretensions to control of the province.[7]

[5] Cited *ibid.,* p. 31.

[6] Juet, a native of Limehouse, England, was an officer on both Hudson's third and fourth voyages to North America. On the fourth voyage, to Hudson's Bay in 1610, Juet was among those rebellious seamen who successfully mutinied against Hudson and set him adrift in the icy waters of the bay. See Franklin Jameson, *Narratives of New Netherland* (New York: Scribner's, 1909), pp. 13–15.

[7] Adriaen van der Donck, *Remonstrance of New Netherland: Addressed to the High and Mighty Lords States-General of the United Netherlands on the 28th July 1649* (Albany: Weed, Parsons, 1856), p. 7.

Hudson never returned to the Netherlands, but his voyage had revealed two things particularly interesting to Dutch merchants. First there was a large, unclaimed tract of North American coast between French Canada and English Virginia that was fortified by neither power. Second, Hudson and his crew had traded with the natives along "the river" for furs. It is uncertain which Dutch entrepreneurial combination was first to follow up Hudson's discovery, but Amsterdam mercantile interest in the area was aroused almost immediately. By 1613 two different Amsterdam-based "companies," one headed by Lambert van Tweenhuysen and one by Hans Claeszoon, were competing with one another for the fur trade along the Hudson River.[8] Before the competition could become ruinous to the trade the van Tweenhuysen and Claeszoon companies, along with two other smaller Amsterdam combinations, amalgamated to form the New Netherland Company in October 1614. Under the terms of a charter from the States-General, the new company enjoyed a monopoly on Dutch trade to the area from January 1, 1615, to December 31, 1617. Very little is known of the company's activities during this time, but evidently it made full use of its monopoly privileges, because it attempted, unsuccessfully, to extend them beyond the deadline. After January 1, 1618, the New Netherland trade was again thrown open by the States-General and, although the New Netherland Company continued to trade to the area and resisted all efforts on the part of its competitors, strong competition for the fur trade did resume.

The vigor with which the New Netherland trade was sought both by the New Netherland Company and by its rivals between 1614 and 1623 is an indication of how valuable it must have been. Only when the West India Company became an estab-

---

[8] It is not my intention to discuss in detail the history of these so-called *voorcompagniën*. See the excellent recent discussions in Simon Hart; Thomas J. Condon, *New York Beginnings* (New York: New York University Press, 1968); and Van Cleaf Bachman, *Peltries or Plantations* (Baltimore: Johns Hopkins Press, 1969).

lished fact, on June 3, 1621, did these private merchants accept the inevitable and turn away from New Netherland. Thus, when in 1623 the W.I.C. turned its attention to the North American portion of its domain, it inherited the experience and knowledge gained by more than a decade of private Dutch mercantile activity in the area. It is therefore worthwhile to inquire what these private merchants had wrought during their decade of activity on American shores.

The sum total of Dutch "colonization" in New Netherland between 1609 and 1623 was represented by one combination fort and trading post, Fort Nassau on Castle Island in the upper Hudson River. It is unlikely that even this meager establishment would have been left behind had it not served the immediate strategic purposes of the van Tweenhuysen Company to erect it in 1614. But such a fortified trading post served a dual mercantile purpose. On the one hand, its arms were a psychological and real deterrent to the invasion of the area by other merchants. On the other hand, it provided a central depot for gathering furs during the entire year and could thereby reduce considerably the length of time a ship had to remain in North America to collect a profitable cargo. When Rev. John Robinson's Pilgrim congregation, living in the Netherlands, appealed to the van Tweenhuysen Company in 1620 to provide it with passage to America, the merchants received the idea favorably because it would strengthen the position of their trading post there.[9]

Thus, out of the jostling of the private Dutch merchants in New Netherland from 1613 to 1623 one striking fact emerges: the Dutch did not originally come to North America to colonize. The Amsterdam mercantile entrepreneurs whose vessels first explored and charted the province had not the remotest notion of establishing there an outpost of Dutch society. Thomas Condon puts it succinctly: "What plans for New Netherland did the private merchants have during the years of their predominance?

---

[9] Hart, p. 37.

With the exception of wanting to extract the greatest possible profit from the area, they had no plans as such. Schooled in the principles of general European and East Indian trade, these private merchants trading to New Netherland had only commercial aims in mind. They were neither colonizers nor empire builders."[10] A lack of any dramatic vision for New Netherland or its future is what characterized this first period of the province's history and defines it rather sharply over against that of New England or even Virginia. Perry Miller reminds us that already in 1608 the Virginia Company had published John Smith's *True Relation* with an anonymous preface in which it was asserted that the ends of the company's labors were "to the high glory of God, to the erecting of true religion among Infidells, to the overthrow of superstition and idolatrie, to the winning of many thousands of wandering sheepe, unto Christs fold, who now, and till now, have strayed in the unknowne paths of Paganisme, Idolatrie, and superstition."[11] No matter how wide the hiatus between the lofty pretensions of the Virginia Company and the crassness of its actual motives, it at least uttered the pretensions. In contrast, not only did the Amsterdam merchants not colonize for evangelistic or theocratic reasons, but an examination of the Dutch documents from New Netherland's first decade reveals clearly that these merchants had no intention of colonizing at all for any reasons.

The transfer of New Netherland into the hands of the gigantic West India Company in 1621 did not mean a change in attitude on the part of the Dutch toward their North American property. It is true that the W.I.C. was conceived as more than a commercial venture by those in the Netherlands who had most ardently worked for its creation, especially Willem Usselincx. In its final form, however, the W.I.C. bore a markedly commercial stamp. For although many and important people in the Netherlands

---

[10] Condon, p. 34.
[11] *Errand into the Wilderness* (New York: Harper and Row, 1956), pp. 101–102.

wished to see a West India Company used primarily in a military way against Spain, the fact remained that the *sine qua non* for the establishment of such a company was capital—and the merchants had that. Particularly in New Netherland the company adopted a commercial posture from the very beginning. There were no Spaniards within hundreds of miles of the area; the province showed little potential for returning a good profit except on the fur trade; and the experience of private merchants over more than a decade indicated that profits could indeed be taken on this trade if the ruinous competition were eliminated. So the coming of the W.I.C. to New Netherland did not imply a sharp break with the first decade of the area's Dutch history. The Dutch continued to ask essentially one question about the province: how could it be made to pay? Their answer also remained the same: furs. Thus from 1623, when the first W.I.C. ship (the *Makreel*) arrived in New Netherland waters, until 1629, when a new approach to the province was adopted, the Dutch still failed to "colonize" the area in any permanent sense.

With these aims, then, the W.I.C. began very gradually to permeate New Netherland. In 1625 an expedition was sent out under a "director," Willem Verhulst, and in the same year the company contracted with an engineer and surveyor, Crijn Frederickszoon, to stake out and construct a substantial fort-trading complex. The instructions given Frederickszoon for the construction of dwelling units within the fort indicate the highly commercial nature of the company's plans: "The second story of all the adjoining houses, 9 feet high and 25 feet square, shall throughout be reserved for the use of the Company, to store therein at first all the provisions belonging to the Company, as well as all the trading-goods and furs and whatever else belongs to the Company."[12] Early in 1626 Verhulst and Frederickszoon selected as a site for the company's headquarters the island of

---

[12] A. J. F. van Laer, ed. and trans., *Documents Relating to New Netherland, 1624–1626, in the Henry F. Huntington Library* (San Marino, Calif., 1924), p. 163. Quoted in Condon, p. 83.

Manhattan, a point located centrally between the Hudson and Delaware fur sources.

The W.I.C.'s plans for this neat, orderly trading establishment in the New World unfortunately proved more impressive on paper than workable in fact. Two problems soon arose. First, it was very difficult to find Dutch natives willing to emigrate to North America on the company's terms. This was a basic impediment, for although the company did not envision a whole province organized as a Dutch society they did need some people to make their trading post work. Furthermore, those emigrants who could be enticed to make a beginning in the New World were generally speaking not a very industrious or trustworthy lot. Any natural tendencies toward inertia or scheming were reinforced by the fact that the realities of life in New Netherland were in rather sharp contrast to the "get rich" propaganda the W.I.C. published at home. Once many of these company employees came to understand that life in New Netherland would be hard and the returns meager, they quite naturally served their own interests at the expense of the company. Since the only immediately profitable enterprise in the province was the fur trade, this trade was pursued illegally by many colonists, driving up the price of furs as relentlessly as had been the case in pre-W.I.C. days.

By 1628 or 1629 it was clear to the directors of the W.I.C. that the course they had adopted for the development of the New Netherland trade was a failure. The venture was not yet paying, and to their merchant minds this was a most serious defect. One alternative was to abandon the area altogether, but such an action would be to abdicate entirely to the English in North America. A second option was to give up the company's monopoly on the fur trade, but this the directors felt would establish a bad precedent and hasten the demise of the company's monopoly in other more important trade areas like Brazil.

The solution finally devised by the W.I.C. directors avoided both of these alternatives. Embodied in a "Charter of Freedoms and Exemptions" promulgated on June 7, 1629, this solution was designed to reserve for the company the valuable fur trade while simultaneously encouraging private participants in the company's capital to establish estates for themselves in New Netherland by promoting and underwriting colonization there.[13] Any person who would agree to establish within the space of four years a colony of fifty or more people fifteen years of age or older was offered the title of patroon (patron) of New Netherland (Art. 3). To each patroon was promised a grant of land that would "extend four leagues along the coast on one side of a navigable river, or two leagues along both sides of a river, and as far inland as the situation of the occupants will permit" (Art. 5). The patroon was to reign supreme on his fief or *leen-goed*.

While the W.I.C. directors as a body hoped that the "Charter of Freedoms and Exemptions" would increase colonization in New Netherland such that the company's trade would become profitable, there is good reason to believe that those who became the colony's first patroons had their own private trade in mind rather than colonization. By January 1630 five Amsterdam merchants had filed notices of intention to establish patroonships in New Netherland, and to a man the five were Amsterdammers and directors of the W.I.C. This gave a slightly contrived appearance to the whole venture, and it was so interpreted by at least some contemporaries. In 1641 David Pieterszoon de Vries, himself more than a little interested in the mercantile prospects of New Netherland, wrote that "when the work [i.e., the proposal to establish patroonships] began to progress, these persons [Kiliaen van Rensselaer and the other later patroons] were directors of the Company and commissioners of New Netherland,

---

[13] The Charter of Freedoms and Exemptions is found in complete translation in A. J. F. van Laer, ed. and trans., *New York State Library Van Rensselaer Bowier Manuscripts* (Albany: University of the State of New York, 1908), pp. 136–152.

and helped themselves by the cunning tricks of merchants."[14]

Of the five merchants who originally announced their intentions to establish patroonships under the charter of 1629, two (Albert Coenraetszoon Burgh and Samuel Bloemaert) never began their ventures and two more (Michiel Pauw and Samuel Godijn) sold their profitless estates back to the W.I.C. in 1636. The jealousy with which the company continued to guard its fur monopoly evidently discouraged these men, who were seeking quick profits. Kiliaen van Rensselaer, however, stuck to his belief that, by building a solid base of colonists pursuing agriculture, the order, stability, and economic balance essential for profitable trade could eventually be developed in New Netherland. He tried to populate his colony of Rensselaerswijck on the upper Hudson with farmers, whose produce he hoped would eventually supply the trading personnel maintained in New Netherland by the company. Rensselaer, however, encountered extreme difficulty in gathering a population for his patroonship. At one point in 1632 he despaired of being able to muster the fifty persons necessary to fulfill the requirements of the charter.[15] He blamed his problems squarely on the restrictive economic policy of the directors, reasoning as follows: "The Company has much discussed certain points which I proposed to them concerning the throwing open of the fur trade, but thus far no decision has been made; what will come of it, time will show. If they wish to keep it to themselves with few people, which is most profitable to them, they cannot defend the country, and with many people they suffer loss; and others will not care to populate the country unless they have the free trade."[16]

---

[14] David Pieterszoon de Vries, *Korte Historael, ende Journaels Aenteyckeninge van Verscheyden Voyagiens in de Vier Deelen des Wereldts-Ronde, als Europa, Africa, Asia, ende Amerika Gedaen.* In Jameson, *Narratives of New Netherland,* p. 210, and quoted in Condon, p. 124.

[15] A. J. F. van Laer, *Van Rensselaer Bowier Manuscripts,* p. 233. Letter of Kiliaen van Rensselaer to Wouter van Twiller, July 27, 1632.

[16] *Ibid.,* p. 230. Kiliaen van Rensselaer to Wouter van Twiller, September 25, 1636. Quoted in Condon, p. 140.

By 1638 the W.I.C. directors were beginning to realize that Rensselaer's estimate of the situation was essentially correct. Even more important, however, was the growing apprehension of the States-General that unless a radical turnabout were effected in the W.I.C.'s New Netherland policy the province might very easily fall prey to the encroachments of the restless New Englanders to the east. "Itinerant Yankee peddlers" Diedrich Knickerbocker was later to label them,[17] and indeed the Dutch had a great deal to fear from their designs on the territory of New Netherland. As early as 1627 William Bradford had communicated to Minuit at Manhattan that it would be wise for the Netherlanders to establish their claim to New Netherland beyond all doubt, for Bradford believed that the English king had granted this province "by patent to divers nobles and subjects of quality." He further urged the Dutch to do this convincingly and with dispatch, "lest it be a bone of contention in these stirring evil times." In conclusion, he pointed out that "it [New Netherland] will be harder and with more difficulty obtained hereafter, and perhaps not without blows," a rather thinly veiled threat. The running dispute between Directors-General Twiller and Kieft and the English settlement on the Connecticut River at Hartford forms a dissonant counterpoint to the whole of New Netherland's history.[18]

The recognized importance of retaining New Netherland in Dutch control was what had prevented the W.I.C. directors from dropping this financial white elephant in 1629. But the measures taken instead, the "Charter of Freedoms and Exemptions," had neither populated the province nor rendered it profitable. Thus in April 1638 the States-General declared in a tone of genuine alarm that: "The population in New Netherland does not only not increase as it ought but even . . . the popula-

---

[17] Irving, *Knickerbocker's History of New York* (New York: Putnam, rev. from 1848 ed.), 1, 296.
[18] O'Callaghan, 1, 109, and passim.

tion which had been commenced is decreasing, and appears to be neglected by the West India Company, so that the inhabitants of foreign princes and potentates, are endeavoring to incorporate New Netherland, and if not seasonably attended to, will at once entirely overrun it."[19] Later the same month the W.I.C. directors conceded that in North America "the right is that of the strongest," and that "the English enclose us from Virginia unto New England." Therefore, they continued, inasmuch as "their High Mightinesses [the States-General] consider it advantageous to preserve the limits of New Netherland, and to establish the population on a better and surer footing," the directors "propose to surrender the trade with the Indians, or something else."[20]

In August of 1638 the company took the desired step. The Amsterdam chamber, acting on behalf of all the directors, presented to the States-General a position paper containing thirteen articles, the ninth of which said in part: "The inhabitants there may, for themselves, or such others as shall instruct or commission them, build all descriptions of craft, either large or small, and with the same and no others navigate all rivers, and prosecute their lawful trade and barter, besides trade therein along the whole coast, from Florida to Newfoundland."[21] The company's trade monopoly, which it had guarded so jealously for nearly twenty years, was finally lifted. The directors now sat back in sanguine expectation of the rapid colonization all of their critics had predicted would follow. But their hopes proved sanguine indeed. At first there were some encouraging signs of settlement, especially in the general area of Manhattan, where "in place of seven farms and two or three plantations which were here before, one now saw thirty farms as well built and as well stocked with animals as in Europe."[22] As time went on, however, it became

---

[19] *Col. Doc.*, 1, 106. Resolution of the States-General urging the colonization of New Netherland.

[20] *Ibid.*, 1, 107, W.I.C. report on the condition of New Netherland.

[21] *Ibid.*, 1, 112. Articles proposed by the W.I.C. for the colonization and trade of New Netherland.

[22] O'Callaghan, 1, 222.

apparent that opening the trade had not had the desired effect of peopling New Netherland and adding to its economic or political stability.

There were basically two reasons why New Netherland's population failed to grow after the W.I.C. dropped its monopoly. The first the company should probably have foreseen. The people in the Netherlands who responded to the freeing of trade were not the sturdy farmers and pioneers the directors had hoped to attract, but profit-seeking private traders who hoped to make a quick fortune by trading for furs with the natives and bilking the colonists for goods from the homeland. The inhabitants of New Netherland soon proposed taxing those "who had drawn excessive profits from the country, by their injurious usury.[23] Furthermore, many of the colonists themselves were unable to resist the lure of quick profits and dropped their agricultural work to push into the interior in search of new sources of fur. By 1643, little more than four years later, the W.I.C. directors were lamenting, with good cause, that "the plan of opening the trade to said place, produces no true effect according to the intent, inasmuch as many will go thither to trade without acquiring a domicile there; and therefore population scarcely increases there, whilst trade is seriously ruined."[24]

Even so, the settling of New Netherland might gradually have begun to progress had it not been for the fact that the colony now became involved in a serious and bloody dispute with the native population. Willem Kieft had been director-general of New Netherland since 1633, when he had replaced Kiliaen van Rensselaer's nephew, Wouter van Twiller. It is not clear how Kieft obtained the post, for as a merchant at La Rochelle he had achieved bankruptcy in 1633 and administratively he was an

[23] *Col. Doc.*, 1, 212. The "Eight men," representing the New Netherland commonalty, to the W.I.C. directors, October 28, 1644.

[24] *Col. Doc.*, 1, 135–136. Agenda of the meeting of the W.I.C. directors, February 2, 1643.

unknown quantity.[25] The gradual expansion of Dutch activities in the area of Manhattan began, about 1640, to create some problems with the neighboring Indians, who had heretofore been friendly. The initial cause of the difficulty is obscure. Evidently some Dutch cows roaming untended through the forest trampled and ate a substantial amount of the Indians' corn. The Indians began to retaliate with a series of raids on Dutch settlers located outside the fort on Manhattan. Level-headed, reasonable action on the part of the director-general could possibly have saved the day, but Kieft reacted otherwise. As was later reported to the directors of the W.I.C., the director-general thought that "the Indians who had waged war against us, should be wholly destroyed and exterminated." To this end he demanded "one hundred and fifty soldiers, armed with muskets and coats of mail, and provided with sufficient munitions of war; inasmuch as he estimated the number of Indians, our enemies, not to be three hundred strong."[26] There were voices of disagreement in the colony, and Kieft bided his time until February 1643. Then suddenly one night an armed expedition was dispatched against a group of unsuspecting Indians encamped on the shores of Pavonia (New Jersey). David Pieterszoon de Vries, who tried to deter Kieft from this mad scheme, recounts the evening: "I remained that night at the governor's sitting up. I went and sat by the kitchen fire, when about midnight I heard a great shrieking, and I ran to the ramparts of the fort, and looked over to Pavonia. I saw nothing but firing, and heard the shrieks of the savages murdered in their sleep." De Vries had accurately foreseen the consequences of this line of action. His final, vain plea to Kieft had been to reconsider because in attacking the Indians he would "also murder our own nation, for there are none of the

[25] Johan E. Elias, *De Vroedschap van Amsterdam* (Haarlem: 1903 and 1904), 1, 188, note.

[26] *Col. Doc.*, 1, 151. Report of the W.I.C. "Board of Accounts" on New Netherland, December 15, 1644.

settlers in the open country who are aware of it."[27] From 1643 until peace was finally reestablished in August of 1645, the Indians proceeded through raid after raid to reduce the Dutch hold on lands surrounding Manhattan.

By the fall of 1644 it was questionable if New Netherland could survive, let alone prosper. A letter from some of the settlers to the directors of the company in October 1644 condemned Kieft's arbitrary maladministration and described the pitiable state of affairs on Manhattan:

Our fields lie fallow and waste; our dwellings and other buildings are burnt; not a handful can be either planted or sown this fall on the deserted places; the crops which God the Lord permitted to come forth during the past summer, remain on the field standing and rotting in divers places, in the same way as the hay, for the preservation of which we, poor people, cannot obtain one man. We are burdened with heavy families; we have no means to provide necessaries for wife or children; and we sit here amidst thousands of Indians and barbarians, from whom we find neither peace nor mercy.

The settlers concluded their long plea to the company with the firm declaration that "it is impossible ever to settle this country until a different system be introduced here, and a new governor be sent out with more people, who shall settle themselves in suitable places, one near the other, in form of villages and hamlets."[28]

To the W.I.C. directors it must have come as bitter frustration indeed to hear from New Netherland that the financial success of that venture depended upon the introduction of still another "different system." Since the W.I.C. had inherited the province in 1621 no fewer than three "different systems" had been experimented with, and all had proved essentially fruitless. The attempt to view New Netherland as simply a fur-trading post foundered on the inability of the Dutch merchants to reach an agreement among themselves to eliminate competition. Patroonships failed

[27] Quoted in Kessler and Rachlis, p. 56.
[28] Quoted in O'Callaghan, 1, 313, 317.

to provide a workable means for populating the province and introducing a stable agricultural economy, because most of the would-be patroons were in reality more interested in a quick profit from furs than in underwriting long-range plantations, and also because there was a serious shortage of industrious Dutchmen who were interested in staking their futures in North America. Finally, even the significant decision of the company in 1639 to throw open the fur trade had failed to make New Netherland a paying venture. Competition again had its deleterious effect as numerous merchants jockeyed for a share of the profits, and not only did these merchants not settle the province but the lure of fast gain attracted many of the earlier settlers away from their farms into the interior. Director-General Kieft's ill-starred attempt to exterminate the neighboring natives nearly administered the *coup de grace* to the struggling little community at the tip of Manhattan. Thus, the harsh reality facing the W.I.C. directors in 1644 was that, after more than twenty years of W.I.C. management, New Netherland was still an economic failure and still awaited a serious Dutch attempt at colonization.

10. The *Predikanten*

The frustration attending Dutch commercial efforts in New Netherland from 1609 to 1647 also plagued the Reformed Church which, as the privileged church in the homeland, naturally accompanied the merchants in their overseas endeavors. Like the merchants, whose basic aim of profit was well-defined, the Reformed Church had a clear view of the ecclesiastical form that should prevail in the Dutch colonies. On June 4, 1636, the Classis of Amsterdam declared, in its formulation of a call for *predikanten* going overseas, that "it is proper, so far as is possible, that the glory of God, and the salvation of the people should be promoted, in all regions and localities where the people may be scattered, or where they may go to pursue their divers kinds of business." Toward the achievement of these ends the classis proposed that religious gatherings "ought to be established and maintained, with the pure preaching of God's Word, the lawful administration of the Sacraments, the public calling on the name of the Lord, and whatever else belongs to regular worship."[1] Thus, as conceived by the Classis of Amsterdam, the church's role in colonial life was to be central and public. This was in all respects consistent with the Calvinist ideal of organic unity between church and state. Furthermore, the church alone was to

[1] Acts of the Deputati ad res Indicas of the Classis of Amsterdam. Translated in H. Hastings, ed., *Ecclesiastical Records of the State of New York* (Albany: James B. Lyon, 1901), 1, 92. The *Ecclesiastical Records* are hereafter cited as *Ecc. Rec.*

be responsible for the content and presentation of public education. On June 7, 1636, the Classis of Amsterdam stated that education was deemed by them to be equally important with worship, for "upon these exercises both the glory of God and the salvation of men are not a little dependent." Schoolmasters for the colonies, who received their commissions from the classis, were to "instruct the youth, both on shipboard and on land, in reading, writing, ciphering, and arithmetic, with all zeal and diligence: and also to implant the fundamental principles of the true Christian Religion and salvation, by means of catechizing."[2]

The Dutch Reformed *predikanten* envisioned the Dutch colonial enterprise as an extension of the organic Calvinist state which supposedly prevailed at home. How far short of this ideal New Netherland had fallen by 1649 was poignantly related by Adriaen van der Donck, former sheriff of Rensselaerswijck, in his *Remonstrance of New Netherland*. It has been shown that, despite any righteous reports from the W.I.C. directors to the effect that their chief aim was the propagation of the Christian gospel, the company always operated in New Netherland in what it at least supposed to be a financially expedient way. Van der Donck scored the company's niggardly attitude toward the church in caustic language. "It is now our time," he said, "to speak of the church property, and to do the truth no violence, we are not aware that there ever has been any, or that the church hath any revenue, except what is given to it. Neither the Company nor the Director ever took the least pains or trouble to obtain or provide any." Furthermore, the company, in van der Donck's estimation, had totally failed in its duty to provide the settlement of New Amsterdam with proper schooling. The inhabitants had tried to rectify this situation, and they had passed the plate on numerous occasions to collect funds for a "Common school." At this point, however, the school had been "built with

[2] The Classis of Amsterdam's "Instructions and Letter of Credential for School-Masters going to the East or West Indies or elsewhere." *Ecc. Rec.*, 1, 98.

words, for as yet the first stone is not laid." Van der Donck's conclusion concerning the degree to which the company had ignored the religious life of the colony was characteristically blunt. It was, he declared, "sufficiently apparent, that scarcely any proper care or diligence has been used by the Company or its officers, for any ecclesiastical property; and, as far as can be ascertained, nothing in the least has been done from the beginning up to the present time."[3]

Between van der Donck and the W.I.C. there was no love lost,[4] and the *Remonstrance* cannot be taken prima facie as an accurate appraisal of the company's efforts in behalf of the gospel in New Netherland. In fact, the directors took real offence at his accusation that they had neglected church property, claiming that the company had erected within the fort at New Amsterdam a church which "cost much more than eight thousand guilders whereof it cannot be proved that the people paid eight hundred; the collection taken up by subscription hath realised the least."[5] Nevertheless, van der Donck's charge contained a kernel of truth, namely, that the company had consistently served first its own financial interests in New Netherland, and all other things including ecclesiastical interests had been relegated to positions of lesser importance. This is borne out by an investigation of the Reformed Church's history in New Netherland prior to 1647.

The first representative of the Reformed Church in New Netherland was the *ziekentrooster* Bastiaen Janszoon Krol. He is a curious figure, who was never finally certain whether his master was God or Mammon, though he clearly gravitated toward the latter. Typical of the generally low level of literacy of the Dutch *ziekentroosters,* Krol had not been able to write at the

[3] Adriaen van der Donck, *Remonstrance of New Netherland,* ed. and trans. by E. B. O'Callaghan (Albany: Weed, Parsons, 1856), p. 32.

[4] See O'Callaghan, *History of New Netherland* (New York: Appleton, 1848), 2, 110–144.

[5] Answer of the W.I.C. to the *Remonstrance of New Netherland.* In *Ecc. Rec.,* 1, 267.

time of his marriage in 1615, and before he submitted himself to the Consistory of Amsterdam in 1623 to be examined for the post of *ziekentrooster* in either the East or West Indies he had been a silk worker.[6] The consistory at first rejected him but later reversed its decision when one of the better candidates became ill. Krol arrived at Manhattan in the spring of 1624 and fulfilled the duties of *ziekentrooster* there until September 1626 when, remarkably enough, he exchanged his ecclesiastical post for that of *kommies* (storekeeper) of the W.I.C.'s trading post at Fort Orange. His further career in New Netherland consisted of being Kilaen van Rensselaer's business agent when the latter established the patroonship of Rensselaerswijck in 1629. Finally, doubtless through the influence of Rensselaer, he attained the position of temporary director-general of New Netherland from Minuit's departure in February 1632 until the arrival of Wouter van Twiller in April of 1633. While this was an achievement of no mean proportion for a man with Krol's qualifications, it can hardly be said that Krol represented a beginning of heroic proportions for the church in New Netherland.

Yet Krol must have possessed a clearer idea of the company's plan (or "non-plan") for New Netherland, and the church's role in this, than did some of his successors. To have gained the trust of a shrewd merchant like van Rensselaer he must have possessed a keen business sense. To have risen from silk worker to director-general of one of the W.I.C.'s territories he must have exhibited a spirit of real enterprise. But at the same time his unschooled piety must have been genuine to have survived, albeit shakily, the rigorous scrutiny of the Calvinist divines in the Consistory of Amsterdam. In the final analysis, however, it is very

---

[6] Eekhof, *De Hervormde Kerk in Noord-Amerika* (*1624–1664*) (The Hague: Nijhoff, 1913), 1, 28. Eekhof, *Bastiaen Janszoon Krol: Krankenbezoeker, Kommies en Kommandeur van Nieuw-Nederland, 1595–1645* (The Hague, 1910). Gerald F. De Jong, "The *Ziekentroosters* or Comforters of the Sick in New Netherland," *New York Historical Society Quarterly,* 54 (October, 1970), 339–360. Krol's wife may have taught him to write.

likely the case that Krol simply did not perceive the depth and seriousness of the question about New Netherland's future. To what extent New Netherland would become a trading post and to what extent it would become a Reformed society are questions he very likely never raised nor bothered himself about. Such was emphatically not the case with Krol's ecclesiastical successor at Manhattan, Jonas Michaëlius. The first ordained *predikant* to serve in New Netherland, Michaëlius's academic credentials came from the University of Leiden where he had studied for six years before taking a pastorate in 1606 in one of the "churches under the cross" in the province of Brabant.[7] His Leiden training, his service in a *kruiskerk* pastorate, and his correspondence with the fierce Counter-Remonstrant Adriaen Smout[8] all point to the likelihood that Michaëlius was a member of that theological circle Jan Wagenaar labeled the "hard Reformed."

Michaëlius arrived at Manhattan on April 7, 1628. There are in existence three letters written to the homeland by Michaëlius between his arrival and his departure from New Netherland in 1632. This is certainly not a wealth of source material, but within this correspondence there are some clues as to what Michaëlius hoped the church in New Netherland would become and what the chief obstacles were to the realization of his hopes.

On August 8, 1628, Michaëlius wrote to Joannes van Foreest, a nobleman and director of the W.I.C. residing at Hoorn. Much of the letter was taken up with a narration of events on the voyage out, a relation of Michaëlius's grief at the death of his wife shortly after arriving in New Netherland, and a description of the countryside and the progress of the settlement at Manhattan. Michaëlius then went on to suggest to Foreest some interesting improvements, which in his opinion would greatly benefit the growth and development of the little community. First, the *predikant* noted that food is "scanty and poor. We need nothing," he

[7] Eekhof, *Hervormde Kerk*, 1, 32–33.
[8] See Chapter 6.

said, "so much as horses and cows, and industrious workers for the building of houses and forts, and to make our farming more profitable, in order that we may have sufficient dairy produce and crops. For to be fed continually from the Fatherland is difficult, expensive, and hazardous." The lack of population in the settlement is a subject to which Michaëlius returned more than once. Remarking that land might be bought cheaply from the Indians, he lamented, "We lack only sufficient people to occupy that country." The building up of the community at Manhattan was retarded chiefly by sparseness of population: "For building purposes there is a greater lack of labourers than of materials." Finally, he protested that the W.I.C. directors had mismanaged the matter of his own salary, for instead of free board they had promised him a portion of land. This promise, however, "is worth nothing. For their Honours themselves knew perfectly well, that neither horses nor cows nor labourers are to be had here for money. And this is the first item of the bill; time will show, what else will follow."[9]

The interesting thing about these observations and suggestions is that they are predicated upon a false assumption, namely, that it was the intention of the W.I.C. to populate New Netherland. This was not at all the plan for the province before 1629, and even thereafter it was adopted only as a means to make the venture profitable. That Michaëlius misread the company's motives in New Netherland (or, at least, that he was animated by quite different ones) is further demonstrated when he comes to speak of his own work. He informed Foreest, "We have begun to found a Christian Church here."[10] This statement is then enlarged upon in a letter written three days later, August 11, 1628, to his ecclesiastical colleague Adriaen Smout in Amsterdam. Michaëlius said that "from the beginning we established a form of a Church." He went on to explain that a consistory had been

---

[9] In Eekhof, *Jonas Michaëlius, Founder of the Church in New Netherland* (Leiden: A. W. Sijthoff, 1926), pp. 107–114.

[10] *Ibid.*, p. 111.

selected and how it would function. Then he moved to a description of the first celebration of the Lord's Supper. He noted with
pride and joy that at the service there were "fully fifty communicants." Many of these "made their first confession of faith before us, and others exhibited their church certificates. Others had
forgotten to bring their certificates with them, not thinking that a
church would be formed and established here."[11] Those who had
not thought that a church (or for that matter, any other sort of
social institution) would be formed in New Netherland were
probably much closer to understanding the W.I.C. than was
Michaëlius.

Farther on in his letter to Smout, the only *predikant* in this
tiny wilderness settlement spoke briefly of what he conceived the
role of the church to be in that frontier situation. As Condon
points out, Michaëlius's elaborate plans for church and social
structure within a motley group of fewer than two hundred persons had its comic aspects.[12] Nevertheless, the Dutch Reformed
Church had a very definite concept of the place and function of
the state and the church within organized society, and Michaëlius
had brought this concept with him to North America. It was not
out of his own theorizing but out of the remembered experience
of the Reformed Church in the Netherlands that he spoke when
he wrote to Smout, "I keep myself as far as practicable within
the pale of my calling, wherein I find myself sufficiently occupied. . . . And I still hope to separate carefully the ecclesiastical
from the civil matters which occur, so that each one may be
occupied with his own subject." Slightly farther on in the same
letter Michaëlius could be mistaken for a Counter-Remonstrant
predikant in the homeland thundering against Oldenbarnevelt's
political meddling in ecclesiastical affairs: "Though many things
are *mixti generis,* and political and ecclesiastical persons can
greatly assist each other, nevertheless the matters and offices,

[11] *Ibid.,* pp. 128–139.
[12] Condon, *New York Beginnings* (New York: New York University
Press, 1968), pp. 110–111.

proceeding together, must not be mixed but kept separate, in or-
der to prevent all confusion and disorder."[13] Unfortunately, Michaëlius was unable to avert the "confusion
and disorder" he so greatly feared. A second letter from Mi-
chaëlius to Foreest, on September 13, 1630, sheds some light on
the earliest frustrations of the church in New Netherland. The
predikant bemoaned to his friend the fact that although "the
beginning of my work seemed to promise something great," all
fond hopes have "gradually vanished through a nefarious enterprise of wicked men, who have created serious tragedies among
us." The "wicked men" were not left unnamed. Michaëlius was
referring to Minuit, the governor, "who is most unworthy of his
office," and the council "that obeys with the same iniquity as he
commands."[14] Minuit is charged with a variety of moral lapses,
among which are lying, fornication, and cheating the company.
But what clearly bothered Michaëlius most about Minuit was
that the governor had used his position as elder in the church
consistory[15] to exonerate himself, "to silence me and make me
hated," and "to eject me out of this place, branded with a mark
of shame." Indeed, as far as Michaëlius was concerned, Minuit
had "resolved to turn everything upside down," and "plots inde-
fatigably to disperse all the fruit of my ministry and of my la-
bours."[16]

Michaëlius's expectations for the church in New Netherland
were frustrated for two reasons. In the first place, his hope for a
well-defined boundary between ecclesiastical and civil spheres
of influence was based on the model of a highly developed society
(the Netherlands), which bore almost no resemblance to New
Netherland. The latter, after all, was by 1630 no more than a
glorified trading post inhabited by several hundred persons,

[13] In Eekhof, *Jonas Michaëlius,* p. 131.
[14] *Ibid.,* pp. 67–68.
[15] Michaëlius had organized a consistory in 1628 and had appointed
Peter Minuit and his brother-in-law Jan Huygen as elders.
[16] Eekhof, *Jonas Michaëlius,* p. 68.

mostly employees of the company. The settlement's raison d'être was almost entirely commercial, and under such circumstances it was not immediately obvious that the "founding of a church" was called for or that a *predikant* should be placed in a position of power within the community—even in a position of ecclesiastical power. And this question of power was the second source of Michaëlius's frustration. Theoretically, the Reformed *predikanten* claimed absolute autonomy only within the bounds of the strictly theological and ecclesiastical. The civil power, however, was inseparably bound together with the spiritual authority in the total organic unity of the state, according to Reformed theology. The magistracy, therefore, was bound to listen carefully to the advice of the church even in civil affairs. Michaëlius had alluded to this point of Reformed doctrine in his earlier letter to Smout, in which he said, "As the Council of this place consists of good people, who are, however, for the most part simple and have little experience in public affairs, I should have little objection to serve them in any difficult or dubious affair with good advice, provided I considered myself capable and my advice should be asked."[17] The trouble was, however, that Minuit and his council neither asked for Michaëlius's advice nor heeded it when it was given. In his 1630 letter to Foreest, Michaëlius relates that when he first realized how Minuit was using his governorship to his own personal advantage he resolved to "be silent, until their affairs being more than transparent enough, they could be absolutely convinced by me and they could not conceal themselves in any hiding places." When Michaëlius finally ventured, however, to advise Minuit against the course he was pursuing, "it is inexpressible with what kind of friendship the governor tried to silence me and to make me hated, in the mean time, through secret complaints by the Lords of the Company."[18]

In 1632, Michaëlius returned to the Netherlands, very likely a disillusioned man. There is an epilogue to his career in New

[17] *Ibid.*, p. 131.
[18] *Ibid.*, p. 68.

Netherland, however, that helps to illumine the ideological aspect
of our story. When Michaëlius arrived in the fatherland he appeared before the Consistory of Amsterdam to evaluate his North
American term of service. The minutes of the consistory for
March 4, 1632, state specifically that Michaëlius related "what
had taken place between him and the governor, being different
kinds of incidents which had happened, whereby his service and
person have been subjected to many disturbances and troubles."[19]
Though the exact nature of his dispute with Minuit remains
mysterious, it is unquestionable that Michaëlius left North America with ill-feeling toward the company. That the feeling was
reciprocal was further documented in 1637. In September the
W.I.C. was looking for another *predikant* to serve in New Netherland, and the Amsterdam classis, noting that Michaëlius was
currently without a pulpit, recommended him for reappoint-
ment.[20] The directors of the W.I.C. responded on October 5,
1637, by saying that, as far as Michaëlius was concerned, "they
would summon him, when they had need of him." The classis
minutes note that this curt reply "greatly displeased the Assembly." The classis decided to force the issue and once more recommended Michaëlius, but on June 7, 1638, the W.I.C. directors said that of Michaëlius's appointment they gave "little or
no hope."[21]

The career of Michaëlius's successor in the church at New
Amsterdam was a stormy one indeed. Spanning the administrations of two directors-general of New Netherland (Wouter van
Twiller, 1633–1638; and Willem Kieft, 1638–1647), the New
Netherland ministry of Everardus Bogardus was marked by a
series of incidents that heightened the church-state tensions already present in the colony. Like his predecessor, Bogardus was a
product of the University of Leiden, where he enrolled in 1627.

---

[19] Reprinted and translated *ibid.,* p. 74.
[20] Reprinted and translated *ibid.,* p. 139.
[21] Minutes of the Classis of Amsterdam, reprinted and translated *ibid.,*
p. 141.

Unlike Michaëlius, however, Bogardus did not complete the full course of study. In 1630 he left the university and was sent to Guinea as a *ziekentrooster* by the Consistory of Amsterdam. At that time he was only twenty-three years old. By 1632, Bogardus was back in Amsterdam where he petitioned the classis to be examined peremptorily for ordination as *predikant*. He preached to the satisfaction of the classis on the text of Galatians 5:16, "But I say, walk by the Spirit, and do not gratify the desires of the flesh," and on June 14, 1632, he received ordination.[22] Almost immediately he was asked by the W.I.C. directors to serve in New Netherland. He agreed and was approved for this appointment by the Amsterdam consistory on July 15, 1632.

Bogardus, along with Director-General Twiller, arrived in New Netherland in April 1633 aboard the ship *Zoutberg*, or *Salt Mountain*. It cannot have been long before these two were at war. Twiller had been a clerk in the W.I.C. warehouse at Amsterdam before his appointment to the New Netherland governorship,[23] and apparently only came into consideration for a post of such responsibility because he was the son of Kiliaen van Rensselaer's sister. That his administrative abilities left much to be desired can be inferred from a scolding letter from Rensselaer to his nephew in 1634 in which the director-general was labeled as hot-headed and proud, always inebriated "if there were wine," lazy and disrespectful, prejudiced against the *predikant,* and no champion of religion.[24] Prejudiced against Bogardus he most certainly was, and the W.I.C. directors even accused him of having stalked the *predikant* in the street "with a drawn knife."[25]

The nature of the issue that first brought the *predikant* and director into conflict is obscure. Once the battle was joined, however, Bogardus proved more than a match for his antagonist. On June 17, 1634, Bogardus wrote a letter to Twiller in which he

---

[22] Eekhof, *Hervormde Kerk,* 1, 51.
[23] *Ibid.,* pp. 52–53.
[24] In van Laer, ed., *Van Rensselaer Bowier Manuscripts,* pp. 266–288.
[25] Eekhof, *Hervormde Kerk,* 1, 52.

used language which, as Twiller's successor Kieft said, was fitting
for "no heathen, let alone Christian, and much less a preacher
of the Word."²⁶ Bogardus labeled the director-general a child of
the devil, a "villain in his hide," and said that "his goats are better than he." Bogardus furthermore informed the governor that
next Sunday in the pulpit he would "clamp him down so tight,"
that "his breastbone would crack."

By 1638 the W.I.C. directors became convinced that Twiller
could not competently administer New Netherland and recalled
him to the homeland. In his place, however, they put another
Amsterdam merchant's son whose credentials were equally, if
not more, dubious. Willem Kieft, son of the Amsterdam merchant Gerrit Willemszoon Kieft, was a financial failure before
he arrived in New Netherland and an administrative failure
shortly thereafter. As van der Donck pointed out in his *Remonstrance* in 1649, Kieft liked to brag that in his own opinion he was
as powerful in New Netherland as the Prince of Orange in the
fatherland.²⁷ He also endeavored to put his words into action,
for in setting up the council that governed New Netherland under his administration he selected three other council members
but kept two votes for himself. Thus his will was virtually un-
opposable.²⁸

Bogardus also had some very definite ideas about the ideal
power structure in a Reformed society, and his ideas included
an important role for the *predikant*. As we learn from the text
of a subpoena issued to Bogardus by Kieft and the council in
1646,²⁹ the friction between the two men dated almost from the
latter's arrival in 1638. In 1639 they had their first clash, but

²⁶ *Ibid.*, 2, xxii of the Appendix. Summons served on Bogardus by Director-General Kieft in January 1646 to answer for his many moral and
civil offenses.

²⁷ Van der Donck, p. 30.

²⁸ *Ibid., passim.* Two of the other council members, *sheriff-treasurer*
Cornelis van der Hoykens and secretary Cornelis van Tienhoven, had no
vote.

²⁹ Eekhof, *Hervormde Kerk,* 2, xxii–xxvii, Appendix.

this was apparently minor and subsequently forgotten. In 1643, however, the trouble began anew. After Kieft's vicious and arbitrary attack on the Indians at Pavonia in February of that year there was a great amount of strong feeling against the governor at New Amsterdam. With this mood prevailing in the settlement, one of the colonists, Maryn Adriaensen, broke into Kieft's office and attempted unsuccessfully to assassinate him. Adriaensen was captured and put into chains, but he had a large number of sympathizers and at the head of these was Bogardus. The *predikant* composed a defense for Adriaensen, but Kieft ignored this and sent the prisoner to Holland. Thereupon, in Kieft's version of it, Bogardus had "wonderfully fulminated" from the pulpit for "nearly fourteen days."[30]

After the debacle of the Indian war had begun, the breach between Kieft and Bogardus steadily widened. Bogardus continually used the pulpit, his house visits, and every other available means to turn the community against Kieft. On December 24, 1645, according to the director-general, Bogardus had said from the pulpit, "in Africa many animals interbreed because of the heat and in this manner many monsters are generated, but in this temperate climate I do not know where such monsters of men come from."[31] "The children could understand," grumbled Kieft, at whom this remark was directed. Nor was this an isolated instance. "Many such sermons," said the governor, had made it necessary for him "to remain out of church."[32]

The crisis in relations between the *predikant* and the director-general, which had been steadily building since 1638, came to a head during the winter of 1645–1646. After Bogardus's sermonic discourse on African monsters Kieft began boycotting church services and ordered several of the provincial officers to follow his example. Furthermore, the governor arranged different kinds of noisy disturbances for the worship hour on Sunday. Several

[30] *Ibid.*, 2, xxiii.
[31] *Ibid.*, 1, 68 [translation mine].
[32] *Ibid.*, 2, xxvi, Appendix [translation mine].

times a military roll was beaten on the drum just outside the church window during a sermon, and sometimes cannons were discharged. The communicants were harrassed and insulted by Kieft's henchmen, but Bogardus would not relax his inflexible opposition to the director-general.[33]

Finally, in near-desperation, Kieft and his council determined to proceed "formally" against the *predikant*. On January 2, 1646, the council informed Bogardus: "Your conduct stirs the people to mutiny and rebellion, when they are already too much divided, causes schism and abuses in the Church, and makes us a scorn and laughing stock to our neighbors."[34] Therefore, by the authority invested in them by the States-General, the Prince of Orange, and the W.I.C. directors, the council ordered the *predikant* to answer all the charges brought against him within fourteen days. Bogardus, however, refused to give way even in face of this frontal assault by the civil authority of New Netherland. His reply to this summons was found by the council, meeting on January 4, 1646, to be "needless and irrational, not answering the document sent to him." The council now decided to employ even blunter tactics and crasser language. Bogardus was ordered "pertinently to answer the accusations in the summons, either postively or negatively, within the time therein prescribed, on pain of being proceeded against as a rebel contumacious toward justice." Now the *predikant* replied with a letter, but this document, according to the council, was so full of "needless subterfuge, calumny, injury, and profanation of God's Holy Word, as well as the contempt of justice and his lawful government, which, as usual, he uses to serve his own passion and obscure the truth,"[35] that the magistrates informed Bogardus on January 18, 1646, that this could not be accepted as a legitimate reply to their summons.

[33] Brodhead, *History of the State of New York* (New York: Harper, 1853), pp. 417–418.
[34] *Ibid.,* p. 418.
[35] Eekhof, *Hervormde Kerk,* 1, 60, 69–70 [translations mine].

Kieft and the council repeatedly demanded a satisfactory response from Bogardus, but to no avail. The *predikant* replied that, as far as he was concerned, he had nothing more to say because in his opinion the government of New Netherland had no authority to try the case. The documents do not state this in so many words, but Bogardus evidently felt that his actions in the pulpit and in the routine of ecclesiastical business were beyond the pale of Kieft's civil authority. The provincial council reconsidered this argument of Bogardus and decided that even though the authority to judge this case had been given to them by the States-General[36] they would put the affair in the hands of a special committee. As the council proposed it, the dispute between Kieft and Bogardus should be arbitrated by a jury composed of Rev. Johannes Megapolensis,[37] Rev. Francis Doughty,[38] and "two or three impartial citizens of the province."[39] Bogardus, however, refused this proposal too, possibly because he feared that Kieft would hand-pick the "impartial citizens." Instead, on April 12, 1646, Bogardus informed the council that he preferred to have the accusations against him considered and judged by Kieft's administrative successor, who had already been appointed by the W.I.C. directors the previous summer.

The conflict was never resolved, but it gradually receded from

---

[36] See the terms of the W.I.C.'s charter, Article 2. In Johannes de Laet, *Jaerlyck Verhael van de Verrichtinghen der Geoctroyeerde West-Indische Compagnie*, ed. by S. P. l'Honoré Naber and J. C. M. Warnsinck (The Hague: Nijhoff, 1931), 1, 8.

[37] In 1646, *predikant* at the colony of Rensselaerswyck, where he was called by Kiliaen van Rensselaer in 1642. After 1649 Megapolensis was *predikant* at New Amsterdam until his death in 1670. See an interesting biographical account by Gerald F. De Jong, "Domine Johannes Megapolensis: Minister to New Netherland," *New-York Historical Society Quarterly*, 52 (January, 1968), 7–47.

[38] In 1646 Francis Doughty was minister to the English Presbyterian congregation at New Amsterdam. Before this he was minister at the settlement of Mespath, and later he preached at Vlissingen on Long Island. He carried on a running financial dispute with Kieft and Stuyvesant.

[39] *Col. Doc.*, 14, 72.

center-stage of the colony's life. Kieft was now a lame-duck governor, and even Bogardus came gradually to feel that he had had enough. He corresponded to the Classis of Amsterdam, earnestly begging them to send a replacement for him. Finally, in the fall of 1647 both Bogardus and Kieft set sail for the homeland aboard *The Princess*. Both were drowned, along with seventy-nine other passengers, when the ship went down in the English Channel on September 27, 1647.[40]

It would be exceedingly difficult to fix the blame for the dispute between Bogardus and Kieft. Kieft's always autocratic and often wrong-headed style of administering provincial affairs must have aggravated Bogardus beyond endurance. But the *predikant* was also far from blameless if even one-tenth of Kieft's accusations are true. The governor repeatedly accused Bogardus of public drunkenness and even of having been inebriated in the pulpit. He also, according to Kieft, was a spreader of vicious lies and rumors.[41] Whatever the truth of these accusations, it should be noted that Bogardus never publicly denied them.

Much more important than establishing blame, however, is noting what the dispute itself meant for the religious life of the settlement. As Kieft himself put it in 1646: "All this tends to the general ruin of the land, both in ecclesiastical and civil matters . . . to the stirring up of mutiny among the people, already split into factions; to schism and contention in the church."[42] Nearly twenty years after the first *predikant* came to New Netherland and fully thirty-five years after the arrival of the Dutch, the intentions of the Reformed Church for the province were still frustrated. Two *predikanten*, Michaëlius and Bogardus, had left for the homeland as disillusioned men. More important, the source of their discouragement and disaffection had not been the roughness of the wilderness or its heathen population so much as the acts and attitudes of the W.I.C. itself.

[40] Eekhof, *Hervormde Kerk*, 1, 72.
[41] *Ecc. Rec.*, 1, 197.
[42] *Ibid.*, 1, 198.

A final area in which the *predikanten* had suffered considerable frustration during these years was that of Indian relations.[43] It will be recalled that in 1628 some of the Amsterdam supporters of the W.I.C. protested to Frederik Hendrik that one of their chief motivations in subscribing capital to the company had been the missionizing of native populations in the Americas. That claim was answered with doubt and cynicism by an anonymous Remonstrant pamphleter, and rightfully so. Although the missionary efforts of the *predikanten* themselves could hardly be called heroic, what efforts they did make were never supported financially or strategically by the W.I.C. Michaëlius was not impressed with the Indians upon first encounter, and he wrote back to the homeland in 1628 that he found them "entirely savage and wild, strangers to all decency, yea, uncivil and stupid as garden poles, proficient in all wickedness and godlessness." Nevertheless, although he knew it would be expensive, he thought that: "we ought, by means of presents and promises, to obtain the children, with the gratitude and consent of the parents, in order to place them under the instruction of some experienced and godly schoolmaster, where they may be instructed not only to speak, read, and write in our language, but also especially in the fundamentals of our Christian religion."[44] Michaëlius announced that he intended to begin to learn the Algonquian language, but by the time of his return to the Netherlands in 1632 had accomplished almost nothing.

A full decade went by before another *predikant,* Johannes Megapolensis at Rensselaerswijck, began to address himself seriously to the problem of missionizing the Indians. Megapolensis tried to learn the Mohawk language—as unsuccessfully as Mi-

---

[43] It is not my intention to outline this problem in detail. See the excellent study of Allen W. Trelease, *Indian Affairs in Colonial New York: The Seventeenth Century* (Ithaca, New York: Cornell University Press, 1960), especially chaps. 2 and 3.

[44] J. Franklin Jameson, *Narratives of New Netherland* (New York: Scribner's, 1909), pp. 126, 129.

chaëlius had tried the Algonquian tongue earlier. And the Mohawk attitude toward the Dutch Reformed brand of worship was also discouraging. "When we pray," Megapolensis said, "they laugh at us. When we deliver a sermon, sometimes ten or twelve of them . . . will attend . . . and afterwards ask me what I am doing. . . . I tell them that I am admonishing the Christians, that they must not steal, nor commit lewdness, nor get drunk, nor commit murder, and that they too ought not to do these things. . . . Then they say I do well to teach the Christians; but immediately add . . . "Why do so many Christians do these things?"[45] The Mohawk had a point. The behavior of the Dutch was frequently a poor advertisement for such lofty religious precepts.

The failure of Dutch Reformed Indian missions in New Netherland can scarcely be blamed solely on the W.I.C. It was the result of a complex variety of cultural and religious factors. But the company had its own peculiar way of looking at the Indian problem, which was succinctly stated by W.I.C. director Johan de Laet in his 1625 publication, *Nieuwe Wereldt:* "With mild and proper treatment, and especially by intercourse with Christians, this people might be civilized and brought under better regulation; particularly if a sober and discrete population were brought over and good order preserved. *They are, besides, very serviceable, and allow themselves to be employed in many things for a small compensation.*"[46] The salvation of Indian souls was conspicuous by its absence from Laet's meditations.

Clearly, during these early years a large gap existed between Reformed and commercial intentions for New Netherland. A qualifying word is necessary, however. Attention has been focused repeatedly on the nature and extent of disagreement between commercial and ecclesiastical plans for New Netherland. It has been argued that while the *predikanten* dreamed of a Reformed society in North America the W.I.C. directors envisioned a trad-

[45] *Ibid.*, pp. 177–178.
[46] *Ibid.*, p. 50, emphasis mine.

ing post, which might at most have to be given a broader agricultural base to make it profitable. All this is true, but it must also be said that the directors of the W.I.C. always gave at least lip service to an establishment of the Reformed religion in New Netherland. As the Dutch church historian Eekhof puts it, "The Dutch Reformed Church, from the moment of its establishment in New Netherland onward, enjoyed the exclusive right of existence in these territories. No other [church] was tolerated."[47] Zwierlein says essentially the same thing: "There was . . . in all New Netherland, except the South Delaware River territory, an absolute prohibition of non-conforming religions outside of the [Reformed] family."[48] The Reformed Church was the official, established church in New Netherland, and all persons emigrating to the province were expected by the W.I.C. to act accordingly. The revised "Charter of Freedoms and Exemptions," published in 1640 by the W.I.C., declared that: "No other Religion shall be publicly admitted in New Netherland except the Reformed, as it is at present preached and practiced by public authority in the United Netherlands; and for this purpose the Company shall provide and maintain good and suitable preachers, schoolmasters and comforters of the sick."[49]

In conclusion, then, it may be said that New Netherland bore, in 1647, the external appearance of a Reformed community planted by Dutchmen in the wilderness of the New World. Internally, however, a great deal of the colony's future hung in the balance. Still to be determined by the merchants was the question of if and how New Netherland might be made to yield profit. Still to be determined by the *predikanten* was the question of what and how great the role of the church would be in the struggling settlement.

[47] Eekhof, *Hervormde Kerk,* 2, 1 [translation mine].
[48] Zwierlein, *Religion in New Netherland* (Rochester, N.Y.: John P. Smith, 1910), p. 5.
[49] *Col. Doc.,* 1, 123.

PART IV

New Netherland, 1647–1664:
The Establishment Challenged

11. The Turning Point

When Peter Stuyvesant sailed into New York Bay on May 11, 1647, he found the settlement at Manhattan in precarious condition indeed. The population of the province had been reduced, by death and emigration resulting from the ruinous Indian wars, to about two thousand persons. The fort at the southern tip of the island was the joke of the town, and cattle grazed on the grass of its ramparts. The church, begun under Kieft's administration in 1642, remained unfinished. Drinking, fighting, and widespread moral and political chaos prevailed among the populace. Hogs and goats roamed the "city" streets. By August 1664 when Stuyvesant reluctantly surrendered his settlement without a struggle to the English Colonel Richard Nicolls, all this chaos had been tamed and transformed beyond recognition, and the population was estimated at ten thousand.[1] The question arising out of these facts is: What had happened in the interim?

Beginning in about 1647–1648 the merchant minds behind the W.I.C. began to take New Netherland seriously as a colonial venture. There were a number of reasons for this, perhaps the most important of which was the simple fact that every earlier attempt to make New Netherland pay as a trading post had failed. For a tiny, unprofitable fur-trading post could, after all, have been entirely abandoned by a gigantic corporation that had the entire western hemisphere as its field of operation. As it hap-

[1] O'Callaghan, *History of New Netherland* (New York: Appleton, 1848), 1, 386; 2, 23, 540.

pened, however, things were not going well for the West India Company in general. The great prosperity of its early years, based to a large extent upon piratical raids against Spanish and Portuguese shipping, reached its zenith in 1628 with Piet Heyn's famous capture of the *zilver vloot* in Havana Bay. Thereafter, this source of income decreased rather rapidly, and it threatened to disappear altogether when Europe began to discuss the possibility of a peace to end the great war of religions.

Already in 1633 the W.I.C. directors submitted a remonstrance to the States of Holland against the negotiation of a peace with Spain. In this document the directors first pleaded the many military services the state had received from the company:

It [the Company] has inflicted . . . excessive damage on the enemy, and caused an indescribable diversion. . . . Laid waste Bahia, which, independent of the incurred damages, cost the King of Spain over ten millions to recover it; and, also, captured, plundered and destroyed Porto Rico, Margarita, Sancta Martha, St. Thomas, Guiana, and sundry other places; prevented the Portuguese, by the continual cruizing of our ships on the coast of Brazil, from bringing over their sugars and other produce. . . . Also, captured [the] fleet from New Spain, and thrice made prize of the rich Honduras ships; took, moreover, in divers parts of Africa and America, over a hundred of [the king of Spain's] vessels, most of which had full freights, including several of his best galleons; and burnt and destroyed nearly as many, if not more, that had ran [*sic*] ashore.[2]

Thus resting their case that the company had benefited the Dutch republic in substantial ways, the authors of the remonstrance went on to describe the spirit with which the W.I.C. would participate in peace negotiations: "This we must, in virtue of our office, lay in all submission, before your Great Mightinesses, that the Company, so far as the interest of its stockholders is concerned, can without great loss, be easily brought to this negotiation, by money or goods for its contracts, such as the case deserves. That the Stockholders also would easily forget their losses,

---

[2] Remonstrance of the W.I.C. against a peace with Spain. In *Col. Doc.*, 1, 63.

if the State might, by that means, be much benefitted; but that the Company would thereby, in time, come to ruin, and be unable to do the State any further service."[3]

The West India Company feared, long before 1648, that conclusion of a peace with Spain would devastate its financial underpinnings. It is a much-mooted point among Dutch historians whether or not the Treaty of Münster which ended eighty years of European religious strife and therefore outlawed piracy against Spanish shipping dealt the *coup de grace* to the W.I.C.[4] Several very respectable authorities have argued that it did. C. Busken-Huet, writing in 1886, declared, "The West India Company was essentially never anything other than a nameless partnership for the plundering of Spanish fleets. As long as the Peace of Münster remained unsigned the Company earned lucrative profits. . . . But it bloomed only from its creation in 1621—when the war with Spain was going to be renewed upon the expiration of the Twelve Year Truce—until 1648 when it was obviously finished with this piracy." Similarly, P. Geyl argued in 1948 that "the Treaty of Münster, which put an end to piracy at the expense of Spain, robbed the Company of all hope of a long-range restoration of her finances."[5]

Whether or not the financial collapse of the W.I.C. in 1671 was predicated on the conclusion of a European peace in 1648 is, for the purposes of this discussion, not an immediately relevant question. The Treaty of Münster did hurt the W.I.C. very badly financially. Even historians who deny that the company was irreparably damaged concede that the end of profitable privateering against Spanish shipping dealt the company a severe

---

[3] *Ibid.*, 1, 64.

[4] See, for example, W. J. van Hoboken, "De West-Indische Compagnie en de Vrede van Münster," *Tijdschrift voor Geschiedenis,* 70 (Groningen: Noordhoff, 1957), 359–368. Van Hoboken assails the view taken on this matter by such giants of Dutch history writing as Busken-Huet and Geyl.

[5] C. Busken-Huet, *Het Land van Rembrandt* (Haarlem: Willink, second printing, 1886), 2, 200; P. Geyl, *Geschiedenis van de Nederlandse Stam* (Amsterdam: Wereldbibliotheek, second printing, 1948), 1, 485.

blow.[6] And, indeed, the directors themselves had already predicted such a result in their remonstrance of 1633.

A second reason—perhaps even more important—why the W.I.C. began gradually to focus more attention on the colonization of New Netherland was the loss of Brazil to the Portuguese in 1652. This was a disastrous turn of events for the company, and one it had done all in its power to prevent. Brazil, with its lush tropical forests and enormous potential for sugar production, had always appeared to the W.I.C. directors as the key to the company's commercial success in the western hemisphere. Despite this interest in Brazil, however, the Dutch had only with great difficulty gained a toehold there and were unable to perpetuate it. The beginning of the end of Dutch influence in Brazil came in 1640, when the Portuguese throne freed itself from the domination of Madrid and reasserted the independence it had not enjoyed since 1580. On paper Portugal now became militarily allied with the Dutch against her Iberian neighbor, but in fact she made common cause with the Portuguese dissidents in Dutch Brazil. The Brazilian situation erupted into open rebellion in 1645 and, despite valiant efforts on the part of the financially beleaguered W.I.C. to head this off, the rebellion culminated in success in 1652. The Dutch were expelled once and for all.

This loss was seen by contemporaries as the most important single cause of the demise of the W.I.C. The Dutch historian L. van Aitzema, who wrote in 1672, introduced his discussion of the attempts undertaken to reorganize the W.I.C. in 1668 with the following statement: "Since the loss of Brazil the West India Company was very much at the end of the line." The French ambassador to the Netherlands, Pomponne, wrote in approximately 1670 while discussing the demise of Dutch Brazil: "The West India Company has never recovered since the loss of a conquest which had constituted the firmest foundation of its

[6] For example, van Hoboken, who argues (pp. 364–365) that privateering against Spanish shipping had already ceased to be an important factor in the W.I.C.'s income by 1640.

elevation and its riches." Later, in the eighteenth century, the historian Wagenaar declared, "She [the W.I.C.] had, since this loss [Brazil], fallen into so deep a pit, that she now not only no longer paid dividends but she paid neither principal nor interest on the money which had been lent her."[7]

Cut off from its privateering and Brazilian revenues, the W.I.C. began to appraise New Netherland with a real view to colonize. Furthermore, it was pressed to do so by an increasingly vocal faction of the settlers themselves—a group in New Netherland that styled itself the *gemeente* or "commonalty" in protests to the States-General. This group, led by such men as Adriaen van der Donck, Jacob van Couwenhoven, and Jan Evertsen Bout composed the famous *Remonstrance of New Netherland* in 1649. In the *Remonstrance* the "commonalty" stressed that the company's failure to colonize the province was at the root of most of New Netherland's ills. They declared: "In the infancy of this country, the Directors adopted wrong plans and in our opinion looked more to their own profit than to the country's welfare, and trusted more to interested than to sound advice." Specifically, continued the *Remonstrance,* the neglect of population had contributed to New Netherland's great poverty in comparison with New England:

Had the Honorable West India Company attended in the beginning to population, instead of incurring great expense for things unnecessary, which might be attended to at more favorable times and then could also be better done, the New Netherland account would not be so large as it is now; first, by the construction of the ship *Nieuw Neerlant,* at an excessive expense; of three costly mills, by making brick, burning tar, manufacturing ashes, salt, and similar undertakings, which through bad management and calculation, came wholly too [*sic*] little or nothing, notwithstanding the excessive ex-

[7] L. van Aitzema, *Saken van Staet en Oorlogh* (1672), 6, 562, quoted in van Hoboken, p. 366; Pomponne, "Relation de mon Ambassade en Hollande," in *Werken van het Historisch Genootschap Gevestigd te Utrecht,* 4th series, no. 2 (1955), p. 91; J. Wagenaar, *Vaderlandsche Historie* (Amsterdam: Tirion, second printing, 1770), 13, 379.

penditure. Had this been applied to colonizing the country, and transporting cattle, the place might now be of considerable importance. This country and its position are much better and more convenient than that occupied by the English, and had not self interest and private speculation been attended to, assuredly, the North or New England would not have outstripped us so much.[8]

As accurate as the critique by the commonalty may have been, it was made, as Condon puts it, from the standpoint of "infallible hindsight." The W.I.C. had certainly been interested in reaping profits, but the company had never, as the commonalty alleged, intended to let the province languish. A plan allowing New Netherland to prosper had not been as clearly visible in 1623, or even in 1639, as it had become by 1649. Furthermore, the situation itself in North America had changed during those years. To quote Condon: "There were now many Europeans dwelling throughout the continent. To the south in 1642 there were ten thousand Englishmen; to the north, perhaps another ten thousand. The activities of these large numbers not only provided a model of what might be done through the development of agriculture but their mere presence meant a market for goods as well."[9]

The company, as a matter of fact, itself realized the necessity and urgency of populating New Netherland at least several years before the commonalty submitted its *Remonstrance*. This was part of the reason why the company reacted so vigorously and polemically to that document.[10] At a cost of much wasted time and capital the W.I.C. gradually discovered a viable long-range plan for making New Netherland pay, and the company now resented being made a scapegoat for the colony's ills by those who had risked nothing. Many documents illustrate the W.I.C.'s

[8] Van der Donck, *Remonstrance of New Netherland,* ed. and trans. by E. B. O'Callaghan (Albany: Weed, Parsons, 1856), p. 28.

[9] Condon, *New York Beginnings* (New York: New York University Press, 1968), p. 164.

[10] See the "Answer of the W.I.C. to the Remonstrance from New Netherland," in *Col. Doc., 1,* 338–346.

new determination to populate New Netherland. The new draft of the Charter of Freedoms and Exemptions exhibited in May 1650, with its many provisions favorable to colonization, is a good case in point.[11] The Company was, however, earnestly discussing the population of New Netherland almost three years before the *Remonstrance*. In a report to the States-General on May 27, 1647, the Board of Accounts of the W.I.C. said:

Respecting New Netherland: That country is considered to be the most fruitful of all within your High Mightinesses' jurisdiction, and the best adapted to raise all sorts of this country [*sic*] produce, such as rye, wheat, barley, peas, beans, etc. and cattle; and that in more abundance than can be done here, were it suitably peopled and cultivated. . . . With a view, then, to give greater encouragement to agriculture, and consequently to population, we should consider it highly advantageous that a way be opened to allow them to export their produce even to Brazil, in their own vessels, under certain dunes, and subject to the supervision both of the Director in New Netherland, and the Supreme Council in Brazil; and to trade it off there, and to carry slaves back in return.

The company considered it especially important to increase New Netherland's slave population "because the agricultural laborers who are conveyed thither at great expense to the Colonists, sooner or later apply themselves to trade, and neglect agriculture altogether."[12]

The inevitable result of the company's enthusiasm to populate New Netherland was diversity. For native Dutchmen remained as reluctant as ever to leave the homeland. As early as 1629 the W.I.C. directors had lamented that "all those who will labor in any way here, can easily obtain support, and therefore, are disinclined to go far from home on an uncertainty."[13] Unable to convince large numbers of natives to emigrate, the W.I.C. turned

---

[11] "Draft of Freedoms and Exemptions for New Netherland," May 24, 1650, in *Col. Doc.*, 1, 401–405.

[12] In *Col. Doc.*, 1, 246.

[13] "Remonstrance of the W.I.C. against a Peace with Spain," in *Col. Doc.*, 1, 65.

to other sources. The first group of real settlers in New Netherland, which had arrived with Cornelis May in 1623, was a group of thirty Walloon families.[14] Nicolaes van Wassenaer, in his *Historisch Verhael* composed between 1624 and 1630, relates a skirmish in 1626 between the settlers at Fort Orange and the Mohawk Indians and he says quite incidentally that only three Europeans survived the encounter, "two Portuguese and a Hollander from Hoorn."[15] When the French Jesuit missionary Isaac Jogues, after his harrowing escape from the Indians, visited Manhattan in 1647 his attention was caught by the diversity of the population on that small island. "On the island of Manhate," he marveled, "and in its environs, there may well be four or five hundred men of different sects and nations; the Director-General told me that there were men of eighteen different languages."[16] After the city of Amsterdam acquired its own colony on the Delaware River from the W.I.C. in 1656, it pursued a policy of recruitment with frank and open disregard for nationality. The commissioners for New Amstel reported to the Amsterdam city council in 1663:

People only must be sent there, who are laborious and skilled in farming. No Hollanders but other foreign nations must be employed and attracted for this purpose, the Swedes and Fins (who are already there in reasonable numbers) being, among others, hereunto particularly fitted, and of whom many families or households are from time to time expected, as they have been notified by their countrymen in the aforesaid Colonie of the good opportunity there. Already some families of them have come from Sweden to the number of 32 souls, who are only waiting for the departure of a ship thither.[17]

Once the colonization of New Netherland was earnestly begun, the theme of diversity became extremely important in the

[14] Jameson, *Narratives of New Netherland* (New York: Scribner's, 1909), p. 75.
[15] *Ibid.,* p. 85.
[16] Isaac Jogues's description of Manhattan. Reprinted *ibid.,* pp. 259–263. This quotation from p. 259.
[17] *Col. Doc.,* 1, 211.

province's social fabric. Diversity was not, however, the only theme to characterize the colony after 1647. The theme of order also became increasingly important and after 1647 was represented by Peter Stuyvesant. Stuyvesant's accomplishments for the cause of physical, political, moral, and religious order in the colony were many, and several of them deserve mention. First, however, it may be of interest to note what the colonists themselves thought of Stuyvesant in this regard. Adriaen van der Donck, articulate spokesman for the New Netherland "commonalty" in the *Remonstrance* of 1649, shows us Stuyvesant "the organizer" from the viewpoint of "the organized." With caustic disdain he says, "His first arrival . . . was peacock like, with great state and pomposity. . . . The word *Myn Heer Generael* and such like titles, were never known here before. He was busy almost every day issuing proclamations of various sorts, most of which were never observed and have long since died, the wine excise excepted, for that was a source of profit."[18] This statement is a strong attestation to Stuyvesant's impact upon the life of the colony. Van der Donck might ridicule Stuyvesant, but he could not ignore him.

Stuyvesant inherited a chaotic situation from Director-General Kieft. At the end of the latter's maladministration in 1647 it was an open question whether New Netherland would collapse under the sheer weight of its own inertia. The W.I.C., however, had finally attained something approximating a clear vision of what New Netherland, and especially New Amsterdam, might become. Stuyvesant now set out to impress this vision upon the colony's inhabitants. The essence of his method was, as van der Donck complained, the proclamation. Soon after he assumed office in 1647, Stuyvesant issued a sharp decree against drinking and fighting on the Sabbath, which read in part: "We see and observe by experience the great disorders in which some of our inhabitants indulge, in drinking to excess, quarreling, fighting,

[18] Van der Donck, p. 42.

and smiting, even on the Lord's day of rest. Whereof, God help us! we have seen and heard sorrowful instances last Sunday . . . to the scandal of our neighbors and finally to the disparagement, yea, contempt of God's holy law and ordinances which command us to sanctify His Rest and Sabbath day to His honor, forbidding all wounding, slaying, and means and occasions whereby the same might arise."[19] The penalties laid down by the ordinance were severe. A tapster selling beer or wine on the Sabbath was fined heavily and had his license revoked, while anyone drawing a knife paid a hundred guilder fine or did a half-year's hard labor on bread and water. If a wound was inflicted with the knife, the penalty was tripled.

Stuyvesant carried his campaign for order into other areas of the settlement's life besides the civil and moral. Especially on Manhattan, he soon began to press for physical improvements. In 1650 he issued the following decree: "Whereas the roads and highways here in New Amsterdam are rendered difficult of passage for wagons and carts on account of the rooting of the hogs— it is ordered, that the inhabitants take care to stick a ring through the nose of all they may own."[20] In 1653 Stuyvesant undertook to build a wall across Manhattan on the north side of New Amsterdam. Fearing the possibility of an attack from New England subsequent to the outbreak of the first Anglo-Dutch war in the previous year, he intended the wall as a line of defense. The director-general's management of this affair reveals a good deal about the vision he held for this first Dutch city in the New World. When the wall was only partially complete, the New Amsterdam city council, which Stuyvesant himself had instituted in 1652, announced that residents would pay for the construction only on condition that the director give up the W.I.C.'s beer and wine excise to the city treasury. Stuyvesant fumed and sput-

---

[19] Quoted in H. H. Kessler and E. Rachlis, *Peter Stuyvesant and His New York* (New York: Random House, 1959), p. 66.

[20] Reprinted in J. Paulding, *Affairs and Men of New Amsterdam in the Time of Peter Stuyvesant* (New York: Casper C. Childs, 1843), p. 7.

tered and finally shot back that the city could have the income
from the tapsters' excise provided that it be used to pay the salaries of the *predikanten* Megapolensis and Drisius, the two Reformed ministers then on Manhattan.[21] New Amsterdam got its
revenue, but the *predikanten* were not paid. A year later an
irate Stuyvesant admonished the city council: "We remind you
to see that the ministers have their salaries paid them, as you
promised on having the revenue from the tapsters' excise granted
to you. If in these things we are forsaken, we wash our hands
before God and the whole world from the calamities that may
come upon ourselves and upon our good subjects."[22]

These events illustrate quite clearly that by midcentury the
W.I.C. was consciously building a colony in North America. The
"trading-post mentality" of earlier days was gone and had been
replaced by an eagerness to sink deep and permanent roots for a
true colonial society. This society, to judge from Stuyvesant's ordinances, should possess compactness, definability, order (both
physical and moral) and the church—the Reformed Church.
When Stuyvesant in 1657 created the privilege of *burgerrecht*,
or citizenship, for residents of New Amsterdam the following inhabitants were granted the *great* citizenship: "*First,* Those who
have been members of the supreme government, or who are at
present, with their descendants in the male line. *Second,* Those
who have been or are yet burgomasters and schepens in this city,
with their descendants in the male line. *Third,* The ministers of
the gospel who have been or are yet in office, with their descendants in the male line. *Fourth,* The officers of the militia, from
the staff to the ensigns included, with their descendants in the
male line."[23] Here Stuyvesant's concept of the ideal city was
clearly stated. The personifications of civil, moral, religious, and
military order should hold the privileged positions in his New
Amsterdam.

[21] *Ibid.,* p. 34.
[22] Quoted *ibid.,* p. 139.
[23] Quoted *ibid.,* pp. 54–55.

12. The Lutherans

The two themes that characterized midcentury New Netherland, and especially New Amsterdam, were diversity and order.
To a certain extent these tended to be incompatible, particularly
in the realm of religion. Our study of church-state relations in the
homeland has already pointed up some of the problems caused
there by this incompatibility and some of the methods adopted
to solve them. By approximately 1650 New Netherland had inherited the homeland's church-state dilemma to a remarkable
degree and went about solving it in essentially the same way.

The Reformed *predikanten*, like Calvin, held an organic view
of society. The sacred and secular aspects of corporate human
existence must, in their view, be harmoniously related, for upon
this harmony depended man's total salvation and—much more
important—the glory of God. The institutional expression of this
harmony was, for the *predikanten,* a state that gave free reign
to the true church (the Reformed, of course) in the areas of
doctrine and polity while protecting it and taking advice from it
in the realm of civil law.

By midcentury, civil and ecclesiastical institutions were beginning to take shape in New Netherland. On the surface, at least,
these developments were favorable to a Reformed establishment.
In 1640 the W.I.C.'s revised Charter of Freedoms and Exemptions stated explicitly that "no other religion shall be publicly
admitted in New Netherland except the Reformed, as it is at

present preached and practiced by public authority in the United Netherlands."[1] Stuyvesant was sworn by oath to uphold the Reformed Church and to permit the public worship of no other religion. The company's second revision of the Charter of Freedoms and Exemptions in 1650 said that "the Patroons and Colonists shall . . . endeavor to devise, in the speediest manner, some means among themselves whereby they will be able to support a Clergyman and Schoolmaster, that the service of God and zeal for religion may not grow cool among them."[2] On the other hand, by 1650 there were storm clouds on the horizon for the establishment. The W.I.C. had finally discovered the key to the profitable operation of New Netherland. That key was population, but few Dutchmen were willing to emigrate and so the company openly encouraged foreign migration under its auspices. To invite the Germans, Swedes, and Finns to participate in this colonial venture was almost certain to introduce problems of religious diversity, and yet the company was forced to this out of financial considerations. The Charter of Freedoms and Exemptions in 1650 also said: "All inhabitants of these United Provinces and other neighboring countries, shall be at liberty to repair to New Netherland in the ships of the company. . . . The aforesaid freemen shall be accepted according to the order of their application, so that whoever comes first shall be accommodated first, without any difference."[3] Such a wholesale method of processing prospective colonists could scarcely be expected to screen out the non-Reformed religious deviants. Nor was it intended to do so.

The result of the W.I.C.'s changed attitude toward colonization in New Netherland was not long in appearing. Spokesmen for both state and church began to make known their intentions for the colony as explicitly as they had previously mani-

[1] Zwierlein, *Religion in New Netherland* (Rochester, N.Y.: John P. Smith, 1910), p. 2.
[2] In *Col. Doc.,* 1, 401.
[3] *Ibid.*

fested their frustrations. The organized dissent of a Lutheran minority provided the first forum for the great debate.

On October 4, 1653, a group of self-styled "adherents of the Augsburg Confession" at Manhattan petitioned Stuyvesant for permission to organize a congregation separately and publicly and to call as its pastor a minister from Holland.[4] How large the Lutheran population of the province was at this time cannot be said with accuracy, but with the company encouraging Swedish, German, and Finnish migration it must have been on the increase. Stuyvesant was disinclined to grant such a request, out of both religious conviction and loyalty to his oath as director-general. Rather than take the full responsibility for such a decision, however, he passed on the petition to the W.I.C. directors in the homeland. The directors did not appreciate being forced by Stuyvesant to state an official position on this matter, and they instructed him the following Spring "not to receive any similar petitions, but rather to turn them off in the most civil and least offensive way."[5] Truly the company was placed in an impossible bind by this kind of situation, for economics dictated that they must colonize New Netherland at all costs while law dictated that they must maintain the Reformed establishment.

The incident might have been smoothed over, but Pandora's box had been opened. Johannes Megapolensis and Samuel Drisius now held a co-pastorate at Manhattan.[6] Two days after the Lutherans filed their petition with Stuyvesant the two Reformed *predikanten* were hard at work on the defense of the establish-

[4] Letter of Johannes Megapolensis and Samuel Drisius to the Classis of Amsterdam, October 6, 1653. In *Ecc. Rec.*, 1, 317.

[5] Letter of W.I.C. directors to Director-General Stuyvesant, March 12, 1654. *Ecc. Rec.*, 1, 324.

[6] Megapolensis had come to the New Amsterdam church from a previous appointment at Rensselaerswyck. Samuel Drisius was appointed to the pastorate at New Amsterdam by the Classis of Amsterdam in 1652. He was born in England of Dutch parents. He could, and upon occasion did, preach in Dutch, French, and English.

ment's prerogatives. On October 6, 1653, they wrote to the Classis of Amsterdam informing it of the request of the Lutherans. Should such a petition be granted by the W.I.C., it would, they argued, "tend to the injury of our church, the diminutions of hearers of the Word of God, and the increase of dissensions, of which we have had a sufficiency for years past. It would also pave the way for other sects, so that in time our place would become a receptacle for all sorts of heretics and fanatics." Then came the punch line—the real reason for the letter. Megapolensis and Drisius of course knew that their position in this matter would be wholeheartedly supported by the classis. Both of them had witnessed the church's struggle in affairs of this kind in the Netherlands. What they could not be certain of was the behavior of the W.I.C. Thus their letter to the classis contained a specific request: "that your Rev. body will use your influence with the Hon. Directors, of the Company, that they may so provide and determine, that the project of our Lutheran friends may be rejected, and thus the welfare, prosperity and edification of the church in this place may be promoted. . . . We have communicated these matters to the Hon. Directors, in whom we have the greatest confidence, but we request your Rev. body occasionally to refresh their memories, lest through want of proper attention to the subject, the requested permission should be given."[7]

The Classis of Amsterdam placed all its zeal at the disposal of the New Netherland *predikanten.* Commending Megapolensis and Drisius for acting "very well and prudently," the classis dispatched its Deputies for Indian Affairs to the January 1654 meeting of the W.I.C. directors to plead the case against the Lutherans. On February 23 the directors resolved "not to permit any Lutheran pastors there, nor any other public worship than that of the true Reformed."[8] Rejoicing in this favorable result,

[7] Megapolensis and Drisius to the Classis of Amsterdam. *Ecc. Rec.,* 1, 317–318.

[8] Minutes of the *Deputati ad res Indicas* of the Classis of Amsterdam, February 23, 1654. *Ecc. Rec.,* 1, 322.

the classis wrote to the New Amsterdam *predikanten,* on February 26, 1654, that "we do not doubt but that the Reformed Doctrines will remain unembarrassed, and be maintained without being hindered by the Lutherans, and other erring spirits."[9] Megapolensis and Drisius received the good news and responded to the classis the following July that they were truly thankful for the assistance rendered in this matter. They further expressed the sanguine expectation that "thus also the way for other sectaries is closed up."[10] The matter of Lutheran worship in New Netherland appeared settled.

A period of months passed with no further developments. The Reformed *predikanten* remained watchful, however, and toward the end of 1655 their attention began to be drawn to the settlement of Middelburg on Long Island. There had previously been an ordained preacher there—an Englishman named Moore—but he had now left and in his absence some people were holding religious gatherings without the benefit of clerical leadership. Knowledge of this situation was passed on to the director-general and his council by the guardians of orthodoxy, who submitted to Stuyvesant that from such activities, "nothing but quarrels, confusion and disorders may be expected in Church and commonalty not only in that place, but also, by giving a bad example, in other places of this Province."[11] Stuyvesant took this admonition very seriously and, true to his character, overreacted. On February 1, 1656, he published an ordinance against unauthorized conventicles which was so severe he had to deal with its repercussions throughout the remainder of his governorship. It is important enough to merit full quotation:

The Director General and Council have been credibly informed,

[9] Classis of Amsterdam to Megapolensis and Drisius, February 26, 1654. *Ecc. Rec.,* 1, 323.

[10] Megapolensis and Drisius to the Classis of Amsterdam, July 15, 1654. *Ecc. Rec.,* 1, 326.

[11] Megapolensis and Drisius to Stuyvesant and the Council of New Netherland, January, 1656. *Ecc. Rec.,* 1, 342.

that not only conventicles and meetings have been held here and there in this Province, but also that unqualified persons presume in such meetings to act as teachers, in interpreting and expounding God's Holy Word, without ecclesiastical or secular authority. This is contrary to the general rules, political and ecclesiastical of our Fatherland; and besides, such gatherings lead to trouble, heresies and schisms.

Therefore, to prevent this, the Director General and Council strictly forbid all such public or private conventicles and meetings, except the usual and authorized ones, where God's Word, according to the Reformed and established custom, is preached and taught in meetings held for the religious service of the Reformed Church, conformably to the Synod of Dort, which is to be followed here, as in the Fatherland, and in the other Reformed Churches of Europe; under a fine of one hundred pounds Flemish [$240], to be paid by all who, in such public or private meetings, except at the usual authorized gatherings on Sundays or other days, presume to exercise, without due qualification, the duties of a preacher, reader or chorister; and each man or woman, married or unmarried, who is found at such a meeting, shall pay a fine of twenty-five pounds Flemish [$60].

The Director General and Council, however, do not hereby intend to force the consciences of any, to the prejudice of formerly given patents, or to forbid the preaching of God's Holy Word, the use of Family Prayers, and divine services in the family; but only all public and private conventicles and gatherings, be they in public or private houses, except the already mentioned usual, and authorized religious services of the Reformed Church. And that this order may be the better observed, and nobody plead ignorance thereof, the Director General and Council direct and charge their Fiscal, and the inferior Magistrates and Schouts, to publish the same everywhere in this Province, and to prosecute transgressors; inasmuch as we have so decreed this for the honor of God, the advancement of the Reformed services, and the quiet, unity and welfare of the country generally.[12]

Stuyvesant treated the new ordinance as no dead letter. Subsequent to its publication some of the Lutheran offenders were even thrown into prison. The director-general's action in this regard was greeted with two very different reactions in the home-

[12] In *Ecc. Rec.*, 1, 343–344.

land. The members of the Classis of Amsterdam rejoiced. Writing to the church in New Netherland, the *predikanten* of the classis stated that without such an ordinance "there would have arisen a very Babel." The classis "could not contemplate, without great emotion of soul, how greatly a pastor's labor would have been increased under such circumstances, and beset with obstacles, and what difficulties would have arisen to interfere with their good and holy efforts for the extension of the cause of Christ." Closing the matter the classis exhorted Megapolensis and Drisius to "employ all diligence to frustrate all such plans, that the wolves may be warded off from the tender lambs of Christ."[13] The W.I.C. directors, on the other hand, received the news of Stuyvesant's stringent measures against conventicles in a very ill humor. On June 14, 1656, they communicated to him their displeasure in a very curt and concise note, the essence of which was that persecuting Lutherans was no way to populate a colony. They would have been more pleased, they said: "if you had not published the placat against the Lutherans, a copy of which you sent us, and committed them to prison, for it has always been our intention, to treat them quietly and leniently. Hereafter you will therefore not publish such or similar placats without our knowledge, but you must pass it over quietly and let them have free religious exercises in their houses."[14]

Again the affair might have rested had it not been for the hypersensitivity of the Classis of Amsterdam and the *predikanten* in New Netherland. One month later, on July 10, 1656, the Deputies for Indian Affairs of the classis reported that they had received intelligence to the effect that "the Lutherans have again requested of the Directors here the privilege of the public exercise of their religion in New Netherland, in conformity with the custom in this country." Furthermore, the deputies reported in an alarmist tone, "this has been granted to them there, as well

---

[13] Classis of Amsterdam to the New Amsterdam church consistory, May 26, 1656. *Ecc. Rec.*, 1, 349.

[14] W.I.C. directors to Stuyvesant, June 14, 1656. *Ecc. Rec.*, 1, 352.

as to all other sects."[15] When the classis received this report the first week in August it was "grieved thereat," and felt it "necessary at the earliest opportunity, even this very day, to wait upon the Directors in regard to this matter."[16] The directors were duly "waited upon" but, as the classis learned the next day, "they said that they knew not of any such complete toleration of the Lutherans there." The *predikanten,* however, were suspicious. The classis discussed the affair and found it advisable that "this matter be more carefully watched and inquired into."[17] Indeed, there was good reason to be suspicious. The company was taking a very vacillating position with regard to the Lutheran question. It was impossible for the classis to find out, and is even now difficult to say with complete certainty, exactly what was promised to the Lutherans in New Netherland. The archives of the Lutheran church in Amsterdam state that individual directors of the W.I.C. were approached by Amsterdam Lutherans. These directors assured the Lutherans that a Lutheran pastor would be tolerated in New Netherland if he were simply sent there without any fanfare.[18] This story is lent plausibility by the fact that at least three directors of the Amsterdam chamber of the W.I.C. at this time were themselves Lutherans. It is difficult to say whether or not a meeting of the W.I.C. formally agreed to permit Lutheran worship in New Netherland. In any case, the situation continued to ferment. On October 3, 1656, it was announced to the Classis of Amsterdam that "in the matter of the Lutheran meeting in New Netherland . . . there was reason to apprehend that there, as well as in all the colonies public worship by Lutherans would be permitted." Predictably, the classis

[15] Minute of the *Deputati ad res Indicas* of the Classis of Amsterdam, July 10, 1656. *Ecc. Rec.,* 1, 354.

[16] Minute of the Classis of Amsterdam, August 7, 1656. *Ecc. Rec.,* 1, 354.

[17] Minute of the Classis of Amsterdam, August 8, 1656. *Ecc. Rec.,* 1, 355.

[18] See H. J. Kreider, *Lutheranism in Colonial New York* (Ann Arbor, Mich.: Edwards, 1942), p. 18.

was "grieved to learn of such a circumstance." It resolved that the W.I.C. directors should be "waited upon, and the injuriousness of this general permission of all sorts of persuasions shall be earnestly deprecated, stating that first of all, and above all, the Church and the glory of God should be cared for."[19] The company, however, remained noncommittal in its replies to the envoys of the classis. The Deputies for Indian Affairs reported back to the classis on November 7 that they had met with the directors "but from all the circumstances, they could only learn that this affair is still unsettled and the settlement a good way off."[20]

In fact, the W.I.C. was stalling for time. The hope of the directors was that Lutheran dissent would gradually come to be quietly accepted in New Netherland as so many different kinds of dissent were accepted in Amsterdam. They reasoned that a combination of time plus constant pressure from the Lutherans would eventually bring about this de facto acceptance of the inevitable by the *predikanten*. In New Netherland, meanwhile, the dissenters kept the pressure on. On October 25, 1656, a group styling themselves "the united adherents of the Unaltered Augsburg Confession" petitioned Director-General Stuyvesant that "henceforth we may not be hindered in our services." They anticipated his favorable reply, they said, because "our friends in the Fatherland, acting in our behalf, have petitioned the Noble, Honorable Lords Directors of the West India Company, our Patroons, in reference to this matter. Upon their petition, they have obtained from their Lordships, as they report to us, in a full meeting, a resolution and decree that the doctrines of the Unaltered Augsburg Confession should be tolerated in the West Indies and New Netherland under their jurisdiction, in the same manner as in the Fatherland under its praiseworthy govern-

[19] Minute of the Classis of Amsterdam, October 3, 1656. *Ecc. Rec.*, 1, 357.

[20] Minute of the Classis of Amsterdam, November 7, 1656. *Ecc. Rec.*, 1, 360.

ment."[21] Stuyvesant probably would have liked to reject this petition out of hand. Loyal servant of the W.I.C. that he was, however, he replied that the request would be forwarded to the directors "by the first ships." But meanwhile he would persist in the enforcement of his ordinance against conventicles.[22]

The Classis of Amsterdam continued to watch the Lutheran affair in New Netherland with a sense of impending doom. On March 19, 1657, the Deputies for Indian Affairs reported that in the new colony on the Delaware (Amsterdam's colony of New Amstel) "other religions, and especially the Lutheran, have crept in." Furthermore, they reiterated their "heavy hearted consideration" that "the Lutherans in New Amsterdam, and principally in New Netherland, are strengthening themselves and are putting forth every effort to establish their position and Forms of worship." The best procedure the classis could devise was once more to "wait on" the W.I.C. directors (and now also the Amsterdam magistrates charged with managing New Amstel) and "seek to persuade them with all serious arguments on the subject in order to check at the beginning this toleration of all sorts of religions, and especially of the Lutherans, lest God's Church come to suffer more and more injury as time goes on."[23]

As well as things seemed to be going for the dissident Lutherans at this point, the situation was in fact neither as bright as they hoped nor as dark as the classis feared. The company, still ultimately concerned to solve the issue of religious diversity in a way that would satisfy all parties and thus increase colonization, decided to pursue a middle course. The directors had considered allowing complete religious toleration to the Lutherans, but probably fearing the severe ecclesiastical repercussions that might fol-

[21] Petition of the Lutherans to Stuyvesant and the Council of New Netherland. *Ecc. Rec.,* 1, 359.
[22] *Ibid.*
[23] Minute of the Classis of Amsterdam, March 19, 1657. *Ecc. Rec.,* 1, 374.

low such a move, they now decided to stop short of that step. They had received Stuyvesant's inquiry of the previous October as to whether or not the Lutheran worship was to be publicly tolerated. Replying on April 7, 1657, the directors stated very simply, "We have by no means the intention to grant to the Lutherans any more liberty regarding the exercise of their religion, than stated in our letter of June 14, 1656, by which we still stand."[24] Thus the directors reiterated that the Lutherans were to enjoy nothing more and nothing less than "free religious exercises in their houses."

The ever-watchful classis was informed of this favorable turn of events three days later by the Deputies for Indian Affairs. The deputies reported that they themselves had been able to dissuade the directors from a previous resolution "tending to permit free worship of the sects, by connivance." Instead, they decided to "abide by the resolution of the preceding year." The classis, however, realized too clearly the company's motives in New Netherland to allow themselves much joy at the latest news. "All these things are fraught with anxious considerations," the *predikanten* grumbled, "and do not place the Assembly completely at their ease."[25] What the classis was uneasy about was the interpretation of the phrase "free religious exercises in their houses." Writing to Megapolensis and Drisius the next month, the classis voiced its concern about this formula. "We observe," they said, "that the Lutherans were permitted the free exercise of their religion in their own houses." This dictum, however, they feared to be open to more than one interpretation: "We cannot interpret this in any other way than that every one must have the freedom to serve God quietly within his dwelling, in such a manner as his religion may prescribe, without instituting any public gatherings or conventicles. When this interpretation is recognized, our complaints will cease. It therefore remains to you, worthy brethren,

[24] W.I.C. directors to Stuyvesant, April 7, 1657. *Ecc. Rec.*, 1, 373.

[25] Minute of the Classis of Amsterdam, April 10, 1657. *Ecc. Rec.*, 1, 374–375.

to be vigilant, lest your congregation, which we learn is at present in a good and encouraging condition, suffer from the liberty which the sects may assume."[26]

While the question was thus being theoretically debated between the Amsterdam Classis and the W.I.C. directors in the homeland, it began to be thrashed out in terms of specifics in the colony. Early in July 1657 Johannes Ernestus Goetwater, an ordained Lutheran minister, arrived in New Netherland aboard the ship Molen. This was the event the Reformed *predikanten* had so long feared, for now, as they put it, they had "the snake in our bosom." Megapolensis and Drisius hardly regarded the presence of Goetwater as a *fait accompli,* however. Immediately addressing themselves to the New Amsterdam city council (the *burgomasters* and *schepens*), they urged six reasons why the Lutheran preacher should be trundled off on the same ship on which he had arrived: the Lutherans had heretofore been granted no permission to hold separate conventicles; contention and discord would result from allowing more than one religious confession in the colony; strife in religious matters would produce confusion in political affairs; the number of participants in Reformed worship would be "perceptibly diminished"; the poor fund treasury of the Reformed would be "considerably diminished"; and if the Lutherans should be allowed public worship, "the Papists, Mennonites and others would soon make similar claims."[27]

The *burgomasters* and *schepens* of New Amsterdam received the protest of the *predikanten* cordially. They summoned Rev. Goetwater and asked him the nature of his mission. The Lutheran pastor "frankly answered, he had been sent on behalf of their Consistory at Amsterdam, to occupy the position of a preacher here, as far as it would be allowed." He also stated that he expected his official credentials from the W.I.C. directors to

[26] Classis of Amsterdam to the New Amsterdam church consistory, May 25, 1657. *Ecc. Rec.,* 1, 381.

[27] Petition of Megapolensis and Drisius to the *burgomasters* and *schepens* of New Amsterdam, July 6, 1657. *Ecc. Rec.,* 1, 387–88.

arrive in New Netherland by the next ship, as well as a letter of permit "giving them freedom of religion as in the Fatherland."[28]

It is unlikely that the W.I.C. had any intention of granting the New Netherland Lutherans "freedom of religion as in the Fatherland." Furthermore, Lutherans in the homeland had no "freedom of religion" as such. They were banned by the letter of the law. What was much more likely was that the company had sent Rev. Goetwater to New Netherland on a trial run. The directors had an aversion to making black and white statements on the subject of religion because such pronouncements had a way of precipitating dispute. If they pronounced openly against the Lutherans they would stand to lose substantial numbers of potential immigrants as well as some colonists already in New Netherland. If, however, they formally endorsed public Lutheran services they would incur the considerable wrath of the Reformed *predikanten,* both at home and in the colony, and theological debate and conflict would almost certainly follow. Under these circumstances, the company had sent Goetwater to the colony to exercise a Lutheran ministry there "as far as it would be allowed." Whether Goetwater was part of the plan, or whether he was a dupe and really believed that his credentials would arrive with the next ship can only be conjectured.

In any case the New Amsterdam city magistrates determined to hold firm. They "could not believe that the Hon. Directors would tolerate in this place any other doctrine than the true Reformed Religion." They were furthermore "under oath to help maintain the true Reformed Religion, and to suffer no other religion or sects." Taking these two things into consideration, they "charged the said Goetwater, not to hold public or private exercise in this city, and not to deliver to the congregation, as he called it, the letters from the [Lutheran] Consistory at [Amsterdam] until further orders."[29] When the action of the city was re-

---

[28] Report of the New Amsterdam *burgomasters* and *schepens* to Stuyvesant and the Council of New Netherland. *Ecc. Rec.,* 1, 389.

[29] *Ibid.*

ported to Stuyvesant, the director-general expressed his approval of "the zeal and desire, shown by the Burgomasters and Schepens of this city for supporting the Reformed doctrine and excluding schismatics."[30]

Goetwater, however, remained in New Amsterdam despite all the official verbiage expended against the legality of his mission. His very presence disquieted Megapolensis and Drisius, who complained to the Amsterdam classis in August 1657 (with very acute insight, it might be added) that: "we suspect that this one has come over to see whether he can pass, and be allowed to remain here, and thus lay the foundation for further efforts." The *predikanten* did all in their power to shake off this "snake in the bosom" before it should bite. They appealed repeatedly to the authorities to "put a stop to this work, which they evidently intended to prosecute with a hard Lutheran head, in spite of and against the will of our magistrates." They asked the New Amsterdam magistrates to open Goetwater's letter from the Amsterdam Lutheran consistory "to learn therefrom the secret of his mission," but the magistrates "have not been willing to do this."[31]

The next ships arrived in September 1657 but the Lutherans received no permit of religious freedom from the W.I.C. In truth, they probably had never expected it. Neither, however, had they expected the order served on Goetwater by the colonial authorities the first week in September. On October 10 the "adherents of the Unaltered Augsburg Confession" complained to Stuyvesant and his colonial council about the edict Goetwater had received ordering him "that he must and shall depart in the ship, *The Waag [Balance]*, now ready to sail." Such a stringent measure the Lutherans had never anticipated. They appealed to the director-general's sense of fairness and justice, and reminded him that "in accordance with your Honor's orders and public an-

---

[30] Stuyvesant's reply to the New Amsterdam magistrates. *Ecc. Rec.*, 1, 390.

[31] Megapolensis and Drisius to the Classis of Amsterdam, August 5, 1657. *Ecc. Rec.*, 1, 394.

nouncements he [Goetwater] has behaved as an honest man, and has never refused obedience to your orders and edicts, but has always given good heed to them; and we too, have behaved quietly and obediently, while we expect from higher authority, the toleration of our religion."[32] As Adriaen van der Donck had so carefully pointed out in the *Remonstrance* of the commonalty, Stuyvesant was not very good at handling opposition to his will, especially when that will had been expressed in an official pronouncement. He now began to suspect that behind this facade of Lutheran cordiality there lay real opposition. Thus on October 16 he shot back to the petitioners that "the Director-General and the Council do not recognize the Unaltered Augsburg Confession, much less any adherents of it." As for Goetwater, Stuyvesant reminded the petitioners that he was in contempt of an order of the provincial government, and that he was therefore "hereby once again commanded to leave with one of the ships ready to sail."[33]

Meanwhile, Goetwater himself had made the dangerous mistake of asking Stuyvesant to explain why he was being banished. In a petition of his own, dated October 15, 1657, he protested that his presence in the colony as a private citizen was perfectly legal, since he possessed a passport from the W.I.C., and furthermore that he was guilty of no *"crimen laesae majestatis."* Therefore, he said, he wished "to be free from charges of disobedience."[34] Stuyvesant answered this plea in the only way he knew; he repeated what he had already said—this time a little louder:

The petitioner, who forgets himself and the truth, is reminded, that the order for his departure was served upon him five or six weeks

[32] Petition of the Lutherans to Stuyvesant and the Council of New Netherland, October 10, 1657. *Ecc. Rec.*, 1, 406.

[33] Stuyvesant's answer to the Lutheran petition, October 16, 1657. *Ecc. Rec.*, 1, 407.

[34] Goetwater's petition to Stuyvesant and the Council. *Ecc. Rec.*, 1, 407–408.

ago, and sent in writing. Since that time two ships have sailed. In one of these he ought to have left, according to order, but the petitioner has neglected to do this, in contempt of the government. He is once more commanded to obey said order by going in one of the two ships about to sail; especially as the Director-General and Council consider it necessary for the honor of God, the advancement of the Reformed Religion, and the common quietness, peace and harmony of this place.[35]

The Lutherans now realized that, with Stuyvesant at the head of the provincial government and the W.I.C. directors unwilling to take an official stand in their behalf, the cause for legal public worship was at least temporarily lost. They still refused, however, to give up hope. Instead of complying with the banishment edict, they secretly removed Goetwater from New Amsterdam to the home of a Lutheran farmer. This maneuver, which Megapolensis and Drisius correctly analyzed as "a stratagem to hold the matter in suspense and gain more time," succeeded in keeping the Lutheran pastor in the colony for nearly two more years. One year later, in September 1658 the New Netherland *predikanten* could only report to the Classis of Amsterdam that "the matter of the Lutherans remains still in a very smoky condition," because Goetwater was still in the province. He had recently been taken ill, however, and the authorities discovered that he was still there, from which fact the *predikanten* hoped that the government would "compel him to leave by one of the earliest ships."[36]

When the ships left, however, Goetwater was still in New Netherland. Even more disturbing, he now began to preach and to hold services, contrary to the orders of Stuyvesant and the provincial council. Again Stuyvesant warned him, but Goetwater paid no heed. The director-general therefore had him summarily arrested in his own house and packed off to Holland in the ship

[35] Stuyvesant's answer to Goetwater's petition, October 16, 1657. *Ecc. Rec.*, 1, 408–409.
[36] Megapolensis and Drisius to the Classis of Amsterdam, September 24, 1658. *Ecc. Rec.*, 1, 433.

Bruijnvisch in the spring of 1659. Heaving an enormous sigh of relief, Megapolensis and Drisius informed the Classis of Amsterdam on September 10, 1659, that "there is now again quietness among the people, and the Lutherans again go to church, as they were formerly accustomed to do."[37]

Thus one phase of the struggle between establishment and dissent came to a close. On the surface, it had ended as a victory for the Reformed establishment, but the *predikanten* did not win the dissident Lutherans back to the fold without paying a fairly high price. The W.I.C. had decided that it stood to lose more than it might gain by trying to force religious toleration on New Netherland. The directors, however, realized that they must find a way of giving religious satisfaction to the sizable Lutheran minority in the colony. Such a way gradually began to emerge.

On May 20, 1658, the directors, supposing Stuyvesant to have banished Goetwater from the province, communicated to the director-general that this action was acceptable to them, "although you might have proceeded less vigorously." They had learned, however, from Lutherans in Amsterdam, that the principal reason why Lutherans in New Netherland had separated from the Reformed Church was "because in the Sacrament of Baptism some words are used there, which are offensive to them and not contained in the new formulary."[38] The item of Reformed procedure which disturbed the Lutherans was the second article of the baptismal formula, which asked the parents of the child if they confessed that "the doctrine which is expounded in the Old and New Testaments and in the articles of the Christian faith, and which is taught in the Christian church *here,* is true and sufficient for salvation."[39] The directors wished to see the offending word, *alhier,* deleted from the formula so that Luther-

[37] Megapolensis and Drisius to the Classis of Amsterdam, September 10, 1659. *Ecc. Rec.,* 1, 449.

[38] W.I.C. directors to Stuyvesant, May 20, 1658. *Ecc. Rec.,* 1, 423.

[39] See Eekhof, *De Hervormde Kerk in Noord-Amerika (1624–1664),* 2, 25.

ans might be more easily induced peacefully to join the Reformed
Church.

We think that the old formulary of baptism is still used in many
churches here, as being less offensive and more moderate, than the
new, and therefore adopted at the beginning of the Reformation as
necessary under the circumstances, in order thereby not to alienate,
but rather to attract people of different belief. We shall leave it to
your prudence and trust, that henceforth you will use the least offensive and most tolerant means, so that people of other persuasions
may not be deterred from the public Reformed Church, but in time
be induced to listen and finally be gained over to it.[40]

The W.I.C. directors were now embarking upon a potentially
explosive course of action. Having failed to procure operating
room for New Netherland's Lutherans outside the Reformed
establishment, they tried to make room for them inside the establishment by theological manipulation. The Arminian struggle of
the second and third decades of the century had already shown
that the Reformed would stoutly resist all such civil meddling in
doctrinal affairs. Nevertheless, the W.I.C. now had too much at
stake in New Netherland to be able to afford rigid religious establishmentarianism.

On August 19, 1658, Stuyvesant and his council decided to
place the request of the directors before the *predikanten* and to
ask for their response. The response was as volatile as might have
been expected. Megapolensis absolutely denied that the formula
of baptism had anything to do with the Lutherans' desire to separate from the Reformed. The "Lutherans," he said, "praise Luther only because they call themselves by his name. They are
Lutherans, and will remain such, because their parents and an-
cestors were Lutherans, as Paulus Schrick their leader in his wisdom once declared." As far as the supposedly objectionable word
alhier was concerned, the *predikanten* doubted that the Lutherans had ever discussed the problem: "As far as our knowledge
goes, there never has been any agitation, or even appearance of

[40] *Ecc. Rec.*, 1, 423.

such, among them in relation to such a question. Indeed, about two years ago one Peter Jansen a stupid northerner, who was neither a Lutheran nor of the Reformed Religion, and who had not intelligence enough to understand the difference between them, nibbled at these questions, but could not give any reasons against them, or receive and try to understand a reason in their favor." Concerning "the advice and proposition of the Hon. Directors of the Company, that we should use the old Formula, which is still used in many churches of Holland, and which is more moderate, and less objectionable to those of other denominations," the *predikanten* promised only that they would refer the matter to the Classis of Amsterdam. They admitted that the Synod of The Hague in 1591 omitted the word *alhier* from the baptismal formula, while the Synod of Middelburg in 1581 made it optional. Nevertheless, they argued, the apostolic churches (Galatians 2:3-4) had never yielded one iota to "the obstinate and perverse," and furthermore, even if *alhier* should be omitted from the formula, by the church would be meant "not Papal church, but the true Protestant and Reformed churches."[41]

Having this response communicated to them by Stuyvesant, the directors decided that it was time for a power play. They felt they had already compromised more than enough on the issue of the Lutherans, and besides they had some ecclesiastical precedent for their position, as even Megapolensis and Drisius had been forced to admit. They therefore informed Stuyvesant, on February 13, 1659, that "our intentions are still the same, as we see no reason, why the preachers there should raise difficulties about it; for it is an order practiced in most of the Reformed Churches here."[42] When the Amsterdam classis sent its Deputies for Indian Affairs to discuss the issue with the W.I.C. directors one week later, "they noticed when they waited upon the Direc-

[41] Megapolensis and Drisius to the Classis of Amsterdam, August 23, 1658. *Ecc. Rec.*, 1, 428-429, 431.
[42] W.I.C. directors to Stuyvesant, February 13, 1659. *Ecc. Rec.*, 1, 441.

tors, that the broaching of this subject would be likely to awaken some displeasure in them."[43]

Later in 1659 the directors communicated to Stuyvesant the precise nature of their positions in the whole Lutheran affair. They told the director-general that they were looking for two or three young *predikanten* to send to New Netherland. They would not, however, send anyone lacking certain qualifications: "It is not sufficient that they lead a good moral life; they must be a peaceable and moderate temperament [*sic*], which depends a good deal on the place of their studies; and not be infected with scruples about unnecessary forms, which cause more division, than edification. The preachers there, Domines Megapolensis and Drisius, do not seem to be free from this kind of leaven, for they make difficulties in regard to the use of the old formula of baptism." The directors understood that many of the Lutherans had now come back into the Reformed fold. This development heartened them, for it implied a return of theological tranquility to the colony, but

care must be taken that this state of affairs continue; that is uncertain as long as such precise forms and offensive expressions are not avoided. It is absolutely necessary, that they be avoided in a Church, which is so weak and only beginning to grow, especially when we consider the difficulties, liable to arise, which might result in the permission to conduct a separate divine service there; for the Lutherans would very easily obtain the consent of the authorities here upon a complaint and we would have no means of preventing it. We find it therefore highly necessary to direct herewith, that you communicate all this to the aforesaid preachers there and seriously admonish and recommend them to adopt our advice and use the old formula of baptism without waiting for further orders from here. That will allay the dissensions in the state and of the church there.[44]

[43] Minute of the Classis of Amsterdam, February 24, 1659. *Ecc. Rec.,* 1, 441.
[44] W.I.C. directors to Stuyvesant, December 22, 1659. *Ecc. Rec.,* 1, 460–461.

Stuyvesant's fierce loyalties to both church and company made this a difficult situation for him. On April 21, 1660, he replied to the directors that he was sorry to hear that they were "displeased, as your expressions make us presume, with the preachers here." Personally, Stuyvesant found them to be of "edifying life and conduct," and he was sure that "neither of them can be suspected of any leaven of innovation or turbulence." He would, however, "not fail, to communicate to them your wishes, while it would help much in observing and carrying out your orders, if some psalm books or special liturgies of the Reformed Church or formularities [sic] of baptism could be found somewhere and sent over, in which the words 'here present' are not used."[45]

The W.I.C. did not let this opportunity pass. In July 1660 the Classis of Amsterdam found that the company had already sent to the colony "some old copies for the use there, in which [the word *alhier*] is not found."[46] When the old formulas arrived in New Netherland, the *predikanten* apparently decided that the struggle was lost this time. On October 4 of the same year Samuel Drisius wrote to the classis that he was about to accede to the directors' demands that he should "meet the Lutherans half way." He had hoped that the classis would be able to intercede with the W.I.C. in this matter, but he gathered that the directors had refused to listen. Indeed, he believed that he was entirely helpless in the matter: "We see . . . that you exhort us to adhere to the Formula; but this does not change the opinion of the Hon. Patroons, that we indulge in no unnecessary precision in matters of indifference; neither does it regain their approbation, or meet the intentions they have expressed. For their Lordships have required the Director-General to declare to us, in their name, that they simply demand that the old Formula should be used by us, without any farther orders from Amsterdam, and without any farther opposition."[47]

[45] Stuyvesant to the W.I.C. directors, April 21, 1660. *Ecc. Rec.*, 1, 475.
[46] Minute of the Classis of Amsterdam, June 1, 1660. *Ecc. Rec.*, 1, 477.
[47] Drisius to the Classis of Amsterdam, October 4, 1660. *Ecc. Rec.*, 1, 486.

What had New Netherland's dissenting Lutherans gained after seven years of struggle? It is not easy to say precisely. Certainly they had not won "religious freedom" in the eighteenth-century American constitutional sense. In the technical, legal sense they had not even gained religious toleration. Their gains, however, had not been insubstantial. They had blunted the sharp cutting edge of the Reformed establishment and proven beyond any doubt that there was place in New Netherland for persons of their religious convictions.

13. The Jews

Another group that challenged the religious order in New Netherland during the second half of the 1650's was the Jews. European Jews had found a congenial home in Amsterdam around the beginning of the seventeenth century. Forced into the ghetto in Eastern Europe and distrusted and persecuted as "Maranos" in the newly reunited Iberian peninsula, European Jewry streamed to Amsterdam and there worked a renaissance of Jewish life and culture. New Netherland enjoyed (or suffered, depending on the point of view) the side effects of this phenomenon.

Some Jews from Holland arrived at Manhattan in the summer of 1654 in order, as the ever-vigilant Megapolensis reported to the Classis of Amsterdam, "to trade." It is possible that this group did not at first intend to remain in North America. In September of the same year, however, they were joined by a new influx of Jewish immigrants cast on New Netherland more or less fortuitously. This second group was composed of Jews who had been involved in the sugar industry in Dutch Brazil. The recapture of Brazil by the Portuguese in 1652 had left them homeless, indigent, and liable to religious persecution, so that their emigration from that place had become necessary. Finally, a third group of Jews arrived at Manhattan the following spring, bringing with them the announcement that more would follow from the homeland.

Domine Megapolensis's vision of the ideal ecclesiastical order in New Netherland had very little room for Lutherans but even less for Jews. On March 18, 1655, he related to the Classis of Amsterdam his version of the latest plague descended upon New Netherland. Using the old argument that diversity could lead only to chaos, he complained that "as we have here Papists, Mennonites and Lutherans among the Dutch; also many Puritans or Independents, and many Atheists and various other servants of Baal among the English under Government, who conceal themselves under the name of Christians; it would create a still greater confusion, if the obstinate and immovable Jews came to settle here." Furthermore, he said, their arrival had caused "among the congregation here a great deal of complaint and murmuring [*een groot knorren ende morren*]." But the worst part was that this appeared to be only the beginning of Jewish immigration, for the most recent group had said that "still more of the same lot would follow, and then they would build here a synagogue."[1]

Megapolensis decided that this problem should be dealt with immediately. It was not feasible to eliminate the Lutherans because there were too many of them in the colony; but there were still only a few Jews. Therefore his plea to the classis went directly to the root of the matter: "We request your Reverences to obtain from the Lords-Directors, that these godless rascals . . . may be sent away from here." Megapolensis probably realized that it would take more than theology to convince the W.I.C. directors to ban the Jews, and he added that "these people have no other God than the unrighteous Mammon, and no other aim than to get possession of christian property, and to win all other merchants by drawing all trade towards themselves. . . . They are of no benefit to the country," he protested, "but look at everything for their own profit."[2]

The Classis of Amsterdam brought the request of the *predikant*

---

[1] Megapolensis to the Classis of Amsterdam, March 18, 1655. *Ecc. Rec.*, 1, 335–336.

[2] *Ibid.*, 1, 335.

before the W.I.C., and the response of the directors was not surprising. They communicated their decision regarding the Jews to Stuyvesant on April 26, 1655. The directors would have liked to agree to Megapolensis's (and apparently also Stuyvesant's) proposal that the Jews should be banned entirely from New Netherland, but that was impossible. After having "weighed and considered" the matter, they had decided such a stringent measure would be "unreasonable and unfair." The Jews could not, in their view, be excluded from New Netherland, because they had sustained such heavy losses in the capture of Brazil by the Portuguese and also "because of the large amount of capital, which they have invested in shares of this Company." Taking all things into consideration, the directors decided it would be best for the Jews to be allowed "to sail to and trade in New Netherland and to live and remain there." Stuyvesant was to govern himself accordingly. The only stipulation placed on Jewish freedom by the W.I.C. was that "the poor among them shall not become a burden to the Company or the community, but be supported by their own nation."[3]

The presence of Jews in New Netherland (especially New Amsterdam) gave rise to all kinds of difficulties. In several ways the New Netherland Jew was relegated to the social position of discriminated-against minority. When in April 1657, Jacob da Cohun Hendricus asked the New Amsterdam *burgomasters* for permission "to bake and sell bread within this city, like other bakers, but with closed door," he was refused.[4] Open retailing was forbidden to Jews even in Amsterdam, but the kind of "closed door" operation of which Hendricus was speaking was common. Already in August 1655, Stuyvesant set up a system by which each Jewish man between the ages of sixteen and sixty could relieve himself of his military obligations by making a

---

[3] W.I.C. directors to Stuyvesant, April 26, 1655. *Ecc. Rec.*, 1, 338.

[4] Minute of the Court of New Amsterdam, April 11, 1657. In Berthold Fernow, ed., *Records of New Amsterdam from 1653 to 1674* (New York, 1897), 7, 154.

monthly payment of approximately three guilders to the New Amsterdam municipal treasury.[5] By providing this option he probably hoped to avoid the argument that Jews should be granted citizenship because they did military duty. Finally, even a separate burial ground within the city limits of New Amsterdam was denied the Jews. This request, which was made July 27, 1655, was refused by Stuyvesant. If the Jews, he said, did not wish to use the general cemetery in New Amsterdam for burying their dead, they could do it "somewhere else on the Company's free land."[6]

In the spring of 1656, Stuyvesant, without having had an official petition to this effect, heard a rumor that the Jews were about to seek permission to build a synagogue. He sought the advice of the W.I.C. directors as to what he should do if and when the request appeared. The directors were hardly about to grant to a handful of Jews the freedom they were hesitant to allow to a much larger number of Lutherans. Replying to Stuyvesant on March 13, 1656, they instructed him that he was by no means to honor such a request should it be forthcoming.[7]

In the opinion of the W.I.C., however, Stuyvesant went too far when in 1655 he forbade the Jews to trade on the Hudson at Fort Orange and on the Delaware River. In a letter dated June 14, 1656, the directors gave Stuyvesant a fairly clear idea of how to deal with the Jews, and what the place of the latter in colonial society should be:

We have learned with displeasure how, contrary to the charter granted by us to the Jewish or Portuguese nation at its request, Your Honor has forbidden to that nation the trade at Fort Orange and on the South River, as well as the purchase of wholesale goods, which is permitted here in the homeland without any difficulty; furthermore, we wish that this had never happened, but that you

[5] Minute of the New Netherland Council, August 28, 1655. *Col. Doc.*, 12, 96.

[6] Eekhof, *De Hervormde Kerk in Noord-Amerika (1624–1664)*, (The Hague, Nijhoff, 1913), 2, 73.

[7] W.I.C. directors to Stuyvesant, March 12, 1656. *Col. Doc.*, 14, 341.

had obeyed our orders with more respect, as you must punctually do in the future. Nevertheless, the Jewish or Portuguese nation there shall not be allowed to undertake any trades or public shopkeeping (for this is not allowed in Amsterdam), but they shall be allowed to do this peacefully and quietly within their own houses.[8]

There was, finally, the issue of whether or not the Jews were to be granted New Amsterdam citizenship. The privilege of citizenship, or *burgerrecht*, was created by Stuyvesant and the colonial council in 1657, but there was considerable sentiment within New Amsterdam that this privilege should not be extended to Jews. Stuyvesant himself had written to the W.I.C. directors in October 1655: "To give liberty to the Jews will be very detrimental there, because the Christians there will not be able at the same time to do business. Giving them liberty, we cannot refuse the Lutherans and Papists."[9] Here Stuyvesant confused civil, commercial, and religious liberty. The directors, however, took a much more moderate position by refusing the Jews the public exercise of their religion, but permitting them free wholesale trade and retail trade behind closed doors, as this was practiced in Amsterdam. Furthermore, the directors informed Stuyvesant that even though the Jews should not be allowed a synagogue, they should be permitted the free practice of their religion in their houses. To this end, their homes were to be built "close together in a convenient place on one or the other side of New Amsterdam—at their own choice, as they have done here [Amsterdam]."[10] This latter stipulation seems to indicate that the directors had in mind the gathering of more than one family at a private home for religious services, as was the practice in Amsterdam.

Stuyvesant, therefore, although he personally would have approved a more stringent policy of anti-Semitism, knew by the

[8] W.I.C. directors to Stuyvesant, June 14, 1656. *Col. Doc.*, 14, 351.
[9] Cited in S. Oppenheim, *The Early History of the Jews in New York, 1654–1664* (New York, 1909), p. 30.
[10] *Col. Doc.*, 14, 351.

summer of 1656 that the W.I.C. wished him to take a moderate stance with the Jews. During the second half of 1656 the Jews apparently acquired more freedom in commerce, because in January 1657 a meeting between Stuyvesant and the New Amsterdam city council discussed "the practice of keeping open store and of selling by retail on the part of Jews and foreigners to the great detriment of the interests of the citizens of the Province."[11] The consequence of this discussion was that, on January 30, 1657, Stuyvesant and the New Netherland colonial council decreed that henceforth only open shop would be kept in New Amsterdam, and this upon condition that the shopkeeper should have procured the New Amsterdam citizenship.[12] The ordinance did not mention the Jews but was clearly aimed at them since it made shopkeeping without citizenship impossible, and it was impossible for Jews to gain citizenship.

The Jews now realized that they must firmly establish their rights in New Netherland on the basis of their February 15, 1655, charter from the W.I.C. They first attempted to gain the right to keep shop "behind closed door," but this was refused to Jacob da Cohun Hendricus in April 1657 by the city council of New Amsterdam. The only remaining option was to seek the full privilege of citizenship, and the Jews believed that their concessions from the W.I.C. were sufficiently broad to win them this right. The issue was precipitated in April by Asser Levy, who appealed for citizenship to the New Amsterdam city council on the grounds that he stood military watch alongside citizens, that he had previously been a citizen of Amsterdam, and that this privilege had been guaranteed by the concessions of the W.I.C.[13] The New Amsterdam *burgomasters* and *schepens* refused the request, but referred Levy to Stuyvesant and the colonial council.

[11] Minute of the Court of New Amsterdam, January 8, 1657. In Fernow, 2, 262.

[12] Minute of the Court of New Amsterdam, January 30, 1657. *Ibid.*, 2, 287.

[13] Oppenheim, p. 36.

Stuyvesant appeared now to vacillate. His position was indeed an uncomfortable one, for he had cooperated with the New Amsterdam authorities to make the lot of the Jew as unpleasant as possible. But on the other hand, he knew that the W.I.C. directors had committed themselves to a program of moderate freedom for Jews in New Netherland and would surely side with them in a showdown. Under these circumstances the director-general finally relented and reversed the decision of the New Amsterdam authorities on Levy's citizenship plea. Later in the same month the *burgomasters* and *schepens* of New Amsterdam were authorized and commanded to admit Levy and his co-plaintiffs Salvador D'Andrada, Jacob da Cohun Hendricus, Abraham de Lucena, and Joseph D'Acosta "with their Nation" to New Amsterdam and New Netherland citizenship.[14]

Several documents suggest that the position of the New Netherland Jews improved considerably subsequent to the pivotal citizenship decision. The New Amsterdam court minutes of June 1658 note that two cases against Jacob Barsimson were processed and "though the defendant is absent yet no default is entered against him, as he was summoned on his Sabbath."[15] When in 1659 New Amsterdam established an oath for the licensing of butchers in the city, a special clause was introduced for the Jews Asser Levy and Moses Lucena exempting them from slaughtering hogs, since it was forbidden by their faith.[16]

The position of the Jews in New Netherland by 1660 can be summarized as follows. As far as the public conduct of their worship was concerned, they had no freedom. The W.I.C. took an explicit stance on the prohibition of a synagogue and thus treated the Jews less favorably than they did the Lutherans. The

[14] Zwierlein, *Religion in New Netherland* (Rochester, N.Y.: John P. Smith, 1910), p. 264.

[15] Minute of the Court of New Amsterdam, June, 1658. In Fernow, 2, 396–397.

[16] Minutes of the Court of New Amsterdam, October 15, and 29, 1660. *Ibid.,* 7, 259 and 261.

order of the company, however, was framed in such a way as tacitly to admit the propriety of conventicles held in private Jewish homes. Jews were allowed to trade within the entire colony on a wholesale basis, and they were permitted to keep retail shop in New Amsterdam where they also enjoyed full citizenship. In short, within a span of five or six years Jews had established beyond any doubt their right to a place within New Netherland's civil, commercial, and religious structure. The Reformed Church had stated its intention in the matter in 1655: "May these godless rascals . . . be sent away from here." The W.I.C. announced its intention the same year: "They [the Jews] shall have permission to sail to and trade in New Netherland and to live and remain there." Between the two intentions there was a wide gulf, but the company was not the loser.

14. The Left-Wing Dissidents

As crucial as were the tests provided by Lutherans and Jews for the Reformed ideal of society's organic unity, the most significant test of all was that presented by the Quakers. This "new unheard of abominable heresy," as Stuyvesant styled it, was the scourge of American colonial authorities. Private spiritual experience, or the "inner light," was the sole source of authority for the Quakers. These people were consequently viewed by civil magistrates on both sides of the Atlantic as seditious anarchists, and by ecclesiastical authorities as "machinations of Satan." No more serious threat could have been posed to the New Netherland established order than that posed by the Quakers. For while other groups challenged the Reformed order in the name of a different kind of social order, the Quakers challenged, or seemed to challenge, the concept of order itself.

The magnitude of the trauma suffered by New Netherland authorities upon encountering their first Quakers can be accurately gauged from the account of the incident given by the *predikanten* Megapolensis and Drisius. On August 6, 1657, a ship suddenly appeared before New Amsterdam "having no flag flying from the topmast, nor from any other place on the ship; only from the foremast a small burgee floated to indicate the wind." No salute was fired before the fort, and those on shore could not be certain whether she was Dutch, French, or English. A W.I.C. official went on board to find out what he could, but "they tendered him no honor or respect." Furthermore, "when the master of the ship came on shore and appeared before the Director-General, he rendered him no respect, but stood still with his hat firm on his head, as if a goat. The Director-General could with difficulty get a word from any of them. He only learned that they had come from London in about eight weeks. When asked as to the condition of Holland, France, etc., hardly a word could be drawn from them. At last information was gained that it was a ship with Quakers on board." When this became known, the New Amsterdam reception must have turned rather chilly because the ship abruptly departed the next day. Megapolensis and Drisius speculated that it sailed for Rhode Island, the "latrina of New England," because "all the cranks of New England retire thither." Before sailing, however, it deposited at Manhattan "two strong young women." Scarcely had the ship disappeared from view,

when these began to quake and go into a frenzy and cry out loudly in the middle of the street, that men should repent, for the day of judgment was at hand. Our people not knowing what was the matter, ran to and fro, while one cried "Fire," and another something else. The Fiscal, with an accompanying officer, seized them both by the head, and led them to prison. On their way to jail, they continued to cry out and pray according to their manner, and continued to do the same when in prison. We perceive from this circumstance that the devil is the same everywhere. The same instruments which he uses to disturb the churches in Europe, he employs here in America.[1]

The hope of the *predikanten* that most of the Quaker menace had been diverted to Rhode Island proved illusory. The new sect suddenly sprang up everywhere in the colony, or so it seemed to the authorities. Later in the month of August 1657 Robert Hodgson, a Quaker, began preaching and holding conventicles with considerable success among the English communities under Dutch jurisdiction on Long Island. Together with two other missionary Friends, Hodgson found among the English "many sin-

[1] Megapolensis and Drisius to the Classis of Amsterdam, August 14, 1657. *Ecc. Rec.,* 1, 399–400.

cere seekers after Heavenly riches . . . prepared to appreciate those spiritual views of religion which these gospel messengers had to declare." At Gravesend and Jamaica the Quakers were "received with gladness," and at Heemstede (Hempstead) Hodgson found colonists who "rejoiced in the spread of those living truths, which were preached among them."[2] Unfortunately for Hodgson, at Heemstede he also found Richard Gildersleeve, a justice of the peace determined to put an early end to these Quaker conventicles.

Gildersleeve swore out a warrant for Hodgson's arrest, and the constable seized the preacher in an orchard one Sunday, where Hodgson was apparently preparing to hold a gathering. The Quaker was confined in Gildersleeve's house while the latter went to church, but instead of bemoaning his situation Hodgson preached through the front window of the house to a large crowd of people "who staid and heard the truth declared." Angered by the audacity of his prisoner, Gildersleeve went to Manhattan and informed Stuyvesant of the situation. The director-general congratulated the magistrate for his efforts to suppress the "Quaker heresy" and dispatched an armed guard to Heemstede to escort the prisoner to Manhattan. Now began the most barbaric act of religious oppression perpetrated by the Dutch during their time in New Netherland—in fact, their only use of physical force to coerce conscience. Hodgson was bound to a cart and dragged most of the way to Manhattan. Upon arrival he was placed in a "dungeon full of vermin and so odious for wet and dirt, as he never saw before."[3] At his trial several days later he was sentenced to a fine of six hundred guilders or two years' hard labor. He tried to defend himself but was given no opportunity to speak and was immediately taken back to his cell.

[2] H. Onderdonck, "The Rise and Growth of the Society of Friends on Long Island and in New York, 1657–1826," in *The Annals of Hempstead, 1643 to 1832* (New York, 1878), pp. 5–6.

[3] Zwierlein, *Religion in New Netherland* (Rochester, N.Y.: John P. Smith, 1910), pp. 216, 217.

Within several days he was returned to court, where his hat was removed (Stuyvesant was particularly offended by the omnipresent Quaker hat) and another sentence was read to him in Dutch, which he did not understand.

About one week later Hodgson was led out and chained to a wheelbarrow and told to work. When he refused, he was twice beaten to the ground by a Negro slave with a four-inch pitched rope, then left chained to the wheelbarrow in the hot sun until he collapsed. This procedure was repeated for the next two days and Stuyvesant informed the prisoner that unless he worked "he should be whipt every day." Hodgson remained obstinate, refused to work, and demanded to know what law he had broken. The director-general refused an answer, continued to have Hodgson chained to the wheelbarrow, and threatened him with sterner punishment if he spoke to onlookers. Hodgson spoke.

The battle of the two wills now moved to a new level of intensity. Hodgson was taken to a room, hung from the ceiling by his hands, and whipped until he was near death. He was then thrown into a dingy cell and left in solitary confinement for two days, after which the whipping was repeated. Hodgson now felt that he would die and asked to have an English-speaking person come to him. The English woman who was allowed to bathe his wounds thought that he could not live another day. Her husband tried in vain to obtain his release. Fortunately for Hodgson, public opinion in New Amsterdam was gradually beginning to swing his way. An anonymous English letter to Stuyvesant asked the director-general whether it might not be wise to send the Quaker to Rhode Island, "as his labor is hardly worth the cost." Finally, Stuyvesant's own sister, Anna, pleaded with him so earnestly that he freed Hodgson on condition that he should leave New Netherland forever.[4]

---

[4] The Hodgson episode is recounted *ibid.*, p. 215–219. Also in Eekhof, *De Hervormde Kerk in Noord-Amerika* (The Hague: Nijhoff, 1913), 2, 78–81; *Ecc. Rec.*, 1, 410; and O'Callaghan, *History of New Netherland* (New York: Appleton, 1848), 2, 347–350.

The battle against the Quakers was going ill for Stuyvesant and the *predikanten*. The director-general had failed in his attempt to make an object lesson out of Hodgson, and meanwhile Quaker enthusiasm had been spreading very quickly on Long Island. Within Dutch jurisdiction on that island, the towns of 's Gravensande (Gravesend), Heemstede, Jamaica, and Vlissingen (Flushing) were all severely smitten by Quaker preaching. To control these "seducers of the people, who are destructive unto magistracy and ministry," Stuyvesant resorted to his old weapon —the ordinance. In the fall of 1657 the director-general issued a proclamation whereby any ship bringing a Quaker into the province of New Netherland should be liable to confiscation. Furthermore, anyone harboring a known Quaker overnight was subject to a fine of fifty Flemish pounds, half of which was to go to the informer.[5] This ordinance was sent to the local magistrates of all towns under Dutch jurisdiction, with instructions to enforce it strictly.

Although the new decree was received obediently in most parts of the province, the town of Vlissingen on Long Island proved obstinate. The inhabitants of Vlissingen previously had been involved in a running dispute with Stuyvesant over religious matters. English settlers, fleeing religious persecution in New England, had come to the town in 1645. To avoid the possibility of again being persecuted because of conscience, they petitioned Director-General Kieft in that same year for religious autonomy. Kieft, who at that time had been desperate to increase the population of the beleagured province, had granted the Englishmen "liberty of conscience," or freedom from "molestacon or disturbance from any Magistrate or Magistrates, or any other Ecclesiastical Minister, that may extend jurisdiction over them."[6] Subsequently, Stuyvesant had by fiat forced the inhabitants of Vlissingen to sign a contract for the ministerial services of Francis Doughty, an

[5] Brodhead, *History of the State of New York* (New York: Harper, 1853), 1, 637.
[6] Zwierlein, p. 161.

English Presbyterian minister of somewhat questionable character who was heavily indebted to the W.I.C.[7] This contract was
never honored by the citizens of Vlissingen, and about 1655
Doughty was obliged to leave New Netherland for Virginia because the English in Vlissingen refused to pay his salary. After
this, there was no minister in the town for several years, and
Megapolensis and Drisius communicated in 1657 to the Classis
of Amsterdam that at Vlissingen "many . . . have become im-
bued with divers opinions and it is with them *quot homines, tot
sententiae*."[8]

Citing the "freedom from molestacon" clause of their 1645
charter from Kieft, the inhabitants of Vlissingen rose in stiff opposition to Stuyvesant's harsh ordinance against Quakers. Under
the instigation of the sheriff, Tobias Feake, and the authorship
of the clerk, Edward Hart, a "remonstrance" was drawn up,
signed by thirty-one townsmen, and presented to Stuyvesant. This
document, known afterwards as the "Flushing Remonstrance,"
is certainly the most important piece of theorizing about religious
liberty that New Netherland produced, and it merits lengthy
quotation:

Right Honorable. You have been pleased to send up unto us a certain Prohibition or Command, that wee shoulde not receive or
entertaine any of those people called Quakers, because they are supposed to bee by some seducers of the people; for our parte wee cannot condem them in this case, neither can wee stretch out our hands
against them to punish, bannish or persecute them, for out of Christ,
God is a consuming fire, and it is a fearful thing to fall into the
handes of the liveing God; wee desire therefore in this case not to
judge least wee be judged, neither to Condem least wee bee Con-
demed, but rather let every man stand and fall to his own. . . . The
law of love, peace and libertie in the states extending to Jews, Turks
and Egyptians, as they are considered the sonnes of Adam, which is
the glory of the outward State of Holland; so love, peace and

[7] *Ibid.*, p. 163. See also *Col. Doc.*, 2, 151.
[8] Megapolensis and Drisius to the Classis of Amsterdam, August 5, 1657.
Ecc. Rec., 1, 397.

libertie extending to all in Christ Jesus, Condems hatred, warre and bondage; and because our Savior saith it is impossible but that offence will come, but woe be unto him by whom they Commeth, our desire is not to offend one of his little ones in whatsoever forme, name or title hee appeares in, whether Presbyterian, Independent, Baptist or Quaker; but shall be glad to see anything of God in any of them: desireing to doe unto all men as wee desire all men should doe unto us, which is the true law both of Church and State; for our Saviour saith this is the Law and the Prophets; Therefore, if any of these said persons come in love unto us, wee cannot in Conscience lay violent hands upon them, but give them free Egresse into our Towne and howses as God shall perswade our Consciences; and in this we are true subjects both of the Church and State; for wee are bounde by the law of God and man to do good unto all men, and evill to no man; and this is according to the Pattent and Charter of our Towne given unto us in the name of the States Generall which we are not willing to infringe and violate but shall hold to our pattent and shall remaine your Humble Subjects the inhabitants of Vlishing.[9]

Stuyvesant swept the "Flushing Remonstrance" aside as so much insolent insubordination. Feake and Hart, along with two other Vlissingen magistrates who had had the temerity to sign the document, were placed under arrest and summoned to New Amsterdam to stand trial. The New Netherland fiscal, Nicasius de Sille, brought the charges, which were, in effect, that these magistrates had violated both the director-general's orders and the 1650 Charter of Freedoms and Exemptions which stated that "no other religion shall be publicly admitted in New Netherland except the Reformed."[10] Under this kind of pressure, all the magistrates except Feake admitted their "error" and humbly asked for pardon. The whole responsibility for the remonstrance was thus placed upon the *schout* (sheriff) of Vlissingen. Feake was summarily tried and found guilty of having instigated "a seditious, mutinous and detestable letter of defiance wherein [he and

[9] In *Ecc. Rec.*, 1, 412–413.
[10] Vlissingen magistrates to Stuyvesant and New Netherland Council, January 9, 1658. *Col. Doc.*, 14, 406–407.

his accomplices] justify and uphold the abominable sect of Quakers, who villify both the political authorities and the ministers of the Gospel, and undermine the State and God's service and absolutely demand, that all sects, especially the said abominable sect of Quakers, shall and must be tolerated and admitted." When Feake admitted his wrongdoing, the court treated him "leniently." Removed from his office, he was sentenced to banishment from New Netherland or a fine of two hundred guilders plus trial costs.[11]

Having crushed his opposition so completely in Vlissingen, Stuyvesant proceeded for the next four years (1658–1662) vigorously to hunt down and eliminate Quakers from their Long Island stronghold. New ordinances aimed particularly at Quakers were promulgated both at a provincial level and at the local level in towns such as Jamaica, Vlissingen, and Heemstede.[12] Nevertheless, the "abominable heresy" seemed to spread rather than disappear. In August 1662 the magistrates of Jamaica were forced to report to Stuyvesant that a majority of that town's inhabitants attended Quaker conventicles. They were powerless to act, however, since the conventicles were not held within their jurisdiction but rather at the home of one John Bowne at Vlissingen. To this man's home came all the Quakers in the area every Sunday.[13]

Stuyvesant moved quickly and decisively against Bowne, but ironically in so doing he sealed the fate of his own establishmentarian policies against the Quakers. The deputy *schout* of New Netherland, Resolved Waldron, was commissioned by Stuyvesant to go to Vlissingen and arrest John Bowne. When Waldron arrived at the Quaker's home he found Bowne nursing his sick wife and child rather than participating in a conventicle, but he nevertheless placed him under arrest. Since the sheriff had no warrant for Bowne's arrest other than Stuyvesant's ordinance

[11] Sentence of Tobias Feake, January 28, 1658. *Col. Doc.*, 14, 409.
[12] See Zwierlein, pp. 225–235.
[13] Minute of the New Netherland Council, August 24, 1662. *Col. Doc.*, 14, 515.

against conventicles, Bowne refused to proceed to New Amsterdam on foot. Waldron therefore conveyed him to Manhattan the
next day by boat, and he was subsequently made to stand trial.[14]

Stuyvesant could not stand Quaker hats, and the first item of
business at Bowne's trial was the forceable removal of his hat by
the sheriff. The director-general himself then read to the prisoner
the articles of the provincial ordinance against conventicles, but
Bowne refused to admit that he had been involved in meetings of
"heretics, deceivers and seducers," since in his view such nomenclature did not apply to "the servants of the Lord."[15] Stuyvesant
refused to argue and instead asked Bowne if he could deny that
he had held conventicles in his house. Although Bowne was at
first reluctant to incriminate himself, he then had a change of
heart and announced he was ready to bear any punishment God
should allow the court to inflict on him. The court found him
guilty both of lodging Quakers overnight and of holding Quaker
meetings in his home. "Thus the abominable sect, that vilifies the
magistrates and preachers of God's Holy Word, that endeavors
to undermine both the State and Religion, found encouragement
in its errors and seduced others from the right path with the dangerous consequences of heresy and schism."[16] Bowne was fined
twenty-five Flemish pounds plus court costs, and threatened with
double that fine for a second offense and banishment for a third.

The case could have ended here, but Bowne refused to pay the
fine.[17] This put Stuyvesant in a very awkward position for, with
the memory of Robert Hodgson still vivid, he was not eager to
resort to harsh physical tactics which might fail anyway. From
September 1662 until January 1663 Bowne was retained in prison

[14] Details in "John Bowne's Journal," partly reprinted in *The American
Historical Record,* 1, no. 1 (January, 1872), 4–8.

[15] *Ibid.*

[16] Minute of the Council of New Netherland, September 14, 1662.
Printed in full in B. J. Thompson, *History of Long Island* (New York,
1843), 2, 77–78.

[17] "John Bowne's Journal."

Chicago Public Library
Harold Washington Library Center
10/5/2006 4:43:52 PM

- PATRON RECEIPT -
- CHARGES -

1: Item Number: R0014576364
   Title: Religion, politics, and
   Due Date: 10/26/2006

2: Item Number: R0011160805
   Title: Religion and trade in Ne
   Due Date: 10/26/2006

------ Please Keep this Slip ------

at New Amsterdam while every sort of device short of torture was employed by the director-general to convince him to accept the sentence of the court. Bowne remained obstinate, however, and on December 14, 1662, the New Netherland provincial council "for the welfare of the community and to crush, as far as it is possible, that abominable sect, who treat with contempt both the political magistrates and the ministers of God's Holy Word and endeavor to undermine the police and religion, resolved to transport from this province the aforesaid John Bowne, if he continues obstinate and pervicatious, in the first ship ready to sail, for an example to others."[18] On January 8, 1663, this resolution was put into effect and Bowne was carried on board the ship *Vos* (Fox) which set sail for Holland the next day.[19] With Bowne, Stuyvesant sent a report of the case to the W.I.C. directors at Amsterdam, and he also announced his intention to use "more severe prosecutions" if Bowne's banishment should fail to work as an effective object lesson.[20]

Bowne, however, was shrewd enough to realize that his banishment could be put to good use. Upon his arrival in Amsterdam he took his version of the incident to the W.I.C. directors and not without success. The company decided that it was time once again to restrain Stuyvesant's Reformed zeal and state explicitly their intention for the colony's religious life. Bowne noted with great joy that the directors, after hearing his story, "were not disposed to take offence at our manners or the like, neither one word against me in particular, nor one word tending to the approval of anything that was done against us."[21] On the contrary, the W.I.C. rebuked Stuyvesant strongly for his handling of the whole Quaker problem. On April 16, 1663, the company sent the director-general a dispatch that aptly summarized its

[18] Minute of the Council of New Netherland, December 14, 1662. In Thompson, 2, 78.
[19] Zwierlein, p. 241.
[20] O'Callaghan, 2, 457.
[21] *Ibid.*

position with regard to the Quakers and religious dissent in general:

Your last letter informed us that you had banished from the Province and sent hither by ship a certain Quaker, John Bowne by name; although we heartily desire that these and other sectarians remained away from there, yet as they do not, we doubt very much, whether we can proceed against them rigorously without diminishing the population and stopping immigration, which must be favored at a so tender stage of the country's existence. You may therefore shut your eyes, at least not force people's consciences, but allow every one to have his own belief, as long as he behaves quietly and legally, gives no offence to his neighbors and does not oppose the government. As the government of this city [Amsterdam] has always practised this maxim of moderation and consequently has often had a considerable influx of people, we do not doubt, that your Province too would be benefitted by it.[22]

From this point forward it was the "maxim of moderation" that prevailed in New Netherland vis à vis the Quakers. No further arrests or prosecution of Quakers were recorded prior to the conquest of the province by the English in August 1664. The Friends, however, were never officially tolerated in New Netherland by the W.I.C., and for a long time the directors refused to allow Bowne to return to the colony except on terms he called "gross and unreasonable."[23]

After 1647 New Netherland's Reformed establishment was challenged successfully by several other groups. For example, when in 1655 the Swedish colony on the Delaware River surrendered to Stuyvesant's small expeditionary force, the Swedes won from the Dutch director-general in the seventh article of the capitulation the concession that "those who will then remain here and earn their living in the country, shall enjoy the freedom of the Augsburg Confession, and one person to instruct them therein."[24]

[22] W.I.C. directors to Stuyvesant, April 16, 1663. *Ecc. Rec.*, 1, 530.
[23] Thompson, 2, 386–387.
[24] Articles of Capitulation, September 25, 1655. *Col. Doc.*, 1, 608.

The most radical threat the New Netherland religious establishment faced, however, was aborted in 1664 when the English
took over the colony. This was the small settlement of Mennonite-
Collegiants led to Zwaanendael on the Delaware River by Pieter
Corneliszoon Plockhoy in 1663.

Plockhoy's name has remained for a long time in the shadows
of American colonial history, but recent research has brought
him to light as a true radical in the fields of religious and economic thought.[25] He was born in the village of Zierikzee ("Zurik-
zee," as he usually spelled it) in Zealand sometime between 1620
and 1625. Not much is known of his life until about 1648 when
he appeared at Amsterdam as the head of a liberal faction within
the Mennonite Church. The parties within the Mennonite
Church were quarreling, and Plockhoy's faction was associating
freely with the Collegiants—a group stemming from the suppression of the Remonstrants at the Synod of Dordrecht in 1619 that
believed the way to an ecumenical Christianity was through the
abolition of church organization, professional ministers, and
creeds. The Collegiants invited all people to attend their meetings, provided only that they believed in the divine inspiration
of the Bible, liberally defined.[26] In addition, they had special concerns in two areas: religious freedom and social justice.

In 1658 Plockhoy took his Collegiant ideas to Cromwellian
England, hoping for a sympathetic hearing from the Lord Protector. In January 1659 he published at London a pamphlet,
The Way to the Peace and Settlement of These Nations, which
consisted of three letters Plockhoy had presented to Parliament

---

[25] The best research on Plockhoy available in English includes Irvin B.
Horst, "Pieter Corneliszoon Plockhoy: An Apostle of the Collegiants,"
and Leland Harder, "Plockhoy and His Settlement at Zwaanendael, 1663,"
both in *The Mennonite Quarterly Review,* 23 (July, 1949), 161–185 and
186–199. Also, Leland and Marvin Harder, *Plockhoy from Zurik-zee*
(Newton, Kansas: Mennonite Board of Education and Publication, 1952)
has an excellent biographical sketch of Plockhoy as well as the full texts
of his most important writings.

[26] Harder and Harder, p. 15.

on the subject of universal religious toleration. Plockhoy's proposals in this pamphlet were unmistakably Collegiant. He said, for example, that the government should "institute . . . in every City and in every County throughout England, Scotland, and Ireland, one general Christian assembling or meeting-place, in such a form, that all people may see one another round about by the help of seats, rising by steps, having before them convenient leaning-places to read and write upon; also one desk aloft on one side or end to hear the holy Scriptures read at a set time, giving freedome after that reading to all people, orderly to confer together concerning the Doctrine and Instruction of their Lord and Master Christ."[27] There is no indication that either Richard Cromwell (Oliver had died in September 1658) or his Parliament of 1659 paid the slightest attention to Plockhoy's proposal for religious toleration, nor, however, is there any indication that Plockhoy was at all daunted. In May of 1659 he published a new pamphlet at London, *A Way Propounded to Make the Poor in These and Other Nations Happy,* which was a fairly detailed plan for the creation of a cooperative community. In this work Plockhoy proposed to bring together four types of people "whereof the World chiefly consists, out of several Sects, into one Family or Household government, *Viz.* Husbandmen, Handi-crafts people, Marriners and Masters of Arts and Sciences, to the end that we may the better eschue the yoke of Temporal and Spiritual *Pharaohs* who have long enough domineered over our bodies and souls, and set up again (as in former times) Righteousness, love and Brotherly Sociableness, which are scarce any where to be found."[28] In this utopian community the gain of merchants would be equitably distributed to all members of society, the society would underwrite and guarantee all capital risks, free medical care would be available to all, widows and their children would be looked after, and happy family life would be promoted.[29]

[27] Horst, pp. 165–166.
[28] Harder and Harder, p. 134.
[29] Horst, p. 171.

By 1662 Restoration politics were in full swing in England and Plockhoy was back in Amsterdam, petitioning the city burgomasters (who had assumed the administration of the Delaware River area of New Netherland from the W.I.C. in April 1657) that he be allowed to establish his projected community at Zwaanendael, near the mouth of the Delaware River. His petition was granted, and on June 6, 1662, a contract was completed with the burgomasters which said, "That he, Pieter Cornelisz. Plockhoy, undertakes to present to us, as soon as possible, the names of twenty-five persons, who will agree to depart by the first ship or ships to the aforesaid colony of this city, to reside there and to work at farming, fishing, handicrafts, etc., and to be as diligent as possible not only to live comfortably themselves, but also that provision may thereby be made for others to come."[30] Before the Amsterdam magistrates granted Plockhoy their approval, they had received from him, in January of 1662, a document containing 117 articles of association that were to govern the proposed cooperative settlement. This document is still extant and forms part of a pamphlet coauthored by Plockhoy and others entitled *Kort Verhael van Nieuw Nederlants*.[31]

The articles of association provide us with enough information about the proposed community to see that it constituted a radical challenge to the organic Reformed society envisioned by the *predikanten* in New Netherland. Not everyone was to be included at Zwaanendael by any means. Article 14 said that "All eccentric persons such as obstinate papists which are strongly attached to the Roman chair, parasitic Jews, Anglican headstrong Quakers and Puritans, and rash and stupid believers in the millenium, besides all obstinate present-day pretenders to revelation, etc., will have to be carefully averted from this Christian civilian society." Nevertheless, the public religious life of the community was to be ecumenical and free from all sectarian establishment, Re-

---

[30] Harder and Harder, p. 51.

[31] The authorship is not certain, but can be reasonably attributed to Plockhoy. See the discussion *ibid.*, Appendix A, pp. 206–213.

formed or otherwise. Article 2 provided that each member of the community

> must also promise upon entering this Christian civilian society to entertain peace and harmony and to abstain from all quarreling about religious matters. He must be completely content with the common religion, with the Sundays and holidays, which will be observed over there as here at home by the reading of Scripture passages by some young or older men from the society, each on his turn, portions fit for the occasion. Psalms will be sung before as well as after the service for instruction and devotion. The convening and leaving will be done in all quietness and reverence.[32]

Plockhoy's group spent a year assembling itself in Amsterdam and sailed for New Netherland on May 5, 1662. On July 28, 1663, the ship *St. Jacob* deposited the 41 persons with their equipment at Zwaanendael on the Delaware River mouth. The settlement never had a chance to get started. Thirteen months later, in August 1664, English naval forces under the command of Sir Robert Carr destroyed all the Dutch settlements on the Delaware River. It was the only military force used by the English in their takeover of New Netherland, and it violated the expressed orders of the Duke of York that the people of the colony were to be treated with "humanity and gentleness."[33] The Zwaanendael community was dispersed, and Plockhoy himself died blind and penniless in about 1700 in Germantown, Pennsylvania.

Thus, the years from 1647 till 1664 witnessed the statement of two fundamentally different intentions for the religious life of New Netherland. Johannes Megapolensis and Samuel Drisius— the two senior *predikanten* in New Netherland—and the Classis of Amsterdam fought valiantly to preserve an organically unified society of the "true" Reformed faith. In their struggle they had the sympathy—and often the considerable help—of Director-General Stuyvesant. But Stuyvesant, the "loyal employee of the

---

[32] *Ibid.*, pp. 189–191.
[33] *Ibid.*, p. 63.

West India Company," was responsible in the final analysis to a group of Amsterdam merchants who had a different intention for the colony. After approximately 1650, the W.I.C. was forced to take new interest in New Netherland, and the company finally realized that only by populating the colony could it be made to pay. The appeal made in 1661 to all of England's Restoration dissenters was typical of the company's point of view: "If any of the English good Christians, who may be assured of the advantages to mankind of plantations in these latitudes above others more southerly, and shall be rationally disposed to transport themselves to the said place, under the conduct of the United States [of the Netherlands], they shall have full liberty to live in the fear of the Lord . . . and shall be likewise courteously used."[34]

[34] O'Callaghan, 2, 446.

15. Conclusion: Connivance, the Dutch Colonial Contribution to American Religious Pluralism

In 1678, fourteen years after the English conquest of New Netherland, Governor Edmund Andros observed of his colony that there were "religions of all sorts, one Church of England, several Presbyterians and Independents, Quakers and Anabaptists, of several sects, some Jews, but Presbyterians and Independents most numerous and substantial." Eight years later his successor, Thomas Dongan, remarked about the religious situation in New York that "Here be not many of the Church of England; few Roman Catholics; abundance of Quakers; preachers, men and women especially; singing Quakers; ranting Quakers; Sabatarians; Antisabatarians; some Anabaptists; some Independents; some Jews; in short of all sorts of opinion there are some, and the most of none at all."[1]

When Richard Nicolls, on August 27, 1664, took New Netherland from the Dutch for his master Charles II, he included in the articles of capitulation the first explicit statement about freedom of religion ever made in that colony. Article 8 said simply that "the Dutch here shall enjoy the liberty of their consciences in Divine Worship and church discipline."[2] Nevertheless, the religious diversity which Andros and Dongan noted in 1678 and

[1] *Col. Doc.*, 2, 262 and 415.
[2] *Ecc. Rec.*, 1, 558.

236

1686 did not date from the English occupation of the colony but was received as a heritage from the Dutch.

Before the end of Dutch rule in New Netherland there were in the colony, in addition to the members of the Reformed Church, a considerable number of Lutherans, a large number of Quakers (especially on Long Island), and a smaller number of Mennonites, Jews, and Roman Catholics. This plain fact becomes enigmatic, however, when it is remembered that throughout the history of New Netherland the Reformed Church alone enjoyed the legal right of existence and public worship. Thus Zwierlein, in his *Religion in New Netherland,* argues that all religions except the Reformed were "absolutely prohibited" in all of New Netherland except the Delaware River territory. He goes on to discuss in three separate chapters the "persecution of the Jews, Lutherans, and Quakers."[3] As we have seen, each of these deviant religious groups had to fight to acquire and consolidate its position in New Netherland, but except in the case of the Quakers this was always accomplished without any real "persecution." That is simply too strong a term to describe accurately the measures taken by the colonial authorities and *a fortiori* those taken by the W.I.C. directors in the homeland. On the other hand, the interpretation of religion in New Netherland that Zwierlein was trying to explode in 1910 was that "New York was the only colony in which perfect religious liberty was to be had. . . . The Dutch granted it to everyone. They had it at home."[4] Such a view, as Zwierlein well knew, totally failed to take into account the manifold legal pronouncements and ordinances against religious dissent in New Netherland.

Most of seventeenth-century American colonial history must be viewed as an extension of European history in order to be seen accurately. This is true of New Netherland perhaps more than of

[3] Zwierlein, *Religion in New Netherland* (Rochester, N.Y.: John P. Smith, 1910), pp. 5, 187–265.
[4] Quoted by Zwierlein in his article "New Netherland Intolerance," *Catholic Historical Review,* 4, no. 2 (April, 1918), 186.

any other American colony. Throughout its history New Netherland's commercial and political life was directly controlled by Dutch merchants in the fatherland, and the Reformed Church, through the Classis of Amsterdam, exerted a vigorous influence on the colony both theologically and institutionally. Zwierlein realized the importance for his topic of a correct view of religious conditions in the United Provinces, and the first chapter of *Religion in New Netherland* was called "The Dutch Background." That chapter argued that the policy of the United Provinces toward non-Reformed religious confessions was, especially after the Synod of Dordrecht, essentially one of repression. Zwierlein put heavy emphasis on the edict of the States-General in 1622 against private Catholic conventicles and against the Jesuits, though he admitted that "there must have been a great deal of connivance, as this placard was renewed in 1624, 1629 and 1641." Summing up, Zwierlein says, "the States General did not recede from its intransigent attitude towards Catholic worship, although the edicts against the Remonstrants and other Protestant dissenters, such as Mennonites and Lutherans, gradually lapsed into desuetude under the moderate policy dictated by the successor of Maurice, his brother Frederick Henry, and supported by the municipal governments, who feared the domination of the Dutch Reformed Church in the event of further repression."[5] The interpretation of the Dutch religious background of New Netherland that has been advanced here differs rather basically from Zwierlein's. But the difference comes at the point of emphasis. It cannot be denied that the States-General issued edicts prohibiting Catholic conventicles in 1622, 1624, 1629, and 1641. In further support of Zwierlein's thesis it could be pointed out that the States of Holland published similar ordinances against "papists" in 1573, 1581, 1588, 1589, 1591, 1594, 1653, and 1659. But the question is what all these ordinances meant; how seriously were they taken?

[5] Zwierlein, *Religion in New Netherland,* pp. 29–31.

The States-General was a weak, almost impotent, central government. Every province held veto power in the States-General, and the provincial delegations in turn were composed of representatives from the municipal governments. Thus the provincial States were in a very real sense more powerful than the States-General, and the policies of each province tended to be dictated by the important town or towns in that province. The question of how to handle religious dissent, and indeed how to handle the militant Reformed *predikanten*, was thus finally decided not at the national but at the local level.

The local municipal aristocracies in the United Provinces were extremely wary of the power and influence of the Reformed *predikanten*. In the first place, many of these aristocrats did not at all share the theological views of the "hard Reformed." They were more attracted to the humanistic, ethical reforms in Christianity proposed by Erasmus or to the milder form of Calvinist theology expounded by Arminius, Uytenbogaert, and the Remonstrants. In the second place, even those local magistrates sympathetic to the Reformed at the theological level were opposed to granting the *predikanten* too much influence in political affairs because such influence could only be granted at their own expense, and the *predikanten* often used their political influence to foment what the magistrates regarded as unnecessary theological dispute. Typical of the first kind of magistrates, the Gouda town council declared in 1583, "The deputies of this city, . . . although the Reformed religion is accepted provisionally, . . . nevertheless do not understand nor would they want to agree that anyone of contrary doctrine should be injured or hindered in his conscience because of his religious views."[6] Less liberal but just as adamant in its opposition to clerical power in political affairs was the refusal of the Leiden magistracy in 1582 to obey the 1581 edict of the States of Holland against Catholic conven-

---

[6] Quoted in H. A. E. van Gelder, *Vrijheid en Onvrijheid in de Republiek* (Haarlem, 1947), p. 90 [translation mine].

ticles. The *predikanten,* said Leiden's magistrates, would upset the precarious political balance by creating unnecessary and meaningless disputes over theology. The Leiden city council complained: "Our illness is doctrinal wrangling and the danger is threatening that the unity with which we have won shall be destroyed."[7]

The hope of the Reformed *predikanten* was that they could capitalize on the extreme anti-Spanish feelings in the United Provinces and convert the war for Dutch independence into a Calvinist crusade at the national level. The weakness of the States-General and the jealousy with which the local regent aristocracies guarded their new-found authority frustrated the *predikanten* in this endeavor. At Amsterdam, however, a third factor was involved in the defeat of the Calvinists' plans. By the middle of the sixteenth century Amsterdam was already an important center of European trade, but after the fall of Antwerp to the Spanish in 1585 and the gradual silting-up of the Scheldt the importance of the city on the Ij increased meteorically. New trade routes were opened that made Amsterdam a world market. Commerce became the central fact of Amsterdam's existence, and this commerce inevitably brought with it a population of wide religious diversity. Amsterdam became, in Andrew Marvell's words, "Turk, Christian, Pagan, Jew—a staple of sects and mint of schism."

Amsterdam's ruling aristocracy during the first half of the seventeenth century was composed, for a large part, of men who were also shrewd merchants. Trade interests therefore assumed an increasingly important role in the city's internal politics, and the interests of trade were decidedly not served by theological strife and religious intolerance. Cornelis Pieterszoon Hooft, perhaps the most articulate of the merchant-magistrates on this subject, said that "our greatest power and welfare derives from the *Imperium maris,* and from foreign commerce." Therefore, Hooft reasoned, "the nature of these lands, and especially of this city (existing,

[7] Quoted *ibid.,* p. 89 [translation mine].

by God's grace, mostly by shipping and commerce) most urgently demands familiar amiability between men." For this reason Hooft was exceedingly impatient with the doctrinally rigid Reformed *predikanten* who were continually exhorting the city magistrates to employ their power of the sword to root out heresy. With disgust he noted that "they [the *predikanten*] exhort the government to proceed against these heresies as against the Canaanites and the priests of Baal . . . [and] they pray also that the matter must be handled with zeal, even though all the trade of the land should be thereby lost."[8]

After Amsterdam's brief flirtation with Reformed orthodoxy at the time of the ending of the Twelve Years' Truce with Spain (1618–1622), it was Hooft's view of the religious situation that prevailed within the city's merchant aristocracy. Remonstrants, Catholics, Jews, Lutherans, Anabaptists, Brownists, and still more bizarre religious groups all pursued their courses relatively unobstructed by civil disabilities. But while all these religious factions were enjoying their de facto freedom, all but the Reformed were prohibited by law. The Amsterdam magistracy made no grand pronouncements about religious liberty abstractly considered, and they did no deep theorizing on the subject; for this, these men of affairs had neither the time nor the inclination. They simply granted religious freedom by default; they failed to implement those national and provincial laws that could deprive the deviant groups of their liberty.

Though Amsterdam undoubtedly stumbled at first into this pattern of dealing with religious dissidents, she soon found that it worked. As the century wore on, she discovered that a decision about the legal status of the dissenters could be indefinitely postponed. They could be dealt with permanently on an ad hoc basis. This manner of dealing with (or ignoring) religious dissent grad-

---

[8] C. P. Hooft, "Memoriën en Adviezen," published in two parts in *Werken van het Historisch Genootschap Gevestigd te Utrecht,* New Series nos. 15 and 16, Third Series nos. 48 and 49. New Series nos. 15 and 16, pp. 236, 30, 96 [my translation].

ually was developed to a fine science by the merchant-magistrates, and the dissenters themselves caught on to the spirit of the city's approach to them and helped promote the system further. Legally, the dissenters did not exist in Amsterdam, but in fact they swarmed over the town, as the *predikanten* indignantly said, "like locusts."

The architectural symbol of this system for reconciling religious establishment and religious pluralism was the *schuilkerk* (hidden church). Located either on the ground floor of a private *grachthuis* (canal house) or in the attic, the *schuilkerk* was totally invisible to the casual passer-by on the street. Inside, however, it was often lavishly ornamented and might even have included a small pipe organ. The size of the *schuilkerken* varied, but some of them were astonishingly large. The Reformed Consistory of Amsterdam noted with chagrin in 1641 that seven contiguous houses had been joined to form one Catholic *schuilkerk* sanctuary. One of these seventeenth-century *schuilkerken* still stands today on the east side of Amsterdam. It occupies the top three stories of a *grachthuis,* and has a seating capacity of at least two hundred persons.

The system Amsterdam evolved for treating its religious dissenters, neither one of intolerance nor one of official sanction, also gradually acquired a name—"connivance" (in Dutch, *conniventie* or *oogluiking*). "Connivance" stemmed from the Latin verb *conniveo,* meaning "to close the eyes" or "blink." Thus it was an appropriate term to describe the policies of the magistrates toward dissent, for they really did "shut their eyes" to the presence of the dissenters. If they had "opened their eyes" the laws of the nation and province would have required them to root out the "heretics" in accordance with the demands of the *predikanten.*

This system of connivance, which was midway between the organic establishmentarianism of the Middle Ages and the pluralism of modern times, developed an appearance of permanence in Amsterdam as the century wore on. Its symbols—the *schuil-*

kerken, the vain protests of the Reformed clergy to the magistrates, the increased use of the term "connivance" by both clergy and magistracy—became distinguishing features of the Amsterdam social landscape. By midcentury, religious connivance had become such an integral part of Amsterdam life that it was quite by chance depicted in the art of Rembrandt. Rembrandt, like Steen, Hals, Vermeer, and other lesser lights of the Golden Age of Dutch art, bolstered his income by painting strictly routine group portraits of Amsterdam's aristocrats in public or professional assemblage. Even the dullness of subject matter could not always obscure the genius of Rembrandt, and several of these group portraits (e.g., *The Night Watch*) became famous art masterpieces. Such a portrait was the one done by the great master in 1662 and entitled *De Staalmeesters* or "The Sampling Officials of the Drapers' Guild." The duty of the sampling officials was to check the quality of cloth produced on Amsterdam looms before it was put up for sale on the Bourse. In Rembrandt's famous painting the gentlemen posing from left to right were: Jacob van Loon, a Roman Catholic who had a *schuilkerk* in his house; Volckert Janszoon, an Anabaptist; Willem van Doeijenburg, Reformed; Jochem de Neve, Remonstrant; and Aernhout van de Mije, a Catholic who also had a *schuilkerk* in his home.[9] The impression Rembrandt's portrait gives, and was supposed to give, is that these gentlemen are not posing but are gathered for the purpose of routine business. No analysis, however brilliant, could say more succinctly than does this portrait that in Amsterdam religious orthodoxy submitted to commercial expediency. To return once more to the words of the Dutch historian Evenhuis: "Amsterdam was, from an external viewpoint, a Reformed city, . . . but there was no city in Holland where more dissenters lived."

Because Amsterdam and Amsterdam capital played such an important role in the founding and governing of the India com-

[9] Private communication from the *Stichting Museum Amstelkring,* Oudezijds Voorburgwal 40, Amsterdam, The Netherlands.

panies, Amsterdam patterns of church-state relations tended to be transported into the far reaches of what became a world-straddling Dutch colonial empire. In Indonesia, Formosa, Japan, Brazil, the West Indies, and New Netherland the pattern was essentially the same. Wherever colonies were established it was more or less expected that the commercial companies would establish the Reformed faith too. The directors of the great India companies for the most part went along with this expectation. They were not great theoreticians on the subjects of church-state relations and religious dissent. To most of them these problems were not even interesting. They proceeded on the generally accepted assumption of the day, which was that one state could not tolerate more than one religion without greatly endangering its political harmony and ultimately its political existence. These merchants, however, did not understand by a Reformed establishment a system so rigid that it would prevent participation in Dutch colonial enterprise by interested non-Reformed groups. The India companies were, in the final analysis, commercial corporations. They were not primarily instruments for the propagation of the Reformed Gospel, though the directors sometimes protested to the *predikanten* that they were, in order to placate the latter's wrath. Where a Reformed establishment was compatible with the profitable operation of a colonial venture, the V.O.C. and W.I.C. directors upheld and nurtured the establishment. Where, however, it appeared that trade and colonization would be hindered by a rigorous pursuit of religious unanimity, the Dutch merchants worked for the moderation of religious establishment without eliminating establishment itself. Their model at this point was the system of the city of Amsterdam—connivance.

New Netherland was, from the moment of its first discovery by the Dutch, a venture based on Amsterdam capital. It was, therefore, always primarily a commercial venture. In due time the Reformed Church made its expected appearance in New Netherland, but the colony was not, in Perry Miller's phrase, a "medieval pilgrimage." It was a hard-headed business venture calculated to wrest profit from the North American wilderness. How to win this profit was a question that occupied the thinking of the W.I.C. directors during the first twenty or tweny-five years the colony was under their supervision. Gradually it became evident that fur trade alone could never make the province profitable. At some point between 1645 and 1650 the company realized that New Netherland must be colonized or given up, and a confluence of economic and political factors made the latter option impossible. Therefore, every possible effort was made to encourage immigration to the province and to sink the roots for a true Dutch colonial society.

The decision to colonize New Netherland raised all the old problems that had characterized the *Kulturkampf* between Reformed Church and merchant aristocracy in the homeland. The Reformed *predikanten* on both sides of the Atlantic demanded that the religious establishment in New Netherland be kept pure. The W.I.C. directors, however, envisioned a moderate religious establishment with operating room for various kinds of dissent. In short, the company intended for New Netherland a policy toward religious dissent similar to the policy of Amsterdam—a policy of connivance. In 1657 a delegation from the Classis of Amsterdam accused the W.I.C. directors of permitting Lutheran worship on the Delaware River "by connivance."[10] When the directors rebuked Stuyvesant for his strong ordinance against conventicles in 1656, they urged him that the best policy toward dissent would be to "sweetly let it pass."[11] Concerning Quaker dissent, the directors advised Stuyvesant in 1663 to "shut your eyes."[12]

The Dutch have a saying: *verscheidenheid maakt verdraagzaamheid,* diversity creates tolerance. So it was that the Dutch

[10] Minute of the Classis of Amsterdam, April 10, 1657. In *Ecc. Rec.,* 1, 274.

[11] Letter of the W.I.C. directors to Director-General Stuyvesant, June 14, 1656. In *Ecc. Rec.,* 1, 352.

[12] Letter of the W.I.C. directors to Director-General Stuyvesant, April 16, 1663. In *Ecc. Rec.,* 1, 530. Also in *Col. Doc.,* 14, 525–526.

colony of New Netherland contributed to a pattern in North America that, more than a century later, resulted in a United States constitutional provision for religious liberty. Philip Schaff noted that the Constitutional Convention in 1787, taking into account the religious diversity then existing in the American colonies, had no choice but to grant religious freedom. When Colonel Richard Nicolls sailed into New York Bay in 1664 he had been confronted with a similar situation.

Bibliographical Essay
and Index

Bibliographical Essay

Only occasional references to unpublished source material occur in the text. The steady conflict that existed between Dutch commercial and ecclesiastical interests, however, can best be verified by extensive reading in the *Acta Classis Amstelodamensis* and the *Protocol van de Kerkeraad van Amsterdam,* both in good condition and located in the Amsterdam Municipal Archives (*Gemeente Archief*). For a foreigner, an assault on these documents will require not only a reading knowledge of Dutch but also some work in sixteenth- and seventeenth-century paleography. Also helpful was the vast pamphlet literature at the Royal Library in The Hague. This enormous treasury of materials on the Dutch Reformation has been charted and catalogued by W. P. C. Knuttel, *Catalogus van Pamfletten Verzameling Berustende in de Koninklijke Bibliotheek,* 8 vols. (The Hague, 1889–1916). Of particular interest were Knuttel No. 621, *Remonstrance of Vertooch by die van Leyden Heeren Ritterschappen ende Steden;* Knuttel No. 3813, *Requeste vande West-Indische Compagnie;* and Knuttel No. 3814, *Ondersoeck der Amsterdamsche requesten.*

Introduction

There are a number of different angles from which one can approach the problem of religion and trade in New Netherland. If one begins with religion, the secondary works are Albert Eekhof, *De Hervormde Kerk in Noord-Amerika (1624–1664),* 2 vols. (The Hague: Nijhoff, 1913), and Frederick Zwierlein, *Religion in New Netherland: A History of the Development of the Religious Condi-*

249

tions in the Province of New Netherland, 1623–1664 (Rochester, N.Y.: John P. Smith, 1910). Zwierlein's interpretation of the Reformed Church in New Netherland is clarified and emphasized in his later article, "New Netherland Intolerance," *Catholic Historical Review,* vol. 4, no. 2 (April, 1918).

Several studies of the economic history of New Netherland have recently appeared. Simon Hart's *Prehistory of the New Netherland Company* (Amsterdam: City of Amsterdam Press, 1959) and Van Cleaf Bachman's *Peltries or Plantations: The Economic Policies of the Dutch West India Company in New Netherland, 1623–1639* (*Baltimore:* Johns Hopkins Press, 1969) pay special attention to the *voorcompagnieën.* S. G. Nissenson, *The Patroon's Domain* (New York: Columbia University Press, 1937), focuses on the patroonship system, while Thomas J. Condon, *New York Beginnings: The Commercial Origins of New Netherland* (New York: New York University Press, 1968), gives an excellent overview of the economic vicissitudes of the colony under the Dutch.

If one considers religion and trade in New Netherland from the perspective of the wider context of Dutch colonial enterprise, a third body of literature opens up. C. R. Boxer's *The Dutch Seaborne Empire* (New York: Alfred A. Knopf, 1965) provides an authoritative and highly readable overview. It is not likely to be surpassed soon in English. O. van Rees, *Geschiedenis der Staathuishoudkunde in Nederland, tot het Einde der Achttiende Eeuw,* 2 vols. (Utrecht: Kemink, 1865–1868), shows how the India companies fit into the broader picture of Dutch economic history. J. Franklin Jameson's "Willem Usselincx," *American Historical Association Papers,* vol. 2, no. 3. (1887), deals with the involved history of the founding of the W.I.C., while W. R. Menkman, *De Geschiedenis van de West-Indische Compagnie* (Amsterdam: Van Kampen, 1947), gives the entire history of the company. The absence of footnotes in Menkman's work is frustrating.

A fourth way to get into the problem of religion and trade in New Netherland is through comparing Dutch colonial motivation with that in other colonies. This is a complex matter, and a number of works apply. Bernard Bailyn, ed., *The Apologia of Robert Keayne* (New York: Harper and Row, 1964), shows an anguished first-generation Puritan caught between commerce and covenant. Sumner

Chilton Powell's excellent *Puritan Village* (Garden City, N.Y.: Doubleday Anchor, 1965), reveals some surprisingly secular Puritans in early Sudbury, Massachusetts. John Winthrop's *History of New England,* ed. by J. K. Hosmer, 2 vols., (New York: Scribner's, 1908), offers an extended glimpse of the ecclesiastical intention for New England which is corroborated by Perry Miller's *Errand into the Wilderness* (New York: Harper and Row, 1956). On the other hand, Bernard Bailyn, *The New England Merchants in the Seventeenth Century* (New York: Harper and Row, 1964), and Darrett B. Rutman, *Winthrop's Boston* (Williamsburg, Va.: University of North Carolina Press, 1965), show how the intention was frustrated. Some examples of various motives for colonizing are presented in E. S. Gaustad, ed., *Religious Issues in American History* (New York: Harper and Row Forum Books, 1968).

Finally, one can talk about what the implications of Dutch colonization were for subsequent church-state relations. Here Anson Phelps Stokes's massive *Church and State in the United States: Historical Development and Contemporary Problems of Religious Freedom under the Constitution,* 3 vols. (New York: Harper, 1950) cannot be overlooked, although Stokes's generalizations are sometimes too simple. William Marnell, *The First Amendment: The History of Religious Freedom in America* (Garden City, N.Y.: Doubleday, 1964), makes many of Stokes' points with less detail and more readability. John Webb Pratt's *Religion, Politics, and Diversity: The Church-State Theme in New York History* (Ithaca, N.Y.: Cornell University Press, 1967) focuses specifically on church and state in New York.

Part I

The problem of church and state in the Netherlands must, of course, be viewed within the context of the Dutch Reformation in general. A good introduction to this topic is provided by T. M. Lindsay, *A History of the Reformation,* 2 vols. (Edinburgh: T. and T. Clark, 1908), although Lindsay's work is now quite out of date in some areas, particularly Anabaptist studies. Better is H. J. Grimm, *The Reformation Era* (New York: Macmillan, 1954), which also has excellent bibliographical suggestions on the Dutch Reformation.

Interesting and interested accounts of the Reformation in the Low Countries by contemporaries of the action are by the Reformed Pieter Bor, *Oorsprongk, Begin ende Vervolgh der Nederlandsche Oorlogen, 1555–1600,* 4 vols. in folio (Amsterdam, 1679–1684), and by the Remonstrant Gerardus Brandt, *Historie der Reformatie, en Andere Kerkelyke Geschiedenissen, in en ontrent de Nederlanden,* 4 vols. (Amsterdam: Jan Rieuwertzoon, Hendrik en Dirk Boom, 1671–1704, 2nd printing, 1677). Both Bor and Brandt contain a great deal of quoted material which was either known to them by oral tradition or has since passed into oblivion. R. B. Evenhuis's work, *Ook Dat Was Amsterdam,* 2 vols. published to date (Amsterdam: ten Have, 1965 and 1967), shows Amsterdam's place in the Reformation with charming narrative style. An excellent source of information on the Calvinist exiles during the pre-Reformation years is H. Q. Jansen and J. J. van Toorenenbergen, eds., *Acten van Classicale en Synodale Vergaderingen der Verstrooide Gemeenten in het Land van Cleef, Sticht van Keulen en Aken, 1571–1589* (Utrecht: Kemink, 1882).

In the matter of Calvin's thinking on church and state I have used as much as possible the original sources, the definitive collection of which is *Joannis Calvini Opera Quae Supersunt Omnia,* ed. by Guilielmus Baum, Eduardus Cunitz, and Eduardus Reuss, 59 vols. (Braunschweig: C. A. Schwetschke, 1863–1900). No one can track such a wilderness without guidance, however, and my guide has been Josef Bohatec, *Calvins Lehre von Staat und Kirche* (Breslau: Marcus, 1937). A fascinating article by H. G. Koenigsberger, "The Organization of Revolutionary Parties in France and the Netherlands during the Sixteenth Century," *The Journal of Modern History,* vol. 27, no. 4 (December, 1955), reprinted in *Estates and Revolutions* (Ithaca, N.Y.: Cornell University Press, 1971), pp. 224–252 traces Calvin's ideas from Geneva to the Netherlands.

Source material for the controversy over the church-order comes mostly from C. Hooijer, ed., *Oude Kerkordeningen der Nederlandsche Hervormde Gemeenten* (Zaltbommel, 1865). The story of this struggle is best narrated in H. A. Enno van Gelder, *Vrijheid en Onvrijheid in de Republiek: Geschiedenis der Vrijheid van Drukpers en Godsdienst van 1572 tot 1798* (Haarlem, Tjeenk Willink, 1947). It is also told in J. Reitsma and J. Lindeboom, *Ges-*

*chiedenis van de Hervorming en de Hervormde Kerk der Neder-
landen* (The Hague: Nijhoff, 1949). The "Coolhaes affair" is treated
at length in H. C. Rogge, *Caspar Janszoon Coolhaes,* 2 vols. (Amsterdam: H. W. Mooij, 1856).

The best thing on the Arminian schism now in English would
appear to be Carl Bangs, *Arminius: A Study in the Dutch Reformation* (Nashville, Tenn.: Abingdon, 1971). Its strength is that it sets
Arminius properly within his broad ecclesiastical and political context; its defect as a treatment of the schism is that it ends with
Arminius's death in 1609. Van Gelder's *Vrijheid en Onvrijheid in de
Republiek* is also relevant to this topic, as is Reitsma and Lindeboom's *Geschiedenis van de Hervorming en de Hervormde Kerk der
Nederlanden*. The depth and complexity of the struggle between
the time of Arminius's death and the Synod of Dordrecht are described in J. C. Naber, *Calvinist of Libertijnsch?* (Utrecht, 1884),
and the synod itself is discussed in H. Bouwman et al., *De Dordtsche
Synode van 1618–1619* (Gereformeerde Traktaatgenootschap "Filippus," 1918).

The problem of religious dissent within the new republic of the
United Provinces can be conveniently studied in the large collection
of printed source materials in J. Reitsma and S. D. van Veen, eds.,
*Acta der Provinciale en Particuliere Synoden Gehouden in de Noor-
delijke Nederlanden Gedurende de Jaren 1572–1620,* 8 vols. (Gron-
ingen: J. B. Wolters, 1892–1899). The unpublished minutes of the
Amsterdam Classis and Consistory are also the repositories of much
valuable information. Van Gelder's *Vrijheid en Onvrijheid in de
Republiek* is again an important secondary work, as is also W. P. C.
Knuttel's article, "Kerk en Burgerlijke Overheid," in *Uit Onzen
Bloeitijd: Schetsen van het Leven onzer Vaderen in de Zeventiende
Eeuw* (Amsterdam, n.d.).

Part II

In studying the seventeenth-century economic history of Amsterdam one is confronted with an embarrassment of riches. A candid
analysis of the Netherlands' mercantile base by a contemporary is
Pieter de la Court, *Interest van Holland ofte Gronden van Hollands
Welvaren* (1662), published in English in 1702 as *The True In-*

terest and Political Maxims of the Republick of Holland and West Friesland and erroneously attributed to Johan de Witt. Amsterdam's many-faceted commercial life is revealed in J. G. van Dillen's massive two-volume collection of source materials, *Bronnen tot de Geschiedenis van het Bedrijfsleven en het Gildewezen van Amsterdam* (The Hague: Nijhoff, 1929). In addition, there are a number of good Dutch secondary works on the subject. The entire second volume of A. Bredius et al., eds., *Amsterdam in de Zeventiende Eeuw* (The Hague: Van Stockum, 1901) deals with Amsterdam's economic life. Very good and statistically documented articles by J. G. van Dillen, "Amsterdam als Wereldstad," and J. C. Westermann, "Beschouwingen over de Opkomst en den Bloei des Handels in de Gouden Eeuw," appear in A. E. d'Ailly, ed., *Zeven Eeuwen Amsterdam*, vol. 2 (Amsterdam, 1946). An interesting description of some aspects of Amsterdam's trade relationship with Scandinavia is J. Schreiner, "Die Niederlander und die Norwegische Holzausfuhr im 17. Jahrhundert," *Tijdschrift voor Geschiedenis*, vol. 49 (1934). Finally, the one English work that covers all this bibliographical ground and much more besides is Violet Barbour's *Capitalism in Amsterdam in the Seventeenth Century* (Baltimore: Johns Hopkins Press, 1950). It is truly difficult to find an adequate superlative for her work.

Much scarcer are materials that reveal how Amsterdam capitalists looked at the world and how they thought. Invaluable here are C. P. Hooft's "Memoriën en Adviezen," *Werken van het Historisch Genootschap Gevestigd te Utrecht*, New Series, Nos. 15 and 16, Third Series, Nos. 48 and 49 (Utrecht: Kemink, 1871 and 1925). H. A. E. van Gelder's doctoral dissertation, *De Levensbeschouwing van Cornelis Pieterszoon Hooft* (Amsterdam: A. H. Kruyt, 1918), throws additional light on this tolerant merchant. The introductory essay in vol. 1 of Johan E. Elias's monumental *Geschiedenis van het Amsterdamsche Regentenpatriciaat*, 2 vols. (The Hague: Nijhoff, 1923), also tells a good deal about the value systems of some of these men. Some things on this subject can be gleaned from Jan Wagenaar, *Amsterdam*, 3 vols. (Amsterdam: Isaak Tirion, 1760–1767), and J. G. van Dillen's article "De West-Indische Compagnie, Het Calvinisme en De Politiek," *Tijdschrift voor Geschie-*

denis, vol. 74 (Groningen: Noordhoff, 1961) should also be consulted.

Amsterdam's treatment of religious dissenters can be observed in detail by reading extensively in the *Protocol* of the Amsterdam Consistory, where the Reformed *predikanten* came to discuss and lament the problem week after week. Much of this *Protocol* material is utilized by R. B. Evenhuis, *Ook Dat Was Amsterdam.* Additional discussions of Jews in Amsterdam are to be found in H. Brugmans and A. Franck, *Geschiedenis der Joden in Nederland* (Amsterdam, 1940); H. I. Bloom, *The Economic Activities of the Jews in Amsterdam in the Seventeenth and Eighteenth Centuries* (Williamsport, Pa.: Bayard Press, 1937): and I. H. van Eeghen, "De Gereformeerde Kerkeraad en de Joden te Amsterdam," *Amstelodamum,* vol. 47 (1960). Additional treatments of the problem of Catholic dissent in Amsterdam are in W. P. C. Knuttel, *De Toestand der Nederlandsche Katholieken ten Tijde der Republiek,* 2 vols. (The Hague: Nijhoff, 1892–1894); L. J. Rogier, *Geschiedenis van het Katholicisme in Noord-Nederland in de Zestiende en Zeventiende Eeuw,* 2 vols. (Amsterdam, 1945); and I. H. van Eeghen, "De Eigendom van de Katholieke Kerken in Amsterdam ten tijde van de Republiek," *Bijdragen Bisdom Haarlem* (1957). The Remonstrant difficulties at Amsterdam are ably related by Wagenaar in the first volume of *Amsterdam.*

The church-state theme in Dutch colonial policy is discussed by Charles R. Boxer in two works: *The Dutch Seaborne Empire* and *The Dutch in Brazil* (Oxford: Clarendon Press, 1957). To pursue this topic in relation to the V.O.C. one should consult Pieter van Dam, *Beschrijvinge van de Oostindische Compagnie,* 4 books in 6 volumes (The Hague, 1927–1954); C. W. Th. Baron van Boetzelaer van Asperen en Dubbeldam, *De Protestantsche Kerk in Nederlandsch-Indië* (The Hague: Nijhoff, 1947); and J. G. van Dillen, *Het Oudste Aandeelhoudersregister van de Kamer Amsterdam der Oost-Indische Compagnie* (The Hague: Nijhoff, 1958). With respect to church-state relations in territories of the W.I.C. there are Johannes de Laet, *Jaerlyck Verhael van de Verrichtingen der Geoctroyeerde West-Indische Compagnie,* ed. S. P. l'Honoré Naber and J. C. M. Warnsinck, 4 vols. (The Hague: Nijhoff,

1937); and W. R. Menkman, *De West-Indische Compagnie*. For the fascinating discussion between van Hoboken and van Dillen about the supposed "Calvinism" of the W.I.C. see W. J. van Hoboken, "The Dutch West India Company: The Political Background of Its Rise and Decline," *Britain and the Netherlands*, ed. by J. S. Bromley and E. H. Kossmann (London: Chatto and Windus, 1960); J. G. van Dillen, "De West-Indische Compagnie, Het Calvinisme en De Politiek," *Tijdschrift voor Geschiedenis*, vol. 74 (1961); and W. J. van Hoboken, "Een wederwoord inzake de Westindische Compagnie," *Tijdschrift voor Geschiedenis*, vol. 75 (1962), which also includes a *"naschrift"* by van Dillen. On the problem of slavery in the Dutch colonial empire, see Gerald F. De Jong, "The Dutch Reformed Church and Negro Slavery in Colonial America," *Church History*, vol. 40, no. 4 (December, 1971) and the sources cited there.

Part III

The territory I have covered in the remainder of the book will undoubtedly be more familiar to the student of American colonial history, so my comments can and will be more brief. No one can work on the early history of New York State without feeling an immense debt of gratitude to Edmund Burke O'Callaghan and Berthold Fernow, who together collected and edited the *Documents Relative to the Colonal History of the State of New York*, 15 vols. (Albany: Weed, Parsons, 1856–1887). The first several volumes contain many documents collected from Dutch archives by O'Callaghan and John Romeyn Brodhead. My interpretative categories of "intention" and "frustration" are borrowed from Sidney E. Mead's brilliant collection of essays on American church history, *The Lively Experiment* (New York: Harper and Row, 1963), particularly from the second chapter, "From Coercion to Persuasion." The earliest, and in some respects still the best histories of New Netherland are E. B. O'Callaghan, *History of New Netherland*, 2 vols. (New York: D. Appleton, 1848), and J. R. Brodhead, *History of the State of New York: First Period, 1609–1664* (New York: Harper, 1853). M. G. van Rensselaer's *History of the City of New York in the Seventeenth Century*, 2 vols. (New York: Macmillan, 1909), looks at the colony from the vantage point of Manhattan, while H. H. Kessler and E. Rachlis, *Peter Stuyvesant and His New York* (New York: Random House, 1959), builds the history of the colony around a character study of Stuyvesant. I do not altogether agree with the criticism that has been leveled recently at Washington Irving's *Knickerbocker's History of New York* (New York: Putnam, revised from 1848 ed.). It is still worth reading. It is not, of course, a "scholarly" history, but it possesses a certain poetic insight into the nature of New Netherland.

My chapter on the frustration of the merchants in New Netherland depends heavily on three already-mentioned secondary works: Simon Hart, *The Prehistory of the New Netherland Company;* Thomas Condon, *New York Beginnings;* and Van Cleaf Bachman, *Peltries or Plantations.* Also important are two collections of source material edited and translated by A. J. F. van Laer: *Documents Relating to New Netherland, 1624–1626, in the Henry E. Huntington Library* (San Marino, Calif., 1924) ; and *New York State Library Van Rensselaer Bowier Manuscripts* (Albany: University of the State of New York, 1908).

The basic collection of materials on religion in New Netherland is to be found in the first two volumes of Hugh Hastings, ed., *Ecclesiastical Records of the State of New York* (Albany: James B. Lyon, 1901) ; the translation and editing of the Dutch documents was done by E. T. Corwin. Important aspects of church life in early New Netherland are illuminated by A. Eekhof's *Jonas Michaëlius, Founder of the Church in New Netherland* (Leiden: A. W. Sijthoff, 1926) and *Bastiaen Janszoon Krol: Krankenbezoeker, Kommies en Kommandeur van Nieuw-Nederland, 1595–1645* (The Hague, 1910). Good recent additions to the literature are Gerald F. De Jong's "The *Ziekentroosters* or Comforters of the Sick in New Netherland," *New-York Historical Society Quarterly,* vol. 54 (October, 1970) and "Domine Johannes Megapolensis: Minister of New Netherland," *New-York Historical Society Quarterly,* vol. 52 (January, 1968). The Reformed Church's futile attempts at Indian missions are recounted in Allen W. Trelease, *Indian Affairs in Colonial New York: The Seventeenth Century* (Ithaca, N.Y.: Cornell University Press, 1960).

Part IV

For an understanding of the W.I.C.'s situation around 1650, W. J. van Hoboken's article, "De West-Indische Compagnie en de Vrede van Münster," *Tijdschrift voor Geschiedenis,* vol. 70 (Groningen: Noordhoff, 1957) is the key work. Van Hoboken calls forth in this article all the views held on the subject by previous Dutch historians. J. Franklin Jameson's *Narratives of New Netherland* (New York: Scribner's, 1909) provides Isaac Jogues's description of Manhattan, as well as many other important original sources, in translation. Many of Stuyvesant's early ordinances in New Amsterdam are reproduced in J. Paulding, *Affairs and Men of New Amsterdam in the Time of Peter Stuyvesant* (New York: Casper C. Childs, 1843), and the common man's view of Stuyvesant and the W.I.C. is given in no uncertain terms by the redoubtable Adriaen van der Donck, *Remonstrance of New Netherland* (Albany: Weed, Parsons, 1856).

On the protracted conflict between the Reformed Church and the Lutherans in New Netherland, I have basically followed the documents in the *Ecclesiastical Records of the State of New York,* with an occasional addition from unpublished materials located in the Amsterdam Municipal Archives. H. J. Kreider's *Lutheranism in Colonial New York* (Ann Arbor: Edwards, 1942) is based in part upon research done in the Amsterdam Lutheran archives and is thus helpful in bringing out the Lutheran perspective on the whole contest. Frederick Zwierlein's *Religion in New Netherland* provides the interpretation of this affair that serves as a foil for my own.

For my discussion of Jews in New Netherland I have once again relied upon the *Documents Relative to the Colonial History of the State of New York* and the *Ecclesiastical Records of the State of New York.* Berthold Fernow, ed., *Records of New Amsterdam from 1653 to 1674,* 7 vols. (New York, 1897), also contains material relevant to this episode, and S. Oppenheim, *The Early History of the Jews in New York, 1654–1664* (New York, 1909), is the basic secondary work.

The sources for the Quaker story are much the same. The establishment version of the story is to be found in the *Ecclesiastical*

Records of the State of New York and the *Documents Relative to the Colonial History of the State of New York.* The Quaker view of the matter is related in "John Bowne's Journal," *The American Historical Record,* vol. 1, no. 1 (January, 1872). H. Onderdonck's "The Rise and Growth of the Society of Friends on Long Island and in New York, 1657–1826," *The Annals of Hempstead, 1643 to 1832* (New York, 1878) narrates these same events. Once again, Zwierlein's interpretation provides a foil for my own. As mentioned in the text, Plockhoy is a fascinating figure, but to date not much work has been done on him in English. As it now stands, Irvin B. Horst, "Pieter Corneliszoon Plockhoy: an Apostle of the Collegiants," and Leland Harder, "Plockhoy and His Settlement at Zwaanendael, 1663," both in *The Mennonite Quarterly Review,* vol. 23 (July, 1949); and Leland and Marvin Harder, *Plockhoy from Zurik-zee* (Newton, Kansas: Mennonite Board of Education and Publication, 1952), are the only and therefore the definitive works.

Conclusion

No new bibliographical ground is broken in the final chapter. I must, however, acknowledge my indebtedness to the administration of the *Stichting Museum Amstelkring* for explaining to me, during a visit to *Onze Lieve Heer op Zolder,* the full religiosociological significance of *Our Blessed Lord in the Attic* and of Rembrandt's *De Staalmeesters.* It was the insight reached in that conversation that provided the interpretative framework for the book.

Index

261